Literature and Learning

Edited by
Elizabeth Grugeon and Peter Walden
for the Reading and Individual Development
Course at The Open University

Ward Lock Educational
in association with
The Open University Press

ISBN o 7062 3768 4 paperback
      o 7062 3769 2 hardback

First published 1978

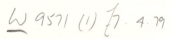

Set in 10 on 11 point Monotype Plantin
and printed by Latimer Trend & Company Ltd Plymouth
for Ward Lock Educational
116 Baker Street, London W1M 2BB
A member of the Pentos Group
Made in Great Britain

Literature and Learning

This reader was prepared by Elizabeth Grugeon and Peter Walden for the fourth module of The Open University Diploma in Reading Development, *Reading and Individual Development.*

Contents

Section Four   Reading and Response

Acknowledgments

The Open University and Publishers would like to thank the following for permission to reproduce copyright material. All possible care has been taken to trace ownership of the selections included and to make full acknowledgment for their use.

Bruno Bettelheim and Theron Raines for 'Fairy tales and the existential predicament', from *The Uses of Enchantment: The Meaning and Importance of Fairy Tales* (1975) published by Alfred A. Knopf Inc; Penny Blackie for 'Asking Questions', from *English in Education 5*, 77–96; Jean Blunt for 'Response to reading; how some young teachers describe the process', from *English in Education, 11*, 3, 35–47; Jeremy Bugler for 'A fine mess they've got you into Olly', from *The Guardian* 10th March 1976; Pat D'Arcy for 'Sharing responses to literature', unpublished report *Children as Readers: The Roles of Literature in the Primary and Secondary School* sponsored by NATE; Anna Davin for 'Historical novels for children', from *History Workshop Journal, 1*, 1, 154–65; Peter Dean for 'Time to get hooked; reading in the middle years'; Agnes Finnegan for 'Story as an adventure for the teenager', (Hart-Davis Educational Ltd); Elizabeth Grugeon and Liz Cartland for 'An approach to analysis', unpublished report *Children as Readers: The Roles of Literature in the Primary and Secondary School* sponsored by NATE; Judy Keiner for 'Learning to read and the TV narrative'; Ralph Lavender for 'Living by fact or fiction'; Heather Lyons for 'Some second thoughts on sexism in fairy tales'; Peter Medway for 'Introducing the poem "Frustrated Virtuoso" by Norman MacCaig'; Jeremy Mulford for 'Comments on traditions of literature teaching'; Sallie Purkis for 'Oral history in the primary school', from *History Workshop Journal 2*, 1, 113–17; Harold Rosen for 'Out there or where the masons went', from *English in Education 9*, 1, 202–11; James R. Squire for 'The responses of Paula while reading a short story', from *The Responses of Adolescents while Reading from Short Stories*, National Council of Teachers of English (USA) Report No 2; Peggy Temple for 'Experience of literacy in working-class life', from Hoyles M. *The Politics of Literacy* (1977) The Writers and Readers Publishing Cooperative; Mike Torbe for 'Modes of response: some interactions between reader and literature', from *English in Education 8*, 2, 21–32; Margaret Walden for 'One class and its reading'; Suzanne Walker for 'Early experiences of reading'.

Introduction

ausmachen

Immediate sense experience constitutes only a vanishingly small fraction of the world we *live* in (as opposed to the local environment we momentarily exist in): the world in which we try to apply the lessons of the past to the moulding of the future, in which we try to provide against the actions of people whom we cannot have continuously within range of our five senses; *this* world, whether we like it or not, is *effectively made of language*; there is no least possibility of ducking past words to the world itself – the world itself *is* words (and word-like things).[1]

We dream in narrative, day-dream in narrative, remember, anticipate, hope, despair, believe, doubt, plan, revise, criticize, construct, gossip, learn, hate and love by narrative.[2]

This Reader is about those particular forms of words that seem to be vital to our learning: the forms that we call narrative and literature. The evidence that we draw on indicates that stories, novels and poetry provide a unique resource. This resource is at its most effective when children's participation in their experience of literature involves their own writing and talking.

But education tends to be geared to facts, and we see about us developments which may lead to learning only being valued when it is required in quantifiable terms. Literature, then, may be out in the cold, an occasional experience of a special kind, unrelated to the rest of education and its objectives.

Many of our chapters relate living and learning to the place of literature in people's lives. We hope that the book itself illustrates the power and centrality of literature. There are passages of autobiographical writing and close studies of children and young people making sense of different kinds of writing. Other chapters deal with the social significance of the narratives that we experience and pass on.

We are not concerned so much with judging the quality of literature, though we do not ignore this, as with the processes involved when the writer, his work and the reader come together. Literature is not an immutable body of knowledge, existing separately from its readers. The nature of the relationship between author, work and reader is a variable one, but one in which all three elements have to be borne in mind, itself a difficult task.

The book concentrates on the experience of literature; our initial approach to the question of 'becoming a reader' is to look at successful examples, to see the process at work. Although everybody lives by fiction, comparatively few actively seek literature as a result of a consciously felt need.

There follow three examples of very different people describing the discovery of their need for literature. The first is Edith Hall, who was brought up in working-class London in a culture full of lively communication, where the corporate building of the family story was of great importance.

Just prior to the Great War of 1914 when I was about six years old, postcards with the then half-penny postage were sent between my relations each day. My grandmother would send us a card each evening which we received by first delivery the next morning. She would then receive our reply card the same evening. If one lived in the same town as one's correspondent, an early morning posted card would be delivered at twelve midday the same day and a reply card, if sent immediately, would be received the same afternoon.

I still have many of these postcards proving what a wonderful service it was; all in one day – and that families like our own could keep in daily touch if they so wished. With such efficiency, who would need telephones, which working-class people did not have anyway?

My greatest and most remembered pleasure was being present at the frequent family reunions; my cousins and myself being put to sleep in a long row in a bed made up on the floor. Guest rooms were unheard of in our extended family.

Trains must have stayed in stations quite a long time in those days because my aunts and other relations living *en route* to my grandmother would be notified that we would be passing through their town, and an aunt and cousin would be on the platform at Grantham and another aunt at Peterborough. We would chat and exchange gifts through the lowered window of the carriage door, then continue on our journey.

Edith Hall's description of her upbringing includes this account of how, despite the almost intolerable condition of her working life, she discovers the novels of Thomas Hardy.

Trying to catch up on one's education after a long day at work was very difficult and I well understood my father's problems as he had left school at the age of twelve to start work. Every evening he would pore over Harmsworth's Encyclopaedia and a self-educator and together we went to a class organized by the Workers' Educational Association. I had some difficulty in that when I was a skivvy in a one servant household, there would be the washing-up to do when I returned from my night class on my evening off which meant changing back into my maid's clothes and washing up the dirty dishes left from the supper I had prepared before leaving for the class.

But now, with what joy, tired out physically but mentally alert did my dear dad and I discuss our class together over supper which mother had prepared for us, and she would additionally help us by washing up afterwards.

On one occasion when dad and I, together with other workers who had been compelled to leave school early, were attending a WEA class, we discussed what books would be interesting and easy to read and would be specially suitable for those who had not read a book since leaving school. Until then I had only read popular periodicals such as *Passing Show, Answers, Tit-bits, Peg's Paper* and cheap novelettes – and then I was introduced to works by Thomas Hardy.

It has to be said that the weekly *Punch* and other publications of that kind showed cartoons depicting the servant class as stupid and 'thick' and therefore fit subjects for their jokes. The skivvy particularly was revealed as a brainless menial. Many of the working class were considered thus and Thomas Hardy wrote in *Tess of the D'Urbervilles* that 'Labouring farm folk were personified in the newspaper-press by the pitiable dummy known as Hodge . . .' and it was in this book that Hardy told the story of Tess, a poor working girl with an interesting character, thoughts and personality. This was the first serious novel I had read up to this time in which the heroine had not been of 'gentle birth' and wealthy and the labouring classes brainless automatons.

This book made me feel human and even when my employers talked at me as though I wasn't there, I felt that I could take it; I knew that I could be a person in my own right.[3]

Our second example of an adult recalling the importance of childhood reading is the writer, V. S. Naipaul. He, too, remembers the discovery of a particular author.

It has taken me a long time to come round to Conrad. And if I begin with an account of his difficulty, it is because I have to be true to my experience of him. I would find it hard to be detached about Conrad. He was, I suppose, the first modern writer I was introduced to. It was through my father. My father was a self-taught man, picking his way through a cultural confusion of which he was perhaps hardly aware and which I have only recently begun to understand; and he wished himself to be a writer. He read less for pleasure than for clues, hints and encouragement; and he introduced me to those writers he had come upon in his own search. Conrad was one of the earliest of these:

Conrad the stylist, but more than that, Conrad the late starter, holding out hope to those who didn't seem to be starting at all.

I believe I was ten when Conrad was first read to me. It sounds alarming; but the story was 'The Lagoon'; and the reading was a success. 'The Lagoon' is perhaps the only story of Conrad's that can be read to a child. It is very short, about fifteen pages. A forest-lined tropical river at dusk. The white man in the boat says, 'We'll spend the night in Arsat's clearing.' The boat swings into a creek; the creek opens out into a lagoon. A lonely house on the shore; inside, a woman is dying. And during the night Arsat, the young man who is her lover, will tell how they both came there. It is a story of illicit love in another place, an abduction, a chase, the death of a brother, abandoned to the pursuers. What Arsat has to say should take no more than fifteen minutes; but romance is romance, and when Arsat's story ends the dawn comes up; the early morning breeze blows away the mist; the woman is dead. Arsat's happiness, if it existed, has been flawed and brief; and now he will leave the lagoon and go back to his own place, to meet his fate. The white man too has to go. And the last picture is of Arsat, alone in his lagoon, looking 'beyond the great light of a cloudless day into the darkness of a world of illusions'.

In time the story of 'The Lagoon' became blurred. But the sense of night and solitude and doom stayed with me, grafted, in my fantasy, to the South Sea or tropical island setting of the Sabu and Jon Hall films. I have, unwillingly, looked at 'The Lagoon' again. There is a lot of Conrad in it – passion and the abyss, solitude and futility and the world of illusions – and I am not sure now that it isn't the purest piece of fiction Conrad wrote. The brisk narrative, the precise pictorial writing, the setting of river and hidden lagoon, the nameless white visitor, the story during the night of love and loss, the death at daybreak: everything comes beautifully together. And if I say it is a pure piece of fiction, it is because the story speaks for itself; the writer does not come between his story and the reader.[4]

Finally, we turn to John Stuart Mill, the prodigious example of a utilitarian education, crammed with information, logic and facts but ultimately, in 1828 at the age of twenty-two, discovering literature as a need.

What made Wordsworth's poems a medicine for my state of mind, was that they expressed, not mere outward beauty, but states of feeling, and of thought coloured by feeling, under the excitement of beauty. They seemed to be the very culture of the feelings, which I was in quest of. In them I seemed to draw from a source of inward joy, of sympathetic and imaginative pleasure, which could be shared in by all human beings; which had no connexion with struggle or imperfection, but would be made richer by every improvement in the physical or social condition of mankind. From them I seemed to learn what would be the perennial sources of happiness, when all the greater evils of life shall have been removed. And I felt myself at once better and happier as I came under their influence. There have certainly been, even in our own age, greater poets than Wordsworth; but poetry of deeper and loftier feeling could not have done for me at that time what his did. I needed to be made to feel that there was real, permanent happiness in tranquil contemplation. Wordsworth taught me this, not only without turning away from, but with a greatly increased interest in the common feelings and common destiny of human beings. And the delight which these poems gave me, proved that with culture of this sort, there was nothing to dread from the most confirmed habit of analysis. At the conclusion of the Poems came the famous Ode, falsely called Platonic, 'Intimations of Immortality': in which, along with more than his usual sweetness of melody and rhythm, and along with the two passages of grand imagery but bad philosophy so often quoted, I found that he too had had similar experience to mine; that he also had felt that the first freshness of youthful enjoyment of life was not lasting; but that he had sought for compensation, and found it, in the way in which he was now teaching me to find it. The result was that I gradually, but completely, emerged from my habitual depression, and was never again subject to it. I long continued to value Wordsworth less according to his intrinsic merits, than by the measure of what he had done for me.[5]

Notes

1 LEMAN, R. (1971) 'Words and worlds', in Bannister, D. (1971) *Perspectives in Personal Construct Theory* Academic Press
2 HARDY, B. (1968) '*The Appropriate Form, an Essay on the Novel*' London: Athlone Press
3 HALL, Edith (1977) '*Canary Girls and Stock Pots*', WEA Luton Branch, Barnfield College, Luton p. 5 and pp. 39–40
4 NAIPAUL, V. S. 'The Reality and the Romance' *The Sunday Times*
5 MILL, John Stuart (1873) *Autobiography* reissued 1924 Oxford University Press pp. 125–6

Section One
Becoming a Reader

Introduction
The first chapters of this Reader look at children's early encounters with
literature and at what kinds of literature they may encounter at home
and at school. To try to move closer to the experience of becoming a
reader we asked Suzanne Walker, herself a compulsive reader from early
childhood, to give an account of her own two children's introduction to
narrative, both inside and outside books. Memories of her own early
experiences fuse with and enrich her observation of the developing
imaginative world of her children, Nicholas and Lucy.

1 Early experiences of reading
Suzanne Walker

It starts on the knee. You have the child close. If he goes to sleep you can meditate, but if he is awake what do you do? Play: toes, fingers, talking games; piggies go to market; which pig is interesting? Not the roast beef eater, but the one who goes 'Wee, wee', all the way home – identification, clearly. Anyway, at this stage there aren't enough teeth to cope with more than roast beef dinner from a little tin. Or the child becomes mock victim, he is attacked and enclosed, can't escape the circling arms. He scrambles out – wins – comes back and tries again. The game gets more sophisticated; protagonist and antagonist are set up in a safe situation. Readiness for actual stories seemed, with my children, to be linked with understanding time, not in a clock-way, such as telling the time, but with the notion that events can be linked; that if I went away, I would come back; that bed comes after bath, which came after tea.

Like other conscientious parents, I read stories too soon, and then, when the books got torn up, went back to the Mothercare catalogue. He wanted objects, learning them as he learned words: spoon, bucket, pantie girdle. The knowledge that objects were connected with activities was the next stage, related, perhaps, to the growth of verbs in the vocabulary. People do things with objects, and the activity itself becomes significant. We bought Richard Scarry for Nicholas at eighteen months: lots of animals rushing around their clean American world. I also used *In the Busy Town*, which has no words, only detailed pictures of the multiple activities of people in a block of flats or a park. Each event could expand into a small story – 'Look, the boy's thrown a ball at him, and he's fallen off his bike'. Actions have consequences in life, too: 'Don't touch the television, you'll break it'; 'If you eat your bread you can have a piece of cake'.

Most published stories for small children are too complex. I had to précis rapidly and filter out all the details that were not firmly centred around 'And then ... and then ...' Two books which needed no cutting were both concerned with tigers: *Little Black Sambo*, and Judith Kerr's *The Tiger Who Came to Tea*. The consequences of actions for the characters were daunting; the outcome rewarded them in terms of food. Little Black Sambo got 169 pancakes fried in tiger butter, while Sophie, eaten out of house, home and bathwater, got sausages and chips and ice cream at the local café. The moral seems to be that those who avoid being eaten shall eat.

I also made up a great many stories about the children, about their toys and their own objects and routines. I used to start in a desperate rush with the first thing that came into my head and hope that a story-line would sort itself out. We developed a series of happenings, for instance, from one opening which began, 'One day Nicholas noticed that a giant had moved in to Number 35 across the road'. He got interested in the problems of inviting a giant to his birthday party, which included making jelly in the bath and borrowing a big silver weather balloon to take home at the end. Sometimes the stories were quite straight in their realism, but these were not as satisfying as the ones that took familiar objects and people and expanded the possibilities beyond the normal.

By three, they had both started story-making themselves, with imaginary friends. Nick had two: Charles and Edward, who varied in age, sometimes being babies, 'very small, only this big'; sometimes children of his own age, or they could be octogenarians or '*hundreds of years old*'. Lucy had more friends, and was more of an impresario, handing me various roles to play. Teddies developed characters: one of them, Henry, is still a bit of a nuisance, after I gave him too much personality in a long queue in Mac Fisheries one day. Henry makes large demands, being an anarchic bear, as opposed to Timothy, who does nothing but cry.

In my own head, as a small child, I made very little distinction between people, animals and toys, assuming them all to be fully conscious. If I had to wear a vest to keep warm, so did my teddy and so, reluctantly, did the family cat. Anthropomorphism is not, I think, imposed on children by adults: they project human characteristics all by themselves. Even at six I was more than half convinced that my toys had independent lives, which was, apart from the humour, why I enjoyed *Winnie the Pooh*. It was perfectly feasible that Pooh and Piglet lived in trees in a real forest and visited a real rabbit and a real boy. I made houses in the garden for assorted pandas and lambs, but could never bring myself to leave them out all night. More than once, after I'd gone to bed and knelt up to look out at the inhospitable darkness, my poor mother had to put on her coat and gather them all up and bring them back, chilly but safe, to my bed.

At seven I read *Alice in Wonderland*, which had the same acceptable mixture of human, toy and animal characters. I was interested recently in Isabelle Jan's idea that the changing size of Alice relates to the child's own growth; he sees parts of the world as larger or smaller as he gets further from his own feet. Also, Alice is surrounded by authority figures, who pick up her words and behaviour and comment on them forthrightly. This felt familiar and especially true of encounters with aunts, bossy creatures with distinctly fishy or froggy characteristics. But the first book I really remember was *Babar*, and what stuck was not the rescue, or the dressing up and standing on two legs, but the death of the mother. I read it sitting in the headmistress's room after I'd fallen over in the playground and banged my lip badly. I was waiting for my own mother to come and take me home, and I can remember being surprised that there could possibly be any story to follow such an event as the death of one's mother; nothing could possibly be significant again, could it?

A little later, when I was six, I read *Ballet Shoes*, by Noel Streatfield. There must have been lots I couldn't have understood, but I did know all about being one of three children, and these were orphans too: orphans were interesting when your own parents had callously abandoned you to school. I wanted to know what happened to them, and, especially, how they got on in their motherless condition, which was the incentive for reading and then rereading the book. To reread is to be reassured: yes, it is always the same, Posy does join the ballet company; Petrova is rescued from the theatre world and can slide under the car with a happy smile and a spanner; poverty is staved off. I felt the Fossil poverty acutely, not, at that time, understanding that people who can employ a cook and maid very probably won't starve.

Books balanced life satisfactorily, especially with regard to time and authority. Life meant an endless wait: for Christmas, for the party, for tea. If you read fast you could get your hero out of a sticky situation and back home with the treasure before lights out. My children get a good deal of their fiction from television, which is not as satisfactory in that it is under the control of the programme planners. The Bionic Man has to wait until Tuesday; you can't have him before breakfast, or on a sunny day half-way up a tree in the garden. Authority was more safely questioned and flouted in books than it could be by me, the youngest of the family and in no doubt as to my place at the bottom of the pecking order. Fairy stories generously provided a larger number of youngest children who got the Prince or the Golden Goose, or who chopped off the Ogre's head. Lucy is also the youngest, and she tends to associate her inferior physical capability not only with youth but with her female status. A greedy child, she enjoys Hansel and Gretel because of the ginger-bread house, but gets profound satisfaction from the fact that it is Gretel who rescues her captive elder brother by stuffing the witch into the oven.

Lucy also enjoys Beatrix Potter's *Tale of Squirrel Nutkin*, perhaps for related reasons. All the other little squirrels take presents to Old Brown the owl, so that he will let them gather nuts on Owl Island. Nutkin is 'excessively impertinent', brings no presents, has no manners, and taunts 'Old Mr B' with riddles. He spends all day playing games while the others are assiduously gathering, and on the very last day gets more and more daring, provokes Old Brown beyond endurance, leaps right on to the owl's head, and ends up in his waistcoat pocket.

'This looks like the end of the story; but it isn't.' Just as Old Brown holds him up by the tail, ready to skin him, Nutkin pulls so hard that his tail breaks, and he escapes. 'And to this day, if you meet Nutkin up a tree and ask him riddles, he will throw sticks at you, and stamp his feet and scold . . .' The riddles and the pictures please, but the story really

5

works as a demonstration of How Far To Go with authority. The Island is Old Brown's, so the trees are under his control. He has to be placated with moles and honey and beetles. Nutkin seems to me to be having a debate with him, treating him as a sleepy god whose limits have to be redefined. I always enjoy reading the story, and Lucy curls up tighter and tighter as the impertinence increases. The satisfaction of the ending confirms power, but it also says something about the possibility, not without danger, of treating it irreverently.

Another parent figure has turned up in Enid Blyton's *The Magic Faraway Tree*. This poor lady, provider of my early staple diet, has suffered wholesale condemnation, some of it certainly justified – the plots and characters in the 'Five' and 'Secret Seven' and 'Mystery' series are almost indistinguishably conventional. In some of the stories for younger children, however, she allowed her imagination to run loose, opening all sorts of possibilities, like magic glue that you can paint on bubbles to turn them into balloons. In *The Magic Faraway Tree* the children encounter Mr Changeabout who is genial, good natured and hospitable. But the moment they won't sit down when they are told to do so, the box of chocolates he offered contains only stones, and he himself turns into a screaming, threatening ogre. I don't think Enid Blyton was making a conscious psychological point, but the incident reproduces vividly the bewilderment and fear that children experience when faced with unpredictable adult behaviour, when privilege is arbitrarily withdrawn or a careless action is punished disproportionately. In her 'realistic' stories the young heroes don't suffer from normal apprehension (it is the mark of an oik or a cad to cringe and flee), but the 'real' villains have to be unrealistic in their behaviour, or they could not be defeated: they are cut-out monsters, set up to be knocked down. In fantasy they can be genuinely frightening, and the fear itself can be recognized and explored creatively.

It has been noticeable that nowadays children's stories admit more disturbing elements than they have done for the last fifteen years or so. Fairy stories which had been rewritten to allow wolves to run away and wicked stepmothers to retire to the country have appeared again in their original form, boiling oil and all. There are even new stories which show that justice does not always prevail, as in *The Cat and Mouse who Shared a House*. In this story the greedy cat tricks the kind and domesticated mouse and eats up all their winter store of butter. When the mouse finds out and reproaches her, she eats the mouse as well. When we read this story to Nicholas he let out a shout of outrage and burst into tears. It clearly cut across the pattern set up by his other source of cat/mouse behaviour, *Tom and Jerry*, where however antisocial the actions of the two animals, neither of them gets killed.

It is exceptional, though, that a picture book should have such an uncompromising ending. Danger and treachery are dealt with less disturbingly in Catherine Storr's *Clever Polly and the Stupid Wolf*. My children have never asked how a big black wolf can be allowed to walk about the town, dress up as Father Christmas or ride on a bus. They accept him as a normal part of Polly's life, and also that he is governed by the same rules – that he can only eat her if the cherry stone pattern comes out right, that he can't pounce on her if she's touching wood. The stories seem to relate to that self-testing phase which almost eagerly postulates beastliness under the bed, and which makes Lucy jump over all the lines in the paving stones on the way home even though she does not know, as I did, A. A. Milne's poem which triumphantly calls out:

'Bears! Just look at me stepping in all these squares!'

My parents looked on stories in much the same way as we tend to regard television, as pleasurable but a bit of a waste of time. Non-fiction was held to be more profitable and likely to fit you for real life; though, on the other hand, books of any kind were quiet and sucked up the endless know-it-all arguments. I read obsessively, addictively. I think, now, that my parents were right in a way; because I read so much I learned to live at second hand, vicariously adopting the enthusiasms of fictional characters where feasible. Perhaps the years of ballet can be traced back to Posy, child-prodigy. I think this is why Arthur Ransome didn't go down well – I knew that the Walkers and Blacketts of this world had no time for the likes of me, and so I gave up before bookreading, story-writing Dick and Dorothea showed up. I regret it for myself, retrospectively, and see this as one of several cases where gentle pressure to persevere would have benefited me. Perhaps a reading adult would have stiffened the rather pulpy diet provided by the local library. We did have a copy of *Palgrave's Golden Treasury*, and I learned a number of the poems by heart, and drifted around the garden intoning 'Fair Daffodils, we weep to see thee fade away so soon'. Poetry offered different satisfaction from fiction, more sensuous, more important: it had to be important, those few words surrounded by all that blank paper. Nicholas's favourite bedtime reading at three and a half was *Excelsior*, not a poem I would have included automatically in an anthology for small children. He liked the mysterious cry uttered in a variety of moods, and the incomprehensible mountain climax. For me, too, that was the other function of literature. If on the one hand it enabled me to identify with people like me, on the other hand it offered an idea of transcendence, otherness, of beauty and mystery. It also provided values other than those of my parents and teachers; it gave me choice, it undermined assumption. But that was later. I can't now remember learning to read, and my own children are vague about the process, recent though it is for them. They still like illustrations, of course, but they are weaned from pictures. Whereas, to start with, words were a bridge that connected and described the things they saw, now it is the words themselves that release pictures and sounds and ideas and emotions inside their heads.

Notes

MITGUTSCH, Ali (1972) *Busy Busy World* Collins

BANNERMAN, Helen (1954) *The Story of Little Black Sambo* Chatto

KERR, Judith (1972) *The Tiger Who Came to Tea* Collins (1973) Armada Picture Lions

MILNE, A. A. (1926) *Winnie the Pooh* Methuen

CARROLL, Lewis (1970) *Alice in Wonderland* Puffin

JAN, Isabelle (1969) *On Children's Literature* English version Catherine Storr (ed) Allen Lane

BRUNHOFF, Jean de (1934) *The Story of Babar* Methuen

STREATFEILD, Noel (1970) *Ballet Shoes* Puffin

POTTER, Beatrix (1903) *The Tale of Squirrel Nutkin* Warne

BLYTON, Enid (1971) *The Magic Faraway Tree* Dean

HURLIMANN, Ruth (1974) *The Cat and Mouse who Shared a House* Longman (1976) Armada

STORR, Catherine (1967) *Clever Polly and the Stupid Wolf* Puffin

Comment

During the last decade teachers, parents and librarians have become increasingly concerned about the content of children's books, in particular reading schemes, textbooks and fiction; sex-role stereotypes, middle class bias and racial prejudice all contribute to the presentation of unacceptable models. This is documented and discussed in Mary Hoffman's chapter, 'Print and Prejudice in Britain Today' in Zimet, S. *Print and Prejudice* Hodder & Stoughton, chapter 10. In **Learning to Read and the TV Narrative,** Judy Keiner questions the assumption that short narrative fictions, as first reading material, will provide children with sufficient interest or stimulus to cope with the laborious task of decoding, which is involved in early reading; she proposes a serious reappraisal of the kind of material we offer to beginning readers in the context of a television-dominated era. She advocates more adventurous approaches to initial reading which pay attention to children's interest in non-fiction. She exemplifies the gulf between the visual literacy fostered by TV and the decoding skills required for reading books. She suggests that the dependence of initial reading material on narrative fiction has serious limitations – and that the assumption that children are predominantly interested in fiction totally neglects important areas of their experience. Among the alternatives she suggests, is a non-fiction and documentary-based approach which could be initiated by teachers and involve children, their parents and various outside agents in producing reading material which comes closer to their own concerns.

2 Learning to read and the TV narrative
Judy Keiner

A few years back now, Neil Postman wrote a very provocative piece called 'The Politics of Reading'. He began by suggesting that teachers of reading, far from being neutral educators, were in effect a sinister politically motivated group. He argued that, in an age when television and other mass media offered readily accessible ways of disseminating information, the insistence on mediating academically respectable knowledge through print amounted to a repressive system of thought control. Far from reading being a liberatory form, the actual reading offered to school pupils inevitably offered a reactionary and conservative account of history, politics and the possibility of social change.

Now Postman was self-confessedly writing a provocative polemic, intended to sting teachers into developing some theory of why and for what purpose schools teach reading. His article seemed too readily to make the assumption of an impending technological takeover; that simply because new electronic technology was in existence, it would supersede and abolish the need for reading. He ignored the question of whether the new technologies would offer anything like the accessibility and openness to control by groups and individuals that print can. The virtual monopoly of films, video and prepared cassette production by multinational conglomerates does nothing to alter reactionary accounts being offered to children, whether of other people's pasts or their own future. But what few writers since Postman have developed further is the whole question of whether the teaching of reading needs to be rethought in the context of a television-dominated era.

Firstly, what sort of content do we offer children in their initial readers? And what sort of justification do we give for the content we do offer?

Almost all first reading material now in use is based on offering short *narrative fictions* to children. I think it would be fair to say that the idea that initial reading should take the form of little complete stories is hardly questioned either by devisers of reading schemes or teachers. If you look back at the history of methods of teaching reading in this country, about which relatively little has been written, you will find two predominant approaches to the selection of material for initial readers developing from the middle of the eighteenth century, as drives towards mass literacy get under way. Firstly, there is the approach through motivation by reward and pleasure; little entertaining stories and attractive woodcuts are seen as important. Secondly, an emphasis on moral instruction produces initial readers which read as admonitions and warnings:

> Boys and girls must not play all day. So comb your hair and wash your hands, and come to school. Stand up in your class; you can read some words now . . .[1]

In the light of examples like the one above, it was hardly surprising that enlightened approaches to the teaching of reading came to reject overt moralism and embrace the conception of materials designed to offer the pleasure of meeting fiction. This tradition of didactic moral and religious instruction seems, with very few exceptions, to have represented the beginning and end of non-fiction content in initial reading material up to the present day. The possibilities of non-fiction offering content which could relate to matters which children themselves are deeply interested in or involved with seem not to have been developed. Nor, of course, is dogmatic moralism in initial readers confined to the primers of nineteenth-century capitalism. I remember being shown an early socialist reader complete with picture of bloated capitalist; it is a tradition which seems to have informed the making of some Soviet initial readers even today. But it is important to remember that discussions of reading material for the education of the poor in the late eighteenth and nineteenth centuries readily proposed the need for teaching reading as a form of political control in the very terms that now seem so outrageous and controversial when expressed by Postman in 1970.

There is a sense in which both the reading-for-pleasure through narrative approach and the moral-and-religious instruction approach were, at least originally, intended to counter the purposes for which the working-class movements of that time saw the teaching of reading – that is the concept of teaching reading from the start as a way of acquiring socially powerful knowledge and of reflecting the social situation of the reader. It is an approach to reading symbolized in the nineteenth-century colophon which the East London-based Centerprise group uses on its publications: 'knowledge is power' as a slogan is blazoned round an image of a printing press which has just printed out the words 'liberty of the press'.

The point I am making, however, is that historically, there is some justification for Postman's charges about the methods and purposes for which reading is taught in state education. But how relevant is such history to the contemporary prevalence of narrative fictions as initial reading matter? Unlike the ideologists and commentators of the eighteenth and nineteenth centuries, most teachers today see education as a neutral process; the teaching of reading may be examined for its potential sexist or racist content, but rarely is the significance of making narrative fiction the base analysed.

It could be argued (and it would have to be a polemical argument rather than a demonstrable case) that the concentration on fiction as initial reading material is one of the ways in which teachers avoid facing the choices that many educators of the nineteenth century seemed rather more ready to put on the agenda. Choosing to offer simple fictions avoids more political questions of what content is to be offered to young children for what purposes. Teachers can avoid decisions as to whether they are preparing children for membership of a docile workforce, or whether they wish to give them 'knowledge for power' – or some sort of eclectic and contradictory combination of the two.

Most reading teachers would of course be outraged at the suggestion that they're avoiding some sort of necessary choice; they're convinced that their work is apolitical and that it's essential that they retain that neutrality. Yet fierce political battles are now being fought about the future of education – and the content and format of the teaching of reading and the context of those activities in school are central to those battles.

In a very searching critique of some of the most cherished tenets of good child-centred progressive teaching, Rachel Sharp and Antony Green suggested that the constant concentration on celebrations of traditional festivals, royal occasions and situations which invite the pupil to place her/himself anywhere but in her/his own time and place are manifestations of what they take to be the characteristic romantic radical conservatism of progressive primary education. That is of course every bit as provocative an interpretation as Postman's, if not more so, since it suggests more strongly than did Postman the lack of a viable alternative in current conceptions of mass education. Stories which never look beyond the admittedly important symbolic psyche of pupils, or the immediate situation in the family have a limitation which needs to be questioned and scrutinized.

But I want as much as anything to question the underlying assumption that such offerings do actually motivate young children or provide them with the excitement and stimulus to cope with the laborious and un-rewarding process of decoding which early reading involves.

Two years ago I wanted to show some students what the reality of the learning-to-read experience offers for the television-oriented child, since I was unable to shake their apparently rooted conviction that, given a 'good' story to read, any child worth her salt would prefer it to the more 'trashy' offerings of television. With the help of some colleagues I began to record examples of the most educationally despised TV offerings – television commercials. Having watched the way in which they not only rooted young children (and myself) to the screen, I was also very inter-ested in the significance of the way in which children would show a great facility for remembering TV commercials and chanting them aloud. They were absorbed so easily into that great repertoire of children's traditional playground chants and games recorded by the Opies; yet you have never found them chanting bits of 'Janet and John', or even the Breakthrough readers.

I also had a tape of an eight-year-old reading aloud a simple work of fiction; I wanted to compare what his experience might be with the experience of watching a run of the sort of TV commercials that are directed at children.

I thought it was important to look more closely at the importance of comparing book-reading with television-watching as a visual experience as well as a verbal decoding experience.

Opposite page 18, then, are a representation of two minutes of fictional narrative as a means of learning to read compared with the experience of watching two minutes of TV commercials. On one side you see a 'story-board' of the TV commercial and its text; on the other an image of the book page as if a TV camera were showing what the child would see, with the transcript of the child reading beneath it.

What to make of this comparison? Does it prove anything? Firstly, if you look at the representation of the reading, it's a record of what a very painful and unrewarding experience learning to read can be, even to attentive and caring adults. The sheer slowness of the process, let alone the number of miscues suggests that it's very unlikely that the child is getting very much meaning or enjoyment out of what he's doing.

Of course, setting up the commercials for comparison isn't to be seen as a simple experiment comparing two equivalent experiences. We don't know what a child would get out of the TV commercials shown here. Yet look at what this set of quite unexceptional commercials does offer in terms of narratives. It's a variety of little complete fictions, attractively presented and enhanced with complex and sophisticated images; three can be completed in the time it takes a child to plough through one page of a book. The narrative formats include a mix of fantasy and reality characters (the Frosties commercial); a moral lesson worthy of the nineteenth-century didactic tradition (the road safety commercial); a letter-as-narrative (the Maltesers commercial) and a complete-the-slogan game which includes word plays on traditional proverbs (the Topic commercial – not shown here).

The question which the comparison poses most strongly for me is whether in this context – and it is the context that most children live in – initial reading based on narrative fictions of the type you find in almost all schemes, sets up reading from the start as a form which offers 'less of the same' compared with other sources of fiction: adults, other children, radio and television. Not, you will note, an argument for ceasing to teach reading, rather an argument for rethinking what alternatives there might be.

By now, I realize that the comparisons I've made, my readiness to suggest that children might be getting something valuable out of TV commercials, will have raised hackles in all ideological directions. Of course, I wouldn't suggest that, just because TV commercials put narrative fictions over well, that that function can in future be left to them. The course of a few hours' viewing offers an extraordinary range of narrative types and formats; from lengthy adventures (old films, etc.), to fantasies (cartoons) and semi-documentaries. In fact, as the German critic Enzensberger pointed out in a very perceptive analysis of the implications of the new media, the TV format effectively abolishes the distinction between fiction, perceived as the invention of a single 'creative' mind, and documentary, made as a collective and collaborative act. It will not escape devotees of the oral tradition that the abolition of the distinction re-establishes the situation in which all the great stories and rhymes that we know through such anthologies as those of Grimm and Halliwell were created. The collective creation of mixed fiction/documentary tales has in any case continued unbroken as *oral* tradition in working-class culture, through its songs and jokes.

I would also question the assumption of a clear moral dichotomy between fictions offered in the cynical commercialism of a TV sales pitch and fictions offered in the wholesome world of 'good' children's literature. The main reason why children's readers are always fiction-based is that they're based on the idea that children are motivated only by things being made 'fun'. So, ironically, children are thereby perceived as seekers after fantasy, gratification and amusement, just as TV advertisers are said to perceive adults. Somehow, fictionalizing matters which are of interest or importance to children is thought to make them more accessible. It may be that this is a rather patronizing view of children, which trivializes their capacity for response and experience. Obviously reading and identifying with a fictional situation can certainly give 'knowledge for power' – but it's an approach which can hardly work for the beginning reader like the one featured in this article; all it can do is teach him that television is a much better resource than books.

Thinking about learning to read in the context of the TV narrative means rethinking both the material we offer to initial readers and the way we use TV in schools. I think we need to look more closely at the work of the nineteenth-century radical groups for whom 'knowledge for power' was the principle on which they based their approach to the teaching of the working class. Fortunately, there's been an increasing amount of work emerging in the last few years from such historians as Richard Johnson, Brian Simon, Barbara Taylor and the group based on *History Workshop Journal*. The interesting thing for me is that working-class radical educators, Owenite feminists, etc., did *not* set themselves up in imitation of or in competition with musical halls, popular novelists and other contemporary popular entertainment forms. It was the Salvation Army which did that. The nineteenth-century radical educators seem to have had much more of a principle of knowledge-for-need, and uncompromisingly offered subject matter based on politics, economics, technology – a very different assumption about the nature of what working-class groups and women will respond to, from all the usual stuff about 'deprived' and 'deficient' home backgrounds which are still assumed to be a barrier to the acquisition of literacy in so much educational literature. It was precisely when Working Men's Clubs turned their emphasis away from knowledge-for-power and towards entertainment for the workers that they began to lose their real radical potential.

Clearly, there's no question of simply transposing the radical-didactic approach of nineteenth-century adult groups onto the situation of learning to read in the state primary schools of the late 1970s.

But the principle of setting out with an idea of teaching children to see literacy as a means of acquiring knowledge for power is one that can be explored further. It means identifying what children are avid to learn about and communicate with others. I want to emphasize the potential of developing a more non-fiction and documentary-based approach. Most children are deeply interested in the lives of the adults they live with, not only in the home situation, but in the work they do; children ask for such accounts over and over again at home. The DES green paper 'Education in Schools' calls for schools to relate more closely to the world of work. In the curious Civil-Service speak of the green paper it comes out as an aim to teach children 'properly to esteem the vital role . . . of industry and commerce' and a few vague gestures of support for the Schools Council's Industry project. Such a suggestion is hardly adequate as a response to children's interest in work and working lives. It is not common for schools to involve parents or other interested adults in producing books for children to read which talk about their work or their personal history though it is increasingly the case that WEA groups up and down the country are producing cheap books on working lives, following the example of Centerprise. It would not be difficult for a school to produce a series of readers on a similar basis, or for a group of interested primary school teachers based on a local teachers' centre to approach the Schools Council for a grant to do a local curriculum project on the production of readers based on the lives of people children know.

There are also one or two useful models in the shape of commercially published books which interested teachers could use as the basis for developing their own approach to non-fiction readers. The Cox and Golden series on workers – *Textile Worker, Hospital Worker, Building Worker*, etc., shows the possibilities of using photo-sequence plus descriptive text to show the relation of working women and men to the process of production. Another related approach is Anita Harper and Christine Roche's *How We Work*, which is based on drawn sequences of people at work and particularly sets out to show how some people (women) have two jobs and some people have one. In my view, it is important in producing readers for children on the topic of work to try to seek out material which does not simply reinforce existing inequalities and stereotypes within work situations. While it may be true that there are relatively few women or blacks in highly skilled manual or managerial jobs, teachers who want to show the possibilities of change or alternatives to the usual conceptions of who does what should be able to widen their range of material by working with local or national ethnic group associations, feminist and single-parent groups and trades councils as well as chambers of commerce and local firms. It goes without saying that the process of producing such materials for pupils could be one in which parents, other interested adults and teachers can potentially work in a more genuinely equal partnership than the ones that so often emerge from more usual forms of PTA activity.

That children are often passionately motivated to learn about the material world is clear enough to any parent or teacher who has been pestered with question after question. As Gwen Dunn suggests in her study of young children's responses to television, *The Box in the Corner*, children acquire complex technical information from their viewing of TV, much of it from programmes not designed for them. While Gwen Dunn, unfortunately in my view, seems to take for granted the idea that some children have 'deprived' and 'deficient' families, and that the role of television and the school alike should be to promote the institution of the family, her study is at least one of the few to make clear how much even very young children do learn and remember through TV. Although she quotes with approval the education officer who suggests that schools without colour TV are themselves depriving children, it is unfortunately still the exception for colour TV to be used in schools – or for children to be encouraged to watch programmes while at school, other than ones specially designed as educational fodder for their age range. It seems to me that the convention of readers as continuous-linear narrative is also one that needs challenging. Again, the evidence of the display of TV commercials suggest that the visual literacy of children is able to cope with much more sophisticated formats. I don't yet recall coming across a discussion of the potential of the format of the Christmas Annual as an approach to initial reading material. Yet the Annual is the one type of book that children actually seem to demand, whether they come from a book-oriented home or not. Such flexible formats could be used by teachers to present children with the sorts of reading material the adults they know have to read – simple labels, captions and instructions, as well as jokes and traditional rhymes. It may be that encyclopaedias and the *Guinness Book of Records*, with their brief gobbets of didactic content have more to offer the initial reader than the full-blown story. And that even the despised comic is a potentially valuable bridge between the skills of visual literacy acquired through TV and the decoding skills needed for reading books.

Of course, it may seem that I am ignoring the child-centred linguistic approach to initial reading for which 'Breakthrough to Literacy' is justly famous. After all 'Breakthrough' supports its initial literacy approach with readers based on children's own language and interests – and these seem to come out as just as the narrative fictions which I've tried to question. I do think that it *is* an excellent approach; yet I am sceptical about whether those readers really do represent children's 'real interests' – or whether they are based on what children know they're supposed to talk to teachers about. It always interested me that, because Piaget chose never to examine children's concepts of politics or the social and economic world, educational discourse seems to have made the assumption that children just don't have them. So it should be revealing to see what research being done by Gella Skouras and Janet Holland in Professor Basil Bernstein's Sociological Research Unit comes up with; they are engaged in investigating young children's and adolescents' conceptions of the social division of labour where a few years ago his assistants were asking children to make up stories about pictures. My feeling about the Breakthrough readers and materials is that they reflect the interests of the creators and the preconceptions of teachers about what children are tuned in to; the now blatantly obvious sexism of some of the booklets is evidence of that, as Glenys Lobban's analysis in *Sexism in Children's Books* suggested.

Finally, it is worth trying to find out more about the experiences of those schools and teachers' centres where work is going on to develop a more adventurous approach to initial readers. A recent issue of the ILEA Centre for Language in Primary Education's *Language Matters* featured an article by Bernard Ashley, a Newham teacher, about the use of a small printing press to produce readers written by the older children for the younger ones. Another East London teacher, Celia Deakin of Princess May Infants' School, has produced readers based on photo-sequences of the children themselves at work and play. But as yet, there seems to be no readily available forum for the dissemination of information about such projects. Perhaps no institution is better placed than the Open University, with its Post-experience courses, to undertake that task. It should after all be second to none in its appreciation of the relationship between learning to read and the TV narrative.

Note

1   Chalmers pp. 31–2

Additional reading and information

Further reading:
1   Background articles
ASHLEY, Bernard (1977) 'Children Writing for Children' in *Language Matters* Vol. 2 No. 2 Centre for Language in Primary Education
CHALMERS, G. S. (1976) *Reading Easy, 1800–1850* London: The Broadsheet King
DUNN, Gwen (1977) *The Box in the Corner* London: Macmillan
ENZENSBERGER, H. M. (1976) 'Constituents of a Theory of the Media' in Enzensberger, H. M. *Raids and Reconstructions* London: Pluto Press; also

in McQuail, D. (ed.) (1972) *Sociology of Mass Communications* London: Penguin

HMSO (1977) *Education in Schools* HMSO

HOYLES, M. (1977) 'History and Politics of Literacy' in Hoyles, M. (ed.) *The Politics of Literacy* London: Writers and Readers Publishing Co-operative

JOHNSON, R. (1976/7) 'Really Useful Knowledge' *Radical Education* Nos 7 and 8

KOHL, Herbert (1974) *Reading, How to* London: Penguin

LOBBAN, Glenys (1976) *Sexism in Children's Books; Facts Figures and Guidelines* Writers and Readers Publishing Cooperative

POSTMAN, Neil (1972) 'The Politics of Reading' in Keddie, N. '*Tinker, tailor . . .*' London: Penguin

ROSEN, H. (ed.) (1976) *Language and Literacy in Our Schools* London: Institute of Education

SIMON, B. (1965) *Education and the Labour Movement* London: Lawrence & Wishart

SIMON, B. (1974) *The Politics of Education and Reform 1920–1940; Studies in the History of Education* Lawrence & Wishart

SHARP, R. and GREEN, A. (1974) *Education and Social Control* London Routledge & Kegan Paul

2   Source materials on work, working class, autobiographies, etc.

COX, S. and GOLDEN, R. (1975)

Car Worker	*Hospital Worker*
Building Worker	*Railway Worker*
Textile Worker	*Mining Worker*

London: Kestrel Books

HARPER, A. and ROCHE, C. (1977) *How We Work* London: Kestrel Books

Centerprise Publications: 136 Kingsland High Street, London E8

Working Lives: Vol. 1 1905–1945
             Vol. 2 1945–1977

BARNES, Ron: A Licence to Live

KNIGHT, Doris: Millfields Memories

LOWE, Rose: Daddy Burtt's for Dinner

NEWTON, Arthur: Years of Change

Readers (large print)
George and the Bus
The Good Old Bad Old Days
Hackney Half Term Adventure

Other working-class autobiographies:
HALL, Edith (1977) *Canary Girls and Stockpots* WEA Luton Branch, WEA Office, Barnfield College, Luton, Beds.

NOAKES, Daisy *The Town Beehive – A Young Girl's Lot* Brighton 1910–34

Bristol People's Publishing Project *Bristol As We Remember It* Bristol PPP, c/o ACCA University Settlement, Barton Hill, Bristol 5

5

VOICE OVER   Hey, Tony, fancy a spell in goal?

TONY   Why, sure, Colin, but first some Kellogg's Frosties

10

— golden flakes of corn with their own toasted in sugar frosting —

VOICE OVER & TONY   They're g-r-r-r-eat!

15

TONY   Take all the time you need . . .

SOUND OFF   (*Ball shooting at goal, ricocheting off*)

20

CHILDREN   (*Cheers*)

25

VOICE OVER   Thanks, Tony—you're great!

30   TONY   Well, at least I saved my Frosties

Reading time in seconds

Just then their younger son,
Arthur, called from the bedroom he

CHILD   *that's hard . . .*
                  . . . Alf

Just then their younger son,
Arthur, called from the bedroom he

. . red *or something . . .*
. . Alf called from the bedroom

shared with his brother Stanley in their
New York home.
   'Hey! Come and look! Hey!'

He sss . . shout — said — um, no . . .

shared with his brother Stanley in their
New York home.
   'Hey! Come and look! Hey!'

oh god! . . um . . shouted with his . .

shared with his brother Stanley in their
New York home.
   'Hey! Come and look! Hey!'

brother—brother . . s . . Stanley

SOUND	(*Traffic noise*) (*Horn blast*)
VOICE OVER	Hey, what . . .

do you think you're doing?

JOE B	Come back here. I tell you what — if you go one like that, you could . . .

be in big trouble. Now look. When you get to the kerb stop. OK?

Make sure the road is absolutely clear. That's part of the Green Cross code. Now let's see you . . .

do it properly. That's better.

Take it from me — be smart — be safe.

Reading time in seconds

shared with his brother Stanley in their
New York home.
   'Hey! Come and look! Hey!'

       in the new York home. 'Hey
       come and look. Hey' . . . . .

shared with his brother Stanley in their
New York home.
   'Hey! Come and look! Hey!'

ADULT   *Good*

CHILD   *Oh, god* . . . . .

Mr and Mrs Lambchop were both very
much in favour of politeness and careful
speech.

       Mr and Mrs Lambchop were both

Mr and Mrs Lambchop were both very
much in favour of politeness and careful
speech.

       very much in . . . .
       . . . .

Mr and Mrs Lambchop were both very
much in favour of politeness and careful
speech.

       for of . . . .

VOICE OVER	Dear Maltesers, Whilst I agree with you that the coating of smooth milk chocolate on Maltesers is absolutely . .

10

SOUND	(*Satellite buzzing*)
VOICE OVER	er, delicious

15

and whilst I realize that you could hardly make Maltesers more . .

SOUND	(*Crunching*)

20

VOICE OVER	. . . crisp and crunchy than they are, I would like to point out that Maltesers' incredibly . .
	light airy centres can cause a few problems in this day and age. Mmmm.

25

SOUND	(*Satellite buzzing*)

30
NEW VOICE OVER	Maltesers. The chocolates with the superlight centres

Reading time in seconds

'Hay is for horses, Arthur, not people,' Mr Lambchop said as they entered the bedroom.

politeness and careful speech, hay is
.. for horses .. nn .. *that's wrong* ..

'Hay is for horses, Arthur, not people,' Mr Lambchop said as they entered the bedroom.

ADULT (*prompting*)   'Hay is' ..

'Hay is for horses, Arthur, not people,' Mr Lambchop said as they entered the bedroom.

CHILD   'hay is for horses' ...

'Hay is for horses, Arthur, not people,' Mr Lambchop said as they entered the bedroom.

.. *what's that?* ......

'Hay is for horses, Arthur, not people,' Mr Lambchop said as they entered the bedroom.

not people, Mr Lambchop said

3 Useful organizations, journals and sources of information and help
Schools Council, 160 Great Portland Street, London W1 has guidelines and information on how to apply for a grant for a local development project.
Community Relations, 15 Bedford Street, London WC2
History Workshop Journal, 1 Rose Lane, Oxford, OX1 4DT
Centre for Language in Primary Education, Sutherland Street, London, SW1 – publishes *Language Matters.*
Ebury English Centre, Ebury Bridge, Sutherland Street, London SW1 has a wide range of useful materials including printed booklets of pupils' stories.
Centre for Urban Educational Studies, 34 Aberdeen Park, London N5 is developing new multicultural reading materials. Also publishes a journal *Junction.*
Oral History Society, c/o Mary Githing, University of Essex, Wivenhoe publishes *Oral History Journal,* also has members interested in developing community-based oral history work in schools.
Spare Rib, 27 Clerkenwell Close, London EC1 regularly publishes articles on current feminist organizations, women working in manual trades, etc.
Equal Opportunities Commission, Overseas House, Quay Street, Manchester M3 3HN keeps a watching brief, among other things, on treatment of sexes in education and should be able to give information on current research and developments.
Photography Workshop, 152 Upper Street, London N1 is useful to contact for sources and advice on photographic material for educational projects.
Childrens Rights Workshop, Writers & Readers Publishing Cooperative, 14 Talacre Road, London NW5 keeps an up-to-date watch on current children's books.
Centre for the Teaching of Reading, 29 Eastern Avenue, Reading – the University of Reading's specialist centre for the teaching of reading has one of the most comprehensive collections in the country of current materials for the teaching of reading.
Society for Education in Film and Television, 29 Old Compton Street, London W1 publishes *Screen Education* which occasionally has articles on TV images and primary education.
British Film Institute, Educational Advisory Service, 81 Dean Street, London W1 has advisers who would be interested to work with teachers on developing the use and study of television images with young children.
Women's Research and Resources Centre, 27 Clerkenwell Close, London EC1 has information on current feminist research and organizations and publishes a newsletter.

Comment

Judy Keiner offers one way of moving away from the stifling effect of narrative restricted by a conventional view of the world. Her proposal that we should make use of children's actual experience will be taken up later, especially in the chapter written by Harold Rosen.

Learning to Read and the TV Narrative has presented the possibility of children being diverted from narrative to reading that relates exclusively to the world around them. They may in the process be able to understand that world more effectively and be in a position to use literacy to further democratic objectives. Their reading must be an integrated part of their daily experience in a way that makes sense of the society to which they belong.

Accepting the need to confront children with the realities of their own lives, we move on to a chapter by Ralph Lavender in which these realities are seen to be mediated through the narratives that we all create for ourselves. He is critical of education that favours factual retrieval to a disproportionate extent, claiming that we live by an internal 'brain fiction' that needs to be fed by relevant narrative experiences. He examines in particular the 'running away and getting lost story' and its many manifestations both in mythologies and in storybooks for children.

3 Living by fact or fiction
Ralph Lavender

Why lit why? [handwritten marginalia]

The psychologist, R. L. Gregory, may have been right when he said, writing about the science of fiction in 1974, that 'we may live more by fiction than by fact'.[1] If so, then his argument has important implications for the teaching of literacy and literature in schools. Education has almost always made fact appear more significant than fiction; assessments of children's performance in reading and other areas of the curriculum tend to concentrate on their ability to retrieve facts. The Bullock Report[2] pointed out how school book collections often concentrate on information books to the neglect of fiction.

Gregory's argument was that 'brain fiction' shows us alternative views of the world and courses of possible action in it, and that it plays an important part both in our perceptions and in intelligent behaviour. 'It is living by fiction which makes the higher organisms special.' Fiction frees us from being merely the subject of our own nervous systems, responding to a stream of stimuli applied from outside sources, 'from the tyranny of reflexes triggered by events'. His argument destroys that model of human conduct which is based on the simple idea of input and output, stimulus and response – that is, it brings about the collapse of the extreme behaviourist position. If Gregory's argument can be accepted, then the fictions we present to children, and which become a part of their own fictions, have to be seen as something very different from a comfortable story for the closing of the day – the quarter-past three polyfilla. For fiction lets us see alternative possible realities, to predict what might happen from what does happen, and therefore to change our reality and the reality in which we live.

This internal 'brain fiction' is what enables us to see and to understand our world. Frank Smith applies the psycholinguistic account of reading[3] to the whole field of human learning, and he argues that the child is like a scientist, constructing a series of hypotheses so as to make sense of the world. This is no different from the 'suppose' of the storyteller, and it is this very ability which enables the child to learn his language. 'The basic learning process of every human being involves the

Source: LAVENDER, R. (1977) 'Living by fact or fiction' *The Times Educational Supplement* 17 September: an expanded version commissioned by The Open University

experimental testing of cognitive hypotheses.'[4] Having formed a theory of the world in order to see and to understand that world, this is the world we live by and live in. Furthermore, this 'theory of the world in the head', as Smith calls it, which can be identified as the same thing as Gregory's 'brain fiction', is not open to inspection, only to introspection. We have, therefore, to take very largely on trust the effect that literature can have on the world we have constructed in our heads and in which we live. This, however, does not mean that there is nothing to be said about the part which literature can play in the child's cognitive, moral and affective development, but it does mean that we must accept the crucial importance of children's own 'storying' as a part of their fantasy lives in the business of building up this world picture. It also means that we should be looking around for some of the fictions we all tell ourselves at some time or another in our lives, and making use of them in order to give power to the teaching of literacy and literature, so that its effects will last.

It appears that one of these fictions we have all told ourselves, as children and probably as adults, too, is the story of running away and getting lost. In the beginning, the story is a moral one: if you run away, you will be punished since running away is an offence. In terms of moral development, of course, this is quite right and only to be expected: at this stage, all transgressors have to be punished, and preferably as permanently as possible. Hence, in the traditional story *Mr Miacca*, Tommy Grimes runs into the dire peril of being boiled and eaten up for supper by the bogeyman; he disobeyed, he was not a good boy, and he did go out into the streets. Beatrix Potter recognized the universality of this experience. Naughty Peter Rabbit goes into Mr McGregor's garden instead of picking blackberries with his sisters as instructed, and he is lucky to escape with his life.

In *Where the Wild Things Are*, the story of running away and getting lost is mixed with the fear of being abandoned – a new and rather later twist. The threat of punishment is sometimes omitted from a story, or else the threat against the escapee is somehow veiled, as it is here. 'That very night in Max's room a forest grew – and grew . . . until his ceiling hung with vines and the walls became the world all around.' Max is only sent as far as his bedroom, it is true, but that is far enough – he is still abandoned there. He answers a threat with a threat. The running away and getting lost story is also an appeal for security at this stage. Even if you do run away, you can always go back home afterwards, and your parents will still love you. Some children actually do it, rather than making a story about it, and their parents sometimes have to be reassured that this behaviour is not totally bizarre. In a recent case, a boy packed his case and went as far as the end of the road before he came back. His elder brother was scornful, saying, 'See, you didn't even get as far as buying an underground ticket, did you?' Max, then, is sent to bed without any supper for being wildly naughty. In the story he makes, he runs away to the land where the real wild things are – there is even a picture on the wall at the bottom of the stairs, when Max frightens the dog by jumping out on him in his wolf suit, it is 'by Max' and it shows a wild thing's head, a foretaste of what is to come. In the land where the wild things are, Max tames them with the magic trick of staring into all their yellow eyes without blinking once. They declare him king; and he orders a wild rumpus. To be able to quell all the bogeys with their roars and teeth and eyes and claws is no mean feat; it also helps if you can do it with a lordly gesture. And there is no king more supercilious than Max, even in his wolf suit. Who has not, at some time or other, wished to impress his powers upon the world? But after the rumpus, Max smells good things to eat, the king of all wild things 'was lonely and wanted to be where someone loved him best of all'. He returns home, and finds his supper waiting for him in his room, 'and it was still hot'. While he has been away, his mother has forgiven him. This is a very satisfactory resolution. The secret of the fascination which Sendak's story holds for children is that everything in it is instantly recognizable to their own 'brain fictions'. The pictures only seem to frighten adults.

Rosie in *Rosie's Walk* does not intend to escape, she just goes for a walk round the farmyard. There is a risk in that, too, of course; you cannot be too careful. Never once does she notice that a fox is following her; not once is the fox mentioned in the story. Some five-year-old children do not understand the fox's purposes, since the nature of foxiness still eludes them: they think he is Rosie's friend, not the archetypal villain, who is cunning, greedy and rapacious. He does a comic turn at every other opening of the book. He steps on the rake, he falls in the pond and the haycock, and he gets stung by the bees. Quite apart from what a child can learn from this book about a book as an object in fact, and about the nature of expectations aroused, there is the fiction that Rosie *also* got back 'in time for dinner'. In 'brain fiction' at least, a mealtime seems to be the moment for discovering that you are not lost, and have not been abandoned, that you have been forgiven, or that you have come home again. Perhaps one of the lessons of this story is that it is wise not to look behind too often. As well as being an appeal for security, a story may also be about how to test out the security you already have, and how to play with the fear.

This quality of reassurance and security is also to be found in Celia Berridge's *Run Away Danny*. Danny's family has moved to a block of flats instead of into the country as he wished, and now he has to go to a new school. But the boys there do not make him feel very welcome, and they will not allow him to join in their game of football. So he runs away (a form of running away not unknown in school, and sometimes acted out in reality) steals a bicycle and gets lost. In the end, however, everything comes right for him. He finds the country, which is actually a park, and exclaims 'millions of grass!' The pictures show a particular set of localities in Greenwich seen from a child's eye-level: but it is the universality of the experience which gives the book its greatest impact.

It is, of course, not surprising that many books for young children use the distancing device of animals to stand for human beings in this running away and getting lost story, as in *The Tale of Peter Rabbit*. Ping, in Marjorie Flack's book of that name, is a duck who leaves his family so that he will not get spanked for being the last over the bridge. Next morning, he has to face the world of the Yangtze River all on his own, and he, too, nearly pays for his rashness with his life. But the reassurance lies in the fact that the life force is such that no one has to face the world alone unless he is equipped for it.

If we begin to look in this way at how we can introduce young children to literature in terms of the recognizability of the experience, all the arguments about the paraphernalia surrounding that experience – whether they and the characters in the story live in a flat or in a detached five-bedroom house with a heated swimming-pool; whether it is dad or daddy; and whether it is fish and chips for dinner or escalope of veal cordon bleu – somehow begin to look like less important arguments.

What makes a story accessible to children is its recognizability in the face of their own experiences and in their own stories, in the face of their own 'brain fictions', rather than the recognizability of the material environment. The fault of too many books aimed at presenting the real environment is that they do not contain recognizable experiences – indeed, some contain no experiences at all, they are not 'stories'. Yet, 'we may live more by fiction than by fact'.

The child and the septuagenerian both have wide-open eyes through which to see and to understand the wonder of the world. For the one, it is still to come: for the other it is past; either still a prospect or still a retrospect. In between childhood and old age, these eyes are covered with a film and people forget that the recognizable experiences count for more than the material environment. Barbara Dockar-Drysdale, the child psychotherapist,[5] talks of the unsung songs and unpainted pictures and unwritten pieces of music most of us still have inside us from the golden age of our early years. We create imaginative, emotional inner worlds, populated by secret and private things, in order to make life tolerable. This is the 'brain fiction', the 'theory of the world in the head', created in what Winnicott called 'the third area'[6] a sort of penumbra cast between the shadows of the inner and the outer. Dockar-Drysdale, however, sees that some people have never had anything to sing about, or else they have forgotten that they ever had. She talks of 'frozen children', who are generalized from Kay in Andersen's *The Snow Queen*, with ice lodged in their hearts. These must be children who have not fully acquired the art of spectatorship, as Harding[7] and Britton[8] define it, where, freed from the necessity of action and participation in the affairs of the world, they are better able to find a harmony between in-here and out-there, between inner necessities and external demands, between what Bruner[9] has called 'the literalities of experience and the night impulses of life'.

24

In order to find this harmony, the running away and getting lost story later shifts its purpose towards responding to the pressure of problems: how to claim independence is one of them. Thus, in *Terry on the Fence* by Bernard Ashley, Terry runs away from home because he can no longer stand being nagged by his mother and bossed about by his elder sister. He falls into the clutches of a gang and he is forced to break into his own school and steal from the headmaster's study. He is terrified by the gang, and is finally caught on the fence by the police – astride a wooden one, not knowing which way to turn, undecided whether to do what he knows is wrong or not and how to balance the risks. There is a complexity of strands in this story; questions to do with honour and the taking of decisions are raised, and the relationship between Terry and the leader of the gang is sensitively drawn. The relevance of this book's theme to this article is manifest.

In Joan Robinson's *Charley*, the heroine claims *her* independence, and more besides, when she camps out in the henhouse behind the hedge at the bottom of her aunt's garden – neither of her aunts wants her anyway, and this one happens to be away on holiday. Through her experiences, Charley learns what it is to live in the world. And again, in the brilliantly witty *From the Mixed-up Files of Mrs Basil E. Frankweiler*, Claudia is bored by the monotony of life and she also knows that there are more beautiful and comfortable places than the corner of a field. She and her brother Jamie claim their independence by camping out for a week in the New York Metropolitan Museum of Art, and they are able to prove the provenance of a piece of sculpture by looking at the mixed-up files of the donor.

Naturally, this theme is one that extends from children's literature into adult literature, where it clearly becomes a part of what Northrop Frye[10] calls the one great story of literature, 'the loss and regaining of identity'. There are four generic plots deriving from this story: romance, tragedy, satire and comedy; and they are all expounded either through the cyclical construct of the seasons or through the dialectical construct of heaven against hell. The journey or quest is a romantic plot, although it may be partly comic; and it is part of the one great story, for no one undertakes an arduous journey without learning about himself and discovering something to do with his identity. Homer knew this: Odysseus knows himself fully when he gets back home and it is even in time for the feast of the suitors. An eleven-year-old boy was heard to say after hearing *The Odyssey*, 'It's a bit far-fetched isn't it?' The running away and getting lost of children's stories must always involve a journey of some kind. This is also why so many traditional stories are about journeys and quests. The story of the green children, first recorded by Ralph of Coggeshall in his medieval chronicle, is one of the more puzzling ones, because there is a question mark over whether the two children do actually find their true identities – one of them dies. The story of the golden goose, and *Henny-Penny*, and the miller and his son who take their donkey to market and do not know whose advice to follow – all are journeys, romantic plots about losing and finding parts of identity. Is not *Cinderella* a journey in three parts? Some of the unhappier traditional stories are about children *sent* away on journeys – *Hansel and Gretel* for instance. Once again, these stories appeal to children from the point of view of security and testing it out.

Understandings like these help us to see children's literature as a part of whole literature. Melville begins *Moby Dick*, thus: 'Call me Ishmael. Some years ago – never mind how long precisely – having little or no money in my purse, and nothing particular to interest me on shore, I thought I would sail about a little and see the watery part of the world.' This one great story stretches from C. S. Lewis's Narnia books and Ursula le Guin's trilogy that began with *A Wizard of Earthsea*, through *The Lord of the Rings* and much of Conrad and Henry James and so on into Russian literature. Some of Conrad's characters run away as a matter of honour; and in Henry James, expatriation amounts perhaps to the same thing. The poignancy of Russian literature is such, whether it is Goncharov's sardonic *Oblomov* or the passionate intensity of Dostoevsky, that the nearer the characters come to rediscovering their identities, the further away they are from actually accomplishing them. If, sometimes, they do run away or get lost, it is all in the cause of the kinds of 'brain fiction' that begin in Beatrix Potter and Maurice Sendak and the others.

Another form of the one great story is finding out how big you are in relation to the world round about you: you cannot know your identity unless you know your size and that of the world. There are many stories about giants and midgets: Jack of both beanstalk and giant-killing fame is one example, and Tom Thumb is another. More recently and less traditionally, there is *The Giant Alexander*. Some stories are about changes of size: there are shrink stories such as *Alice in Wonderland* and *The Shrinking of Treehorn*. Perhaps the most remarkable story about changes in size is *Gulliver's Travels*, which, if it appeals at all to children, does so because of the needs of their experience, and not on account of Swift's barbs. These stories are about the relationship between puniness and immensity, and those nascent powers which the child feels within himself may enable him to make his own mark on his world. At the beginning of his experience the child is sure of his unique quality; only later does he realize that he is a representative of common humanity as well, and it was this decline of egocentricity and growth of compassion to which Chukovsky, the Russian folklorist, referred as the goal of the storyteller.[11]

These themes serve to show that, even though there may be differences between literature for children and adult literature, in many more important respects there is continuity. They are similar literatures. After all, there is continuity between the stories children tell themselves and those adults tell themselves. Having understood the truth of this, it then becomes clear that children should have the chance of being 'taught literature', not because they have to be educated but because they are alive. And then it also becomes possible to avoid the Scylla of selling the literature known as 'kids' stuff' as if it were some sort of cheap offer which might even come with trading stamps; and the Charybdis of thinking about the 'real stuff' as literature for an élite.

The art of the storymaker is common to all, as is the urge to make and to receive story: writers, whether they be Sendak or Tolstoy, pluck from their experience what speaks to all men; the rest of us pluck from our experience what speaks mainly to ourselves alone. Barbara Hardy tells us:

> Nature, not art, makes us all story tellers. Daily and nightly we devise fictions and chronicles, calling some of them daydreams or dreams, some of them nightmares, some of them truths, records, reports, and plans. Some of them we call, or refuse to call, lies. Narrative imagination is a common human possession . . . [12]

William Labov, the American linguist, carried out stringent analyses of oral narratives given by Negro adolescents in New York, looking at them syntactically and semantically.[13] In the second analysis, he argues that an oral narrative must contain an orientation, giving the person or the time or the place or the situation; a complication, which skilled storytellers would be able to multiply; an evaluation, which betrays the storyteller's view and gives the story a point; and finally a resolution. Labov's work seems to give a linguistic confirmation to the literary critic's faith, because he is saying that there are fundamental narrative structures, and that we all understand and can operate these formal properties in the stories we receive and those we produce. The child who writes 'Once upon a time, they all lived happily ever after' has already acquired some of these structures.

If, then, literature can be taught with these kinds of understanding, children will come to recognize, gleam by gleam, that just as story is for living with and not being educated by, so is reading. Once they have seen themselves as readers, once they have become readers, and because they know what they can do with stories, they are much more likely to remain lifelong readers; and they will know that the learning is never over. If we want children to learn to read, we must begin where they are: and literature is where they are.

As teachers of literature with people of any age, it is by searching out the themes of all our storyings and by bringing to our teaching an awareness of the wholeness of our literature and what it is for, that we can best help our pupils to see and to understand their world, to construct 'a theory of the world in the head' through their 'brain fictions'. There will then be less danger that they will live by a theory received that they have not managed to make their own. As Carl Rogers puts it, 'Too much education means learning to live your life by other people's standards.'[14]

Notes

1 GREGORY, R. L. (1974) 'Psychology: Towards a Science of Fiction', *New Society*, 23.5.74. Also in Meek, M., Warlow, A., Barton, G. (1977) *The Cool Web* Bodley Head
2 DES (1975) *A Language for Life* (The Bullock Report) HMSO
3 SMITH, Frank (1971) *Understanding Reading*, Holt, Rinehart & Winston
4 SMITH, Frank (1975) *Comprehension and Learning* Holt, Rinehart & Winston Inc.
5 DOCKAR-DRYSDALE, Barbara (1968) *Therapy in Child Care* Longman
6 WINNICOTT, David (1971) *Playing and Reality* Tavistock
7 HARDING, D. W. (1963) *Experience into Words*, Chatto & Windus (1974) Penguin
8 BRITTON, James (1970) *Language and Learning* Allen Lane (1972) Penguin
9 BRUNER, Jerome (1962) *On Knowing: Essays for the Left Hand* Harvard University Press
10 FRYE, Northrop (1957) *Anatomy of Criticism* Princeton University Press
11 CHUKOVSKY, Kornei (1963) *From Two to Five* University of California Press
12 HARDY, Barbara (1975) *Tellers and Listeners* Athlone Press
13 LABOV, William and WALETZKY, Joshua (1970) 'Narrative Analysis: Oral Version of Personal Experience' in Helm, J. *Essays on Visual and Aural Narrations* University of Washington Press
14 ROGERS, Carl (1961) *On Becoming a Person* Constable

Children's books referred to in the text

JACOBS, Joseph (1968) 'Mr Miacca', in *English Fairy Tales* Bodley Head (1970) Puffin
POTTER, Beatrix (1902) *The Tale of Peter Rabbit* Warne
SENDAK, Maurice (1967) *Where the Wild Things Are*, Bodley Head (1970) Puffin
HUTCHINS, Pat (1968) *Rosie's Walk* Bodley Head (1970) Puffin
BERRIDGE, Celia (1975) *Runaway Danny* Deutsch
FLACK, Marjorie and WEISE, Kurt (1935) *The Story of Ping* Bodley Head (1970) Puffin
ANDERSEN, Hans (1975) *The Snow Queen* Hodder and Stoughton
ASHLEY, Bernard (1975) *Terry on the Fence* Oxford University Press
ROBINSON, Joan G. (1969) *Charley* Collins (1971) Armada Lions
KONIGSBURG, E. L. (1969) *From the Mixed-up Files of Mrs Basil E. Frankweiler* Macmillan (1974) Puffin
CROSSLEY-HOLLAND, Kevin (1966) *The Green Children* Macmillan
STOBBS, W. (1970) *The Golden Goose* Bodley Head
STOBBS, W. (1968) *Henny-Penny* Bodley Head
WILDSMITH, Brian (1969) *The Miller, the Boy and the Donkey* based on a fable by La Fontaine
PERRAULT, Charles (1970) *Cinderella* Bodley Head
GRIMM Brothers (1970) *Hansel and Gretel* Bodley Head

LE GUIN, Ursula (1971) *A Wizard of Earthsea* Gollancz (1971) Puffin
TOLKIEN, J. R. R. (1968) *The Lord of the Rings* Allen & Unwin
GONCHAROV, Ivan (1970) *Oblomov* Everyman
JACOBS, Joseph (1975) *Jack and the Beanstalk* Bodley Head
JACOBS, Joseph (1970) *Jack the Giant Killer* Bodley Head
GRIMM Brothers (1976) *Tom Thumb* Pelham Books
HERMANN, F. (1964) *The Giant Alexander* Methuen
CARROLL, Lewis (1970) *Alice in Wonderland* Puffin
HEIDE, F. P. (1975) *The Shrinking of Treehorn* Puffin
SWIFT, J. (1970) *Gulliver's Travels* Penguin

Comment

Bruno Bettelheim's study of fairy tales grew out of his dissatisfaction with the shallow content of books being used to teach reading, 'the acquisition of skills, including the ability to read becomes devalued when what one has learned to read adds nothing important to one's life ... The idea that learning to read may enable one later to enrich one's life is experienced as an empty promise when the stories the child listens to, or is reading at the moment, are vacuous.' This observation, coinciding with his discovery that fairy tales seemed to offer an enriching and satisfying literary experience for the children he was working with, inspired his lengthy study of the meaning and importance of fairy tales. In his introduction to *The Uses of Enchantment*, he echoes Ralph Lavender's assertion that, 'if we want children to learn to read, we must begin where they are ...' 'The more I tried to understand why these stories are so successful at enriching the inner life of the child, the more I realized that these tales, in a much deeper sense than any other reading material, start where the child really is in his psychological and emotional being.'

In *The Uses of Enchantment, The Meaning and Importance of Fairy Tales*, Bruno Bettelheim offers a psychoanalytical interpretation of familiar tales to support his hypothesis that fairy tales are powerful agents affecting children's maturation, whether or not they 'understand' their meaning in an adult way. Fairy tales, he maintains, reassure, because they demonstrate that others have the same kind of fantasies; children possess an inner world of fantasy, which is irrational, emotional, subjective, sensual, violent and often frightening. Fairy stories, he believes, can bring order to the child's inner life by offering symbolic solutions to his difficulties. Bettelheim stresses the positive effect of fairy stories upon children: they both reflect the child's inner life and convey a sense of order. In chapter 5, Bettelheim looks at what fairy tales have to offer, that modern stories written for young children tend to avoid: 'The fairy tale ... confronts the child squarely with the basic human

29

predicaments'; modern writers, publishers and parents sometimes prefer to avoid this kind of confrontation. Hodder and Stoughton have broken some of the taboos in their series by the Swedish writer and illustrator, Gunilla Wolde. Her books for under-fives deal head on with the realities of Thomas, Sara and Emma's preschool lives. In *Thomas and Sara are different* (Gunilla Wolde, Hodder and Stoughton 1975) Thomas and Sara play unashamedly in the nude; the text is explicit: 'Thomas has a penis'. In *Emma and the measles* sex roles are reversed, father takes little brother's temperature, and gives him 'little sips of cool juice'. The doctor is a woman and adults behave like adults – 'Mummy gets angry with Emma for screaming. And Daddy gets cross with Mummy for being cross with Emma'. Emma's understandable jealousy is finally recognized and resolved.

The books in this series seem to answer a real need but when Hodder published the first books in a series for slightly older children, dealing with larger and more potentially disturbing issues, they met with criticism; not of the content as such but the manner in which it was presented.

4 A fine mess they've got you into Olly
Jeremy Bugler

Birth, divorce, disease, death. The main phases of the modern life-cycle as viewed by misanthropic Muggeridge? Perhaps, but they are also the broad subject-matters of an unusual quartet of children's books that has just been published. Taken together, the books break new ground in writing for children.

The quartet deals with the traumas of childhood, seen through the eyes of a small boy, Olly. All the books, published by Hodder and Stoughton, bear a strapline: Olly Sees It Through. If two of the books are ordinary enough in dealing with Olly's experiences in going into hospital and when he gets a new baby brother, the other two take hold of the Untouchables of children's literature.

One concerns divorce, in this case of the parents of Olly's playmates; the other is titled: *When Olly's Grandad Died*. More books in the series, dealing with other childhood traumas or crises, are planned.

The books are written by two Swedes, child psychologist Monica Gydal, and a maker of children's television programmes, Thomas Danielsson. Based on a Swedish TV series, the books are carefully if slightly flatly written, and have two predominant attributes: an on-the-level manner of talking between adults and children, and a habit of not funking the issue, what Danielsson described as 'not bullshitting the children'.

Or rather, those are the attributes you notice if you can read 'Sa var det nar Ola kom pa sjukhus.' But if you pick up *When Olly went into Hospital*, you get something much more old fashioned. English publishers have rewritten the books, deeming the Swedish originals too progressive for the British. Passages have been dropped or cut, whole paragraphs inserted, sentences rephrased, and motives ascribed where none was present before. A children's literature Thomas Bowdler has been at work.

The Swedes are furious. Learning about the changes rather late, Gydal and Danielsson want Hodder to pulp the whole series. The publishers have refused outright, saying they bought the rights and the freedom to rewrite from a Danish agent. Gydal and Danielsson are now contemplating suing the Swedish Broadcasting Corporation for allowing

Source: *The Guardian* 10 March 1976

what they consider a mangling to happen. Thomas Danielsson is sending some advice to Hodder and Stoughton about what they should do with their series, advice that Partridge's *Dictionary of Historical Slang* describes as 'a low colloquial vulgarism, nineteenth and twentieth centuries'.

While it is refreshing to find that children's writers can be every bit as angry with bowdlerizing as any other species of writer, what is really interesting is to study the changes that Hodder and their text writer Charles Ellis felt they had to make.

To begin with, the Swedish originals' blurring of the traditional roles of the sexes has been refocused. A picture of Olly making cakes with his Grandma in *When Olly's Grandad Died* has gone. In the hospital book the text accompanying a picture of Olly sitting on his bed with his mother and his father, who is reading to him, has been quite changed.

The Swedish version, in a literal translation, says: 'Then Olly's mum and dad come to visit him. Because it's the visiting hour, the other children have visitors, too. Olly's mum and dad talk to him a little and his dad reads a story. But Olly is tired and doesn't really understand what the story is all about. Then Olly's mum says that Olly has a temperature and that's why he's tired . . .'

In the English edition, the passage reads: 'But when his Dad came in the evening, and read him a story, he was so pleased that he got up and sat between them. It almost made it worthwhile being in hospital, to have his Dad, who was generally *very* busy, tell him a story.'

Much more noticeable, though, is a pervasive authoritarianism in the English rewrite. There are scores of changes, some major and some tiny, in which the tone of the adult relating to the child has been altered, and the familiar sense of *de haut en bas* restored.

Here is an incident in the hospital. Swedish original: 'Ulf tips all the toys onto the floor and laughs with all his might. The playsister tells Ulf to pick all the toys up again. She helps him too.'

English version: 'Roy (Ulf) tipped the trolley over. The lady was very angry. "If you don't pick all those toys up this minute I shall see you have no more toys today or any other day." Roy made a face but picked them up all the same.'

Here's an incident in the divorce book in which Olly, having just heard that his friend's parents are getting divorced because they are so unhappy together, comes home and hears his own parents arguing. Worried, Olly stands by the door, where his mother finds him. Swedish original: ' "What's the matter Olly?" she asks. But Olly just stands there and cannot answer. "Answer me, Olly. Are you unhappy about something?" she asks as she picks him up.'

English version: ' "What's the matter, Olly?" she said. Olly stood and said nothing. "What's up darling? Have you been naughty or something like that?" Still Olly couldn't answer and Mum picked him up in her arms.'

The English versions all strive to make Olly accept the situation he happens to be in, and if possible to approve of it. Here's Olly in hospital again (English version): 'As he settled down to sleep that night, Olly decided that hospital wasn't too bad. He still wanted his Mum to stay all night but he was too tired to argue, and when she left it didn't seem worth crying about.'

The Swedish Olly, though, is allowed his right to object to what is happening to him: 'After a while Olly falls asleep. Then his mum and dad go away. It is difficult to fall asleep in the evenings. Everything is so boring. And Olly is cross with his mother who's not there with him.'

'He still wants to go home.'

In five pages of numbered objections sent to Hodder and Stoughton, Monica Gydal and Thomas Danielsson assert the child's own rights shouldn't have been written away. For example: page 13 – ' "He wasn't afraid any more." Why this remark that he is not afraid any more?; he has the right to be afraid.'

Broadly, the English versions also lack precision and detail. They include, on the other hand, more colloquial conversation and much more story line.

This is quite deliberate, says Charles Ellis, who has been working for Hodder's for two years. The books should be read by children in the eight to nine age bracket, he says, and by younger children through an adult. Especially, the books needed to be made more dramatic to retain the interest of the adults who have to do the reading to the children.

Hodder's managing director, Clifford Hufton, stoutly defends Charles Ellis's treatment: 'Charles Ellis went to an extraordinary degree of research to establish what the English market would accept . . . British parental attitudes are not as liberal as those in Sweden, and we do not think the function of the books is carried out if we step too far in advance of accepted thinking.'

Clifford Hufton then lists a number of reasons for the changes, including the tradition of British picture books always using less text than those on the Continent 'so material just had to be cut'. He also says: 'The present tense is unacceptable for books in this age group.'

The key to Hodder's changes is fairly obvious: the market. Gydal and Danielsson's Swedish originals are aimed specifically at a narrow age range of five- to six-year-olds. 'There are no books on these subjects for children of this age in any language,' says Danielsson.

Hodder, on the other hand, want a much broader appeal, a larger market and larger sales. Hence the aim at the eight- to nine-year-olds and the younger children. To this end, all the English versions take out any mention of Olly's age in the belief that nine-year-olds would disdain reading about a four- or five-year-old. 'It's just the old commercialism' says Danielsson.

Hodder and Charles Ellis do regret some changes. They say, for example, that the 'playsister' in the hospital did turn out a little too ferocious with the little boy Roy. Otherwise, they fight their corner.

33

But what most annoys the Swedes is the contention that the books are too advanced for the British. 'It's the old myth again that the Swedes are so progressive—as untrue as the myth that the Swedes are always committing suicide' says Danielsson. Some of his early inspiration, to write children's books, he says, came from browsing in the Children's Book Shop in Notting Hill Gate, London. He remembers taking a bundle of Leila Berg's Nipper books back to Sweden, long before they were published so successfully there.

The Olly books, argue the authors, are not at all revolutionary or startling provided you accept that the best way to talk to a child is not as a miniature adult or growing-up baby, but as a human being.

Two more Olly books have already appeared in Sweden: in one, Olly witnesses a road accident and in the other, Olly moves house. It's these two that Hodder want to publish, but Danielsson says they won't be allowed to.

When the dust settles, the best outcome will be the arrangement that ensures that Gydal and Danielsson get their books published in Britain more or less as they are written. The books so far are pretty remarkable, and the two dealing with divorce and death are outstanding for sensitivity and their honesty with difficult subjects.

Comment

The problem has, in fact, been resolved and the books which deal with divorce and death have been published. It is unfortunate that some publishers still retreat from contemporary material which they see as potentially disturbing, hiding behind market research into parental (*not* children's) attitudes. Fortunately, perhaps in ignorance, they continue to publish fairy tales, myths and legends which deal head on, albeit symbolically, with the darker aspects of life. As Bettelheim observes, in the following chapter, ' "Safe" stories mention neither death nor ageing, the limits to our existence, nor the wish for eternal life. The fairy tale, by contrast, confronts the child squarely with the basic human predicaments.'

5 Fairy tales and the existential predicament
Bruno Bettelheim

In order to master the psychological problems of growing up – over-coming narcissistic disappointments, oedipal dilemmas, sibling rivalries; becoming able to relinquish childhood dependencies; gaining a feeling of selfhood and of self-worth, and a sense of moral obligation – a child needs to understand what is going on within his conscious self so that he can also cope with that which goes on in his unconscious. He can achieve this understanding, and with it the ability to cope, not through rational comprehension of the nature and content of his unconscious, but by be-coming familiar with it through spinning out daydreams – ruminating, rearranging, and fantasizing about suitable story elements in response to unconscious pressures. By doing this, the child fits unconscious content into conscious fantasies, which then enable him to deal with that content. It is here that fairy tales have unequalled value, because they offer new dimensions to the child's imagination which would be impossible for him to discover as truly on his own. Even more important, the form and structure of fairy tales suggest images to the child by which he can structure his daydreams and with them give better direction to his life.

In child or adult, the unconscious is a powerful determinant of be-haviour. When the unconscious is repressed and its content denied entrance into awareness, then eventually the person's conscious mind will be partially overwhelmed by derivatives of these unconscious elements, or else he is forced to keep such rigid, compulsive control over them that his personality may become severely crippled. But when unconscious material *is* to some degree permitted to come to awareness and worked through in imagination, its potential for causing harm – to ourselves or others – is much reduced; some of its forces can then be made to serve positive purposes. However, the prevalent parental belief is that a child must be diverted from what troubles him most: his form-less, nameless anxieties, and his chaotic, angry, and even violent fantasies. Many parents believe that only conscious reality or pleasant and wish-fulfilling images should be presented to the child – that he should be

Source: BETTELHEIM, B. (1975) *The Uses of Enchantment. The Meaning and Importance of Fairy Tales* New York: Alfred J. Knopf Inc. pp. 6–11 (re-issued London, Thames & Hudson Ltd 1977)

exposed only to the sunny side of things. But such one-sided fare nourishes the mind only in a one-sided way, and real life is not all sunny.

There is a widespread refusal to let children know that the source of much that goes wrong in life is due to our very own natures – the propensity of all men for acting aggressively, asocially, selfishly, out of anger and anxiety. Instead, we want our children to believe that, inherently, all men are good. But children know that *they* are not always good; and often, even when they are, they would prefer not to be. This contradicts what they are told by their parents, and therefore makes the child a monster in his own eyes.

The dominant culture wishes to pretend, particularly where children are concerned, that the dark side of man does not exist, and professes a belief in an optimistic meliorism. Psychoanalysis itself is viewed as having the purpose of making life easy – but this is not what its founder intended. Psychoanalysis was created to enable man to accept the problematic nature of life without being defeated by it, or giving in to escapism. Freud's prescription is only by struggling courageously against what seem like overwhelming odds can man succeed in wringing meaning out of his existence.

This is exactly the message that fairy tales get across to the child in manifold form: that a struggle against severe difficulties in life is unavoidable, is an intrinsic part of human existence – but that if one does not shy away, but steadfastly meets unexpected and often unjust hardships, one masters all obstacles and at the end emerges victorious.

Modern stories written for young children mainly avoid these existential problems, although they are crucial issues for all of us. The child needs most particularly to be given suggestions in symbolic form about how he may deal with these issues and grow safely into maturity. 'Safe' stories mention neither death nor ageing, the limits to our existence, nor the wish for eternal life. The fairy tale, by contrast, confronts the child squarely with the basic human predicaments.

For example, many fairy stories begin with the death of a mother or father; in these tales the death of the parent creates the most agonizing problems, as it (or the fear of it) does in real life. Other stories tell about an ageing parent who decides that the time has come to let the new generation take over. But before this can happen, the successor has to prove himself capable and worthy. The Brothers Grimm's story 'The Three Feathers' begins: 'There was once upon a time a king who had three sons . . . When the king had become old and weak, and was thinking of his end, he did not know which of his sons should inherit the kingdom after him.' In order to decide, the king sets all his sons a difficult task; the son who meets it best 'shall be king after my death'.

It is characteristic of fairy tales to state an existential dilemma briefly and pointedly. This permits the child to come to grips with the problem in its most essential form, where a more complex plot would confuse

37

matters for him. The fairy tale simplifies all situations. Its figures are clearly drawn; and details, unless very important, are eliminated. All characters are typical rather than unique.

Contrary to what takes place in many modern children's stories, in fairy tales evil is as omnipresent as virtue. In practically every fairy tale good and evil are given body in the form of some figures and their actions, as good and evil are omnipresent in life and the propensities for both are present in every man. It is this duality which poses the moral problem, and requires the struggle to solve it.

Evil is not without its attractions – symbolized by the mighty giant or dragon, the power of the witch, the cunning queen in *Snow White* – and often it is temporarily in the ascendancy. In many fairy tales a usurper succeeds for a time in seizing the place which rightfully belongs to the hero – as the wicked sisters do in *Cinderella*. It is not that the evildoer is punished at the story's end which makes immersing oneself in fairy stories an experience in moral education, although this is part of it. In fairy tales, as in life, punishment or fear of it is only a limited deterrent to crime. The conviction that crime does not pay is a much more effective deterrent, and that is why in fairy tales the bad person always loses out. It is not the fact that virtue wins out at the end which promotes morality, but that the hero is most attractive to the child, who identifies with the hero in all his struggles. Because of this identification the child imagines that he suffers with the hero his trials and tribulations, and triumphs with him as virtue is victorious. The child makes such identifications all on his own, and the inner and outer struggles of the hero imprint morality on him.

The figures in fairy tales are not ambivalent – not good and bad at the same time, as we all are in reality. But since polarization dominates the child's mind, it also dominates fairy tales. A person is either good or bad, nothing in between. One brother is stupid, the other is clever. One sister is virtuous and industrious, the others are vile and lazy. One is beautiful, the others are ugly. One parent is all good, the other evil. The juxtaposition of opposite characters is not for the purpose of stressing right behaviour, as would be true for cautionary tales. (There are some amoral fairy tales where goodness or badness, beauty or ugliness play no role at all.) Presenting the polarities of character permits the child to comprehend easily the difference between the two, which he could not do as readily were the figures drawn more true to life, with all the complexities that characterize real people. Ambiguities must wait until a relatively firm personality has been established on the basis of positive identifications. Then the child has a basis for understanding that there are great differences between people, and that therefore one has to make choices about who one wants to be. This basic decision, on which all later personality development will build, is facilitated by the polarizations of the fairy tale.

Furthermore, a child's choices are based, not so much on right versus wrong, as on who arouses his sympathy and who his antipathy. The more simple and straightforward a good character, the easier it is for a child to identify with it and to reject the bad other. The child identifies with the good hero not because of his goodness, but because the hero's condition makes a deep positive appeal to him. The question for the child is not 'Do I want to be good?' but 'Who do I want to be like?' The child decides this on the basis of projecting himself wholeheartedly into one character. If this fairy-tale figure is a very good person, then the child decides that he wants to be good, too.

Amoral fairy tales show no polarization or juxtaposition of good and bad persons; that is because these amoral stories serve an entirely different purpose. Such tales or type figures as 'Puss in Boots', who arranges for the hero's success through trickery, and Jack, who steals the giant's treasure, build character not by promoting choices between good and bad, but by giving the child the hope that even the meekest can succeed in life. After all, what's the use of choosing to become a good person when one feels so insignificant that he fears he will never amount to anything? Morality is not the issue in these tales, but rather, assurance that one can succeed. Whether one meets life with a belief in the possibility of mastering its difficulties or with the expectation of defeat is also a very important existential problem.

The deep inner conflicts originating in our primitive drives and our violent emotions are all denied in much of modern children's literature, and so the child is not helped in coping with them. But the child is subject to desperate feelings of loneliness and isolation, and he often experiences mortal anxiety. More often than not, he is unable to express these feelings in words, or he can do so only by indirection: fear of the dark, of some animal, anxiety about his body. Since it creates discomfort in a parent to recognize these emotions in his child, the parent tends to overlook them, or he belittles these spoken fears out of his own anxiety, believing this will cover over the child's fears.

The fairy tale, by contrast, takes these existential anxieties and dilemmas very seriously and addresses itself directly to them: the need to be loved and the fear that one is thought worthless; the love of life, and the fear of death. Further, the fairy tale offers solutions in ways that the child can grasp on his level of understanding. For example, fairy tales pose the dilemma of wishing to live eternally by occasionally concluding: 'If they have not died, they are still alive.' The other ending – 'And they lived happily ever after' – does not for a moment fool the child that eternal life is possible. But it does indicate that which alone can take the sting out of the narrow limits of our time on this earth: forming a truly satisying bond to another. The tales teach that when one has done this, one has reached the ultimate in emotional security of existence and permanence of relation available to man; and this alone can dissipate the fear of death. If one has found true adult love, the fairy story also tells, one doesn't need to wish for eternal life. This is

39

suggested by another ending found in fairy tales 'They lived for a long time afterward, happy and in pleasure.'

An uninformed view of the fairy tale sees in this type of ending an unrealistic wish-fulfilment, missing completely the important message it conveys to the child. These tales tell him that by forming a true inter-personal relation, one escapes the separation anxiety which haunts him (and which sets the stage for many fairy tales, but is always resolved at the story's ending). Furthermore, the story tells, this ending is not made possible, as the child wishes and believes, by holding on to his mother eternally. If we try to escape separation anxiety and death anxiety by desperately keeping our grasp on our parents, we will only be cruelly forced out, like Hansel and Gretel.

Only by going out into the world can the fairy-tale hero (child) find himself there; and as he does, he will also find the other with whom he will be able to live happily ever after; that is, without ever again having to experience separation anxiety. The fairy tale is future-oriented and guides the child – in terms he can understand in both his conscious and his unconscious mind – to relinquish his infantile dependency wishes and achieve a more satisying independent existence.

Today children no longer grow up within the security of an extended family, or of a well-integrated community. Therefore, even more than at the times fairy tales were invented, it is important to provide the modern child with images of heroes who have to go out into the world all by themselves and who, although originally ignorant of the ultimate things, find secure places in the world by following their right way with deep inner confidence.

The fairy-tale hero proceeds for a time in isolation, as the modern child often feels isolated. The hero is helped by being in touch with primitive things – a tree, an animal, nature – as the child feels more in touch with those things than most adults do. The fate of these heroes convinces the child that, like them, he may feel outcast and abandoned in the world, groping in the dark, but, like them, in the course of his life he will be guided step by step, and given help when it is needed. Today, even more than in past times, the child needs the reassurance offered by the image of the isolated man who nevertheless is capable of achieving meaningful and rewarding relations with the world around him.

Comment

Bettelheim's enthusiasm for the fairy tale does not reflect current attitudes. Compare the two paragraphs below. The first paragraph comes from Bettelheim's detailed analysis of the story of Cinderella, in which he looks at the tale as told by the Brothers Grimm as well as the better known version by Perrault.

> On the surface, *Cinderella* is as deceptively simple as the story of *Little Red Riding Hood*, with which it shares greatest popularity. *Cinderella* tells about the agonies of sibling rivalry, of wishes coming true, of the humble being elevated, of true merit being recognized even when hidden under rags, of virtue rewarded and evil punished – a straightforward story. But under this overt content is concealed a welter of complex and largely unconscious material, which details of the story allude to just enough to set our unconscious associations going. This makes a contrast between surface simplicity and underlying complexity which arouses deep interest in the story and explains its appeal to the millions over centuries.
>
> (*The Uses of Enchantment* Bruno Bettelheim Thames & Hudson (1977) p. 239.)

The second paragraph is taken from a recent American publication:

> Unless we want to discard most of the books in our libraries these days, we'll need to learn to live with some old favourite children's books, and learn to use them in new ways. Let's consider some classics for children: to begin with, Cinderella. What are the sexually-stereotyped elements in this story and how could they be 'de-stereotyped'? If we were to revise this story, applying the new consciousness of sex-role stereotypes, how could we do it in such a way so that ultimately it would be supportive of sexual equality and would also work as a good story as well?'
>
> (*A Child's Right to Equal Reading. Exercises in the liberation of children's books from the limitations of sexual stereotypes* Verne Moberg A National Education Association Publication.)

Given that the view that we should rewrite or revise traditional stories which present women in stereotypical roles is an extreme one, it is an expression of a very strong feeling that parents and teachers should be aware of the need to identify books which do and do not contribute to the positive self-image of girls. Since 1974 The Children's Rights Workshop has been working to help develop a more critical approach to children's books (see *Print and Prejudice* Sarah Goodman Zimet pp. 107–8).

It is in this context that Heather Lyons has written **Some second thoughts on sexism in fairy tales.**

6 Some second thoughts on sexism in fairy tales

Heather Lyons

In recent years hitherto established reputations of bodies of children's literature have been subject to increasing criticism from a number of different quarters. Criticisms seem to have been directed indiscriminately at old classics, prize-winning contemporary novels for children and at fairy tales as familiarly presented. Thus parents and teachers, and increasingly publishers and writers, who are concerned not to mediate sexist, racist and class stereotypes to young readers have had to think twice about offering some old childhood favourites of their own, which on inspection now yield unmistakeable traces of unacceptable attitudes. The literature on the middle classness of children's literature has been a growing one, though there have been conscious attempts over the last few years to rectify the dearth of available stories in which ordinary children can recognize themselves unpatronizingly presented.[1]

More recently still has been the move largely from within the women's movement to rewrite fairy stories, for broadly similar reasons. Though entirely in sympathy with the concern that informs such attempts, I want to argue here that in the case of fairy stories in particular and folk narratives in general the attempt to rewrite stems from a number of misconceptions about the tales themselves. The first of these would seem to be that such tales are always about passive heroines; the second that women's viewpoint is unrepresented, and the third that what is wrong can be straightforwardly remedied by rewriting. As a preliminary to my discussion of these misconceptions however, I shall include just a few words on what is meant here by the term fairy tale.

Subject matter and audience of the fairy tale

Fairy tales, popular preconceptions notwithstanding, are often neither about fairies nor exclusively intended for children. In the introduction to her scholarly and comprehensive collection of British folk tales,[2] Katherine Briggs identifies the fairy tale as one of a number of kinds of folk narrative, itself to be distinguished from folk legend. Generally we are told the distinction is a straightforward one: 'folk narrative is folk fiction told for edification, delight and amusement; folk legend was once believed to be true.'[3] In what follows I propose to include reference to stories which strictly speaking should not be regarded as fairy tales though they all fall under the heading of folk narrative. The fairy tale –

the equivalent to the German *Märchen* though no really good substitute term exists in English – is generally a magical tale. The magical element may be provided by supernatural personages – fairies, enchantresses, demons and so on – or by magical properties of ordinary objects or people. Thus talking beasts are common, or heroines from whose lips toads or gold fall at every word, or magic apples which lead the way, or tables which once laid produce a feast. Variants of such tales where the magical element is lacking altogether exist in sufficient numbers to have merited the separate designation of *novelle* by Briggs, following the practice of the Aarne-Thompson tale-type index.[4] In addition, under the heading of folk narrative we may find the jocular tale, 'a great body of drolls, noodle stories and bawdy tales'[5] and the nursery tale, 'such stories as "Henny-Penny" and "The Old Woman and the Pig" . . . obviously invented for small children and of a type to be appreciated by the very young.'[6]

On the question of the child audience, J.R.R. Tolkien has described the association of children and fairy stories as 'an accident of our domestic history'.[7] In eighteenth-century Europe, the age of enlightenment cast such manifestations of popular belief and custom as the folk tale at best as curious antiquities and at worst as relics of worn-out superstition, as such to be consigned to the status of old wives' tales fit only for the nursery. Yet when a shift in the climate of opinion occurred towards the end of the century and the scholar collectors – the Grimm brothers foremost among them – began publishing their collections, they preferred first-hand to literary sources and upheld a new principle of faithfulness to the spirit, the manner and the language in which they were told, however rough or unpolished they seemed at the time, or adorned with barbarous detail. Among the most eager members of their audience, or so the accounts indicate, were children, seizing as they always must have done on what was not intended specially for them, in preference to what was.

The passive heroine

To return to the stereotype of the fairy tale. As commonly encountered it seems to go something like this:

> Heroes succeed because they act, not because they are. They are judged not by their appearance or inherent sweet nature but by their ability to overcome obstacles, even if these obstacles are defects in their own characters. Heroines are not allowed any defects, nor are they required to develop, since they are already perfect. The only tests of most heroines require nothing beyond what they are born with: a beautiful face, tiny feet and a pleasing temperament.[8]

A wide reading of tales both confirms and denies this description. There are tales, it is true, where the princes do the rescuing, and the princesses wait to be rescued or are simply on offer at the end as part of a package reward for the displays of masculine resourcefulness and feats of strength or daring with which the tale is taken up. But familiarization with the traditional components of tales and an awareness of how they can combine and recombine to quite different effect in different versions reveals that this is far from true of all tales. There are many others – admittedly less familiar to most of us today – which portray resourceful strong heroines roaming the world and braving dangers as well as any hero with nothing but their wits and the occasional magical aid to help them. 'East of the Sun and West of the Moon' is one such tale, and the 'Black Bull of Norroway' another (also called the 'Brown Bear of Norway'). They belong to a tale-type where a sister or a woman seeks for her brothers or her lover and asks directions of the moon, sun and stars, finally finding them on a glass mountain, or in the face of some other severe test.

The robber-bridegroom group of tales include variants where a spirited bride-to-be discovers a potentially murderous or in some way deceptive intention on the part of her future husband and by verbal or physical challenge defeats and even destroys him. 'Mr Fox' is one of the best of numerous English versions, and Flora Annie Steel collected a popular one in the Punjab towards the end of the last century, called 'Bopoluchi'. The more familiar version of this group of tales is of course 'Bluebeard', though the pallid heroine forlornly calling 'sister Anne, sister Anne' is a mere shadow of Lady Mary, the heroine of 'Mr Fox', or of 'Bopoluchi' brandishing a bill hook and challenging her captor to fight it out.

Other tale-types which feature non-passive heroines are the girl who rescues her sisters; the girl as helper in the hero's flight; the clever peasant girl; the strong woman as bride; the change of sex; and the reinstatement of the slandered and banished woman. It is important to emphasize here that each tale-type listed will include a number of tales often collected from all over the world under its head, not just an isolated example. In addition, variants of other tale-types exist where either a boy or a girl carries out a comparable set of acts. Thus 'Mollie Whuppie' can be seen as a variant of 'Jack and the Beanstalk' or 'The Dauntless Girl' of the Grimm tale 'The Boy Who wanted to Know what Fear Was'. Versions of 'Puss in Boots' exist where it is a mistress rather than a master whose interests puss serves and for whom he wins the ogre's castle. A particularly interesting tale-type to look at in this connection is that of the three sisters rescued. Two major variants of this exist. In one, the rescue is done by a sister (tale-type 311); in the other by a brother (tale-type 312). The Aarne-Thompson tale-type index listing shows that of the two, tale-type 311 is both the most widespread and the most numerous, occurring in thirty-one out of a possible forty countries covered in the index, with a total of 464 versions. This can be compared with tale-type 312 occurring in twenty-six of the forty countries with a total of 217 versions.

Fairy tale and the printed word

One is driven to speculate that the predominance of the notion that there are rigid kinds of depiction of male and female characters in fairy tales may have something to do with their mediation in modern times by the printed word, and with the narrowing-down of common knowledge of tales to a mere handful of the multiplicity of which there are records. The reason for the emergence of certain tales in certain versions as the ones everyone knows is itself interesting to speculate on. Does the equation of 'Cinderella' with the version which has become widely known in its Perrault telling, or adaptations from it, account for the unnatural frozen-ness which seems to have overtaken it? And has the newly frozen form been determined in part at least by the person of the collector, inevitably all too often white, male and middle class however sympathetically orientated to his peasant respondents? Why is it that we remember not the names of the tellers from whom the Grimms first had 'The Elves and the Shoemaker', 'The Twelve Dancing Princesses', 'Rumpelstiltskin' or 'The Frog-Prince', but only the name of the collectors? It is as though these stories which had passed so freely from mouth to mouth had come to belong only to the two brothers.

Working with student teachers it has been interesting to note how introduction to versions other than Grimm or Perrault can precipitate an irritable or even outraged response: 'it isn't the *right* version'. Of the versions of 'Cinderella' collected in China, Finland, Estonia, Livonia, Lithuania, Lapland, Sweden, Norway, Britain, France, Spain, Germany, Italy, Poland, the West Indies, India, Indonesia and from among American Indians and Spanish Americans, which is the right one? Where the traditional tales have become the property of the famous collectors and the rightness of all other recorded versions become determinable by reference to them, the essential nature of the stories is in my view altered. Essentially they are unowned and unownable. Tolkien speaks of the human capacity for 'appropriating' the things of the world, and how, once appropriated they are locked up, hoarded and cease to be seen. For him fairy stories can open the cage doors 'and let all the locked things fly away'. Moreover, 'the gems all turn into flowers or flames, and you will be warned that all you had (or knew) was dangerous and potent, not really effectively chained, free and wild; no more yours than they were you'.[9]

Kay Stone's study[10] of the availability of the Grimm collection of fairy stories to North American children today throws further light on the general point being made here about the mediation of what are now the most familiar tales. It shows that of the hundred and twenty-nine tales in the original collection, twenty-five or fewer generally appear in present-day selections. Thus of the forty heroines appearing in the original number of tales ('not all of them passive and pretty') an inevitably much reduced number feature in the selections. Indeed, Stone estimates that the proportion of passive heroines rises from an original 20 per cent to as much as 75 per cent in present-day North American versions. She goes on to identify Walt Disney as a key mediator of 'the already popular stereotype of the innocent beauty victimized by the wicked villainess' through his film versions of just three tales: 'Sleeping Beauty', 'Snow White' and 'Cinderella'. Moreover she is able to report a general interest expressed among her forty women interviewees aged seven to sixty-one in more diversity, even where no dislike of passive heroines was expressed. Many were interested to hear of tales searched out by Stone from five major Anglo-American collections, of the kind discussed here. Examples include, tales where women destroy threatening male villains, a tale where a girl does not need her father to convince her that frogs make interesting bedfellows, tales where mother and daughter cooperate in escaping from a giant and destroying him, where the heroine leaves home voluntarily ('Mossycoat') or in protest over her father's rejection of her lover.

Narrative and narrator

When we turn to the question of the women's viewpoint in fairy stories and whether or not it is represented, some consideration has to be given to the identity of the teller of the folk narrative. The teller of tales, as already suggested above is likely to be a key mediator of the form in which they occur. We know that to tell a story, itself known only from other tellings, is to make something both new and not new. Its newness may be a product of chance: a detail is forgotten; other material known from a different source is inserted. In considering the contribution that the narrator makes to both the preservation and variation of the tale, Tolkien has this to say:

> Fairy stories are by no means rocky matrices out of which the fossils cannot be prized except by the expert geologist. The ancient elements can be knocked out, or forgotten and dropped out, or replaced by other ingredients with the greatest ease: as any comparison of a story with closely related variants will show.[11]

He accounts for retentions and insertions by a general 'sense of significance' among narrators, whether or not the significance is capable of being explicated by them, or remains mysterious and symbolic.

Perhaps we can only speculate how it might be that the identity of the teller affects a telling. We know that women, children and men have all been tellers of tales the world over. Flora Annie Steel, collecting Punjabi tales in the 1870s and 1880s, found expert child narrators telling tales to child audiences in the open air through the long hot Indian night.[12] An occasional footnote in a scholarly collection will indicate the currency of a tale primarily among the women of a community; and J. F. Campbell in his introduction to *Popular Tales of the Western Highlands* describes how the old men would gather to hear and tell tales among themselves. Surely such circumstances must have contributed to the colouring and variety of such tales as they have come down to us? Unfortunately, systematic recording of the names of the tale-teller was not the order of the day in the great era of tale collection from the 1870s to the First World War, though increasing emphasis is laid on the importance of it in modern researches.[13] So it is only rarely possible to ascribe particular tales to women tellers thus making it difficult to look at possible differences in emphasis in women's tales. We are left with the tantalizing question: was it the women tellers in particular who liked to include in their repertoire those variants of a tale which featured a Molly rather than a Jack? How far might they have been responsible for generating the variants in the first place? For instance, the widespread tale of the man who did his wife's work comes in at least two major variants. In one, the man and his wife agree to do each other's work for a day.[14] The woman completes her labour in the fields without trouble; the man is quite unable to coordinate the variety of household tasks that constitute his wife's work and his day is marked by a whole series of mishaps. The moral explicitly drawn is that the wife's work is as hard if not harder than the man's. Alternatively, of a pair of newly-weds, either the man is driven to do domestic tasks by a wife who proves shrewish, and berated for his incompetence; or the young wife unused to household management undergoes a series of similar domestic mishaps for which she is reproached by her husband. Might not the presence of a preferred version in an individual teller's repertoire have had as much to do with his liking for a sly joke at the expense of women, or hers for one at the expense of know-all husbands? Impossible as the question is to answer, to ask it at least draws attention to the variety of folk narrative and to the diverse readings of human experience which different combinations of its basic elements provide.

On origins

What then are the objections to rewriting? I would want to say first given the availability of alternatives it may simply be unnecessary. But there is more to it than that. The question is made more difficult to answer when lack of space as here inhibits any detailed discussion of the question of origins of the folk tale, so hotly debated by the great nineteenth-century folklorists in this country and elsewhere. For some, folk tales were degenerate cosmic myths; for others, they were the regeneration and reworking of ancient and worn-out traditional elements, in a vigorous form expressive of the conditions of ordinary folk. Conflicting theories of origins and of diffusion and mode of transmission remain with us to this day. Nevertheless, we do know from the labours of scholars and collectors over many years that there is a remarkable world-wide scattering of the same tales or elements of tales. I would want to say that a fiction proceeding from an individual consciousness will have another flavour altogether from that of such folk narratives, containing as they do some very ancient shared concerns of the human race as a whole, shaped, modified and passed on by countless tongues over great periods of time. No single imagination has dressed these tales; however various in detail or different in combination of elements, the bones remain. John Ruskin had this to say on the subject in his Introduction to the 1892 reprint of the original English selection from Grimm appearing under the title *German Popular Stories:*

> Every fairy tale worth recording at all is the remnant of a tradition possessing true historical value; – historical, at least in so far as it has naturally arisen out of the mind of a people under special circumstances, and risen not without meaning ... It sustains afterwards natural changes from the sincere action of the fear or fancy of successive generations; it takes new colour from their manner of life, and new form from their changing moral tempers. As long as these changes are natural and effortless, accidental and inevitable, the story remains essentially true, altering its form indeed like a flying cloud, but remaining a sign of the sky; a shadowy image as truly a part of the great firmament of the human mind as the light of reason which it seems to interrupt.

Tolkien himself draws our attention to the importance of the tale as historically shaped, and to the particular effect this must have on a modern audience.

> For one thing [the tales] are now *old*, and antiquity has an appeal in itself. The beauty and horror of The Juniper Tree (Von dem Machandelbloom), with its exquisite and tragic beginning, the abominable cannibal stew, the gruesome bones, the gay and vengeful bird-spirit coming out of a mist that rose from the tree, has remained with me since childhood; and yet always the chief flavour of that tale lingering in the memory was not beauty or horror, but distance and a great abyss of time, not measurable even by 'twe tusend Johr'. Without the stew and the bones – which children are now too often spared in mollified versions of Grimm – that vision would have been lost ... Such stories have now a mythical or total (unanalysable) effect.[15]

I would want to add that this effect is likely to be lost in translation to modern moralities. By way of fuller illustration of some of these general points, I would like to describe some of the kinds of story I have mentioned in more detail. In what follows I will consider role reversal, the exchange of conventional attributes in male and female characters, the question of whether fairy tales are misogynist or not, and the presentation of beauty and goodness.

Role reversal

Stories can be found with female equivalents to the male counterparts of more familiar versions. A good example of this is 'Mollie Whuppie',[16] or 'Mallie Whuppie' as it is sometimes called, a generally little known version of 'Jack and the Beanstalk' although it is not difficult to get hold of it. The story starts more like 'Hansel and Gretel', with the three children abandoned in the forest because the parents are too poor to keep them. It is the youngest, Mollie, who by her efforts extricates them from subsequent dangers and looks after their interests. First, a giant's wife takes the girls in and puts them to sleep overnight in the same bed as the giant's daughters. Mollie notices golden chains on the necks of the giant's daughters, and she sees that ropes have been put round her own and her sisters'. She exchanges them, and in the night the giant enters, feels for the ropes, and murders his own daughters. After this escape, the three sisters turn up at the king's court where Mollie tells their story. She strikes a series of bargains with the king, who is full of admiration for her. She promises to steal an object from the giant and bring it back; her reward is to be a king's son in marriage for each of her sisters and finally for herself. On the third and last occasion Mollie is caught by the giant. A battle of wits ensues, and it is only by means of further ingenuity, courageousness and nimbleness that Mollie manages to escape and receive her just reward.

Stories can also be found with male equivalents of female counterparts. A particularly interesting case in point is what seems to be in part at least a male version of Cinderella, entitled 'The Princess on the Glass Hill'.[17] In this story it is Cinderlad, the youngest son who is despised and ill-treated because of his ugly, dirty appearance from sitting among the ashes, but who, as a result of magical intervention, is enabled to appear transformed by a suit of silver or gold at a royal occasion where a great company is assembled. Word of both the appearance and subsequent mysterious disappearance of the splendid stranger is brought home by two elder brothers who have declined to have Cinderlad in their company.

> 'Oh, I should have liked to see him, that I should,' said Cinderlad, who was as usual sitting by the chimney among the cinders. 'You indeed!' said the brothers, 'you look as if you were fit to be among such great lords, dirty lout that you are to sit there!'
> Next day the brothers were for setting out again, and this time too Cinderlad begged them to let him go with them; but no, they said he was not fit to do that, for he was much too ugly and dirty.[18]

Although the princess in this story seems to be the archetypal stereotype – passively seated on the top of her glass mountain waiting to be won –

this should not be allowed to detract from the interest of the tale in the context under consideration here.

Exchange of conventional attributes in male and female characters

Too often, according to the conventional notion of story content, the men have both the brawn and the brains. But there are a number of stories where resourceful girls and women extricate themselves and their men from tricky situations by dint of sheer brain-power. Two such stories are 'Pottle O' Brains'[19] and 'The Barber's Clever Wife'.[20] 'Pottle O' Brains' revolves round a fool's attempt to buy himself the brains his mother tells him he'll need when she is gone. When neither his pig's nor his dead mother's heart buy him the brains from a wise woman – she has required the heart of what he loves the best in payment – a kind girl takes him on. The story continues:

> 'I'll look after thee,' says the lass. 'They say fools make the best husbands . . .' So they were wed, and she cooked and worked and made the house so clean that at last the fool said: 'Lass, I'm thinking I like thee best of everything.' Then he looked a bit sad-like, and said: 'Does that mean I'll have to kill thee, and take thy heart up to the wise-woman?'
>
> 'Not a bit of it,' says she. 'Just take me up, heart and all, and mebbe I'll help thee with the riddles.'
>
> 'I reckon they're too hard for women-folk,' says he.
>
> 'Just try me,' says she.[21]

He does, and the girl answers all the wise woman's riddles. The fool goes away happy on being told that he's got his pottle of brains already – in his wife's head.

Then there is the very widespread tale of the fool saved by a member of his family who substitutes a goat or a sheep's head for the body of the man he has killed. Katherine Briggs gives a version in her *Dictionary of British Folk Tales*, entitled 'Silly Jimmy and the Factor' where it is the mother who carries out the substitution, thus saving her foolish son who tells all to whoever comes asking.

A splendid and very common tale from the Punjab is called 'The Barber's Clever Wife'. It tells how a stupid barber loses all his money and how his clever wife tells him to beg from the king. The king gives him a piece of waste land, which the wife induces some thieves to dig up for her by a clever trick. As a result she has a fine harvest which she sells for a crock of gold pieces. The thieves repeatedly attempt to gain possession of this. The first time they get a crock of goat's droppings instead, the second time they are stung by hornets, the third time they get the tips of their noses cut off, the fourth time their chief gets the end of his tongue bitten off and finally, by sheer force of argument, the barber's wife wins the lawsuit which the thieves bring against her in court. All the defeats suffered by the thieves are a result of her resourcefulness and quick-wittedness.

Brains all well and good, readers may be thinking, but what about physical strength? But even brawn turns out not to be a male prerogative. There are a number of tales where women's physical strength is put to the test as a means of detecting who they are, when for some reason their sex is ambiguous. The tests depend on the assumption that the women's identity will be revealed by their less than manly strength. But the women pass the tests successfully, and are only found out by trickery. One such tale, 'Bellucia', appears in the seventeenth-century Italian collection of Giambattista Basile, generally known as *The Pentamerone*. The tests of masculinity include riding a wild colt, and firing a fowling piece, both of which tasks the disguised heroine performs in a manner in no way distinguishable from a man's. A tale which includes similar tests is Grimm's 'The Twelve Huntsmen'. A characteristic motif of the Brunhilde tale-type (the strong woman as bride) is the suitor test. This can entail matching the woman in strength, lifting the woman's giant weapon, and riding the woman's horse, which needs a strong hand.

In considering the exchange of attributes as a characteristic of folk narrative, it is interesting to note the widespread tradition of numbskull stories, particularly strong in Britain, and well represented in Jewish culture. Katherine Briggs names forty-five different places in the British Isles reputed to be inhabited by simpletons.[22] These range from the Lincolnshire fens to the Isle of Wight, and take in Cambridge and no fewer than six Yorkshire villages. These stories purport to be about particular small communities – the wise men of Gotham; the sages of Chelm – but are nearly always told about the men, who invariably engage in lunatic solutions of problems which are often misconceived. Thus when a cheese by chance rolls down the hill, another is sent after it to fetch it back; or the villagers set about trying to rake the moon out of the pond since it has fallen out of the sky, or seek to light the new town hall – inadvertently built without windows – by collecting sunlight in buckets and pails and carrying it inside. The point of the stories is the foolishness of men – a foolishness put on display for all to relish and laugh at. It is important to emphasize here that I am not suggesting that the stories are or should be against men; the mockery is affectionate and implicit and from a feminist point of view reveals the possibility of a world not entirely made up of capable men and incapable women, but of human beings equally capable of error and foolishness. Since British fools are so well represented in Katherine Briggs *Dictionary of British Folk Tales* in the large section of jocular tales, I choose to give a Jewish story here as an example of the type.

The Rabbi's Golden Clogs

In Chelm, the village of fools, there was none greater among them

C

than their own rabbi. So highly did the sages of Chelm esteem their rabbi that they wished to make him a gift as a mark of their high regard. But what to give?

Now Chelm like most Polish villages became remarkably muddy underfoot from Succoth to Purim, so what better than a pair of clogs as a gift to protect the rabbi's shoes? 'And,' said the chief of all the sages, 'let them be made of gold to show how the sages of Chelm value their rabbi'. So the golden clogs were bought and much admired. But now the sages saw a mighty problem to tax their wits: how to keep the mud from besmirching the golden purity of the rabbi's clogs. Day and night the sages disputed the matter in the houses of study and the synagogues.

In the end of course it was the rabbi himself who was inspired with the solution. He would indeed wear the golden clogs, but henceforth would walk upon his hands.[23]

Are fairy tales misogynist?

There are some tales – often of ancient and mythological origin – which in the form that they come down to us today, redolent of centuries of Jewish and Christian tradition, seem intensely misogynist. 'Pandora's Box' is one such tale; 'Cupid and Psyche' could be construed as another. Both these tales seemingly reveal the ills loosed upon the world by the woman's insatiable curiosity, before which even the sternest patriarchal abjurations or tenderest of loving entreaties count for nothing. Thus I was very interested to come across a number of variants of the Cupid and Psyche story in a nineteenth-century collection of Italian tales that happened to come into my possession.[24] In them both Cupid and Psyche or their counterparts in Italian dress are freely translated into each other's roles. It appears that the search for the lost husband and the man on the quest for his wife are both recognizable types of the folk tale. The impact is not quite the same; we are all too imbued with Adam and Eve as part of our cultural heritage for the man's misdemeanour to excite quite the same misapprobation. Nevertheless, I have felt less inclined ever since to see Psyche and Pandora as oppressively universal symbols.

To look at the matter from a slightly different angle, it would be easy to interpret the famous Grimm story of 'The Fisherman and his Wife' as a classic put-down of women.

A poor fisherman catches a magic flounder, but doesn't think to ask for a reward for his kindness in releasing it. The fisherman's wife sets out to maximize their good fortune and sends her husband back to make a succession of requests. First, the hovel on the shore becomes a cottage, then a castle, and it is the woman who begins to wish for herself (since her husband doesn't want it) an even more powerful status. Her imaginings take her from being a busy bourgeoise running a household to becoming king, emperor, pope, and finally to becoming God. The hubris of this last wish precipitates the denouement of the story; all returns to how it was before. Throughout, the husband, timorous and increasingly hesitant about his wife's wishes (they seem to him 'not right'), scuttles to and from the shore, where he summons the flounder with the words:

Flounder, flounder in the sea,
Come to me, O come to me!
For my wife, good Ilsebill,
Wills not what I'd have her will.[25]

Ilsebill's will: another tract on the downfall of womankind? In the story the downfall is heralded by the increasingly ominous voice of nature; the sea and sky become ever more stormy at each visit to the shore. And yet there's a tremendous tension created within the tale between the rumbling warnings of conscience indirectly suggested and the marvellousness and daring of Ilsebill's transformations.

'What does she want now?' asked the flounder.
'Alas, flounder,' he said, 'my wife wants to be emperor.'
'Go home,' said the flounder. 'She is that already.'
So the fisherman went home, and there he saw the whole castle was made of polished marble, ornamented with alabaster statues and gold. Before the gate soldiers were marching, blowing trumpets and beating drums. Inside the palace were walking barons, counts and dukes, acting as servants; they opened the door, which was of beaten gold. And when he entered, he saw his wife upon a throne which was made out of a single block of gold, quite six cubits high. She had on a great golden crown, three yards high and set with brilliant and sparkling gems. In one hand she held a sceptre, and in the other the imperial globe, and on either side of her stood two rows of halberdiers, each smaller than the other, from a seven foot giant to the tiniest little dwarf no higher than my little finger. Many princes and dukes were standing before her.
The fisherman went up to her quietly and said, 'Wife, are you emperor now?'
'Yes,' she said, 'I am emperor.'
He stood looking at her magnificence, and when he had watched her for some time, said, 'Ah, wife, let that be enough, now you are emperor.'
'Husband,' said she, 'why are you standing there? I am emperor now, and I want to be pope too. Go down to the flounder.'

'Well, what does she want now?' asked the flounder.
'Alas,' said the fisherman, 'she wants to be pope.'
'Go home, then. She is that already,' said the flounder.

Then he went home, and there he saw, as it were, a large church surrounded by palaces. He pushed his way through the people. The interior was lit up with thousands and thousands of candles, and his wife, dressed in cloth of gold, was sitting on a much higher throne, and she wore three great golden crowns. Round her were numbers of church dignitaries, and on either side were standing two rows of tapers, the largest of them as tall as a steeple, and the smallest as tiny as a Christmas tree candle. All the emperors and kings were on their knees before her.

'Wife,' said the fisherman looking at her, 'are you pope now?'

'Yes,' said she, 'I am pope.'

He stood staring at her, and it was as if he were looking at the bright sun. When he had watched her for some time he said, 'Ah, wife, let it be enough now that you are pope.' But she sat as straight as a tree and did not move or bend the least bit. He said again, 'Wife, be content now that you are pope. You cannot become anything more.'

'We will think about that,' said his wife.

But the woman was not content; her greed would not allow her to sleep, and she kept thinking and thinking what she could still become. The fisherman slept well and soundly, for he had done a great deal that day. But his wife could not sleep at all and turned from one side to the other the whole night long and thought, till she could think no longer, what more she would become. When she saw the red dawn she went to the window and as she was watching the sun rise, she thought, Ha! Could I not make the sun and moon rise?

'Husband,' said she, poking him in the ribs with her elbow, 'wake up. Go down to the flounder. I will be God.'[26]

Anyone still unconvinced by my account should look at Maurice Sendak's inspired illustration in the recent two-volume selection of Grimm tales entitled *The Juniper Tree*,[27] which I think reflects something of the same feeling for the story.

Messages in tales of this kind are never simply transmitted. I like to think that within the voice of the prevailing culture in 'The Fisherman and his Wife' – prevailing as it does in the end – there is a strong note of dissonance, the resulting mismatch leaving resonances behind long after the final moral has been enunciated.

The presentation of beauty and goodness in women

A seemingly intractable feature of fairy tales from a feminist point of view could be said to be the valuing of beauty in women above all else, both in itself and as a moral virtue. Too many tales for comfort counterpose the good and beautiful girl with the wilful, lazy or ugly one; the first always rewarded, the second punished. I propose to discuss this notion in relation to two stories, 'Puddocky'[28] and 'The King Who

Wanted a Beautiful Wife',[29] and to try to show how a moral ambivalence adheres to the idea of beauty in them.

In both stories the possession of beauty or the lack of it has disturbing effects. 'Puddocky' begins rather like 'Rapunzel'; the beautiful Parsley goes to live with a witch in whose garden the parsley she craves for grows. As a grown girl she sits at a window, singing and combing her hair. Three passing princes, out to seek their fortunes, instantly fall in love with her and immediately draw their swords on each other out of jealousy. The witch, hearing the uproar, thinks that Parsley's beauty is at the bottom of this, and curses Parsley who is transformed into a toad. The princes at once put up their swords, make friends and go home to their father. The second part of the story takes the form of a series of trials for the princes, whereby the ageing king intends to decide which of his sons shall inherit the kingdom. The first trial requires a bale of linen to be found fine enough to go through a ring; the second a dog small enough to fit in a walnut shell, and the third (inevitably) the most beautiful bride. After wandering the world the youngest son finds himself under a bridge at the world's end, where a little toad called Puddocky crawls out of a marsh and offers her help. By proving her ability to help the prince succeed in the first test, she wins his confidence to try her for the second. Again he succeeds, but when on the third visit her offer of help is to follow him herself to his father's house in her pumpkin coach drawn by rats, he is unable to refuse out of respect and feeling for her former kindness. Becoming transformed once more into the beautiful Parsley, Puddocky fans the prince's feeling for her into love, and easily wins the final contest. But an uncomfortable detail of the story remains; the rejected bales, little dogs and beautiful women – brought in succession in cart and coachloads by the prince's brothers – are ordered by the king to be thrown into a pond and left to drown. The injustice of the fate of the rejected brides – discarded like so many dogs or parcels – strikes a sour note at the very end of the story.

'The King Who Wanted a Beautiful Wife' also revolves round seemingly arbitrary extremes in the treatment of women. A king desires a beautiful wife; a fruitless search takes him to the door of two old women – sisters – whose hands are soft and white as young girls' from being shut away from the light of day all their lives. Deceived by the whiteness of the hand that passes him the requested glass of water, the king imagines a sequestered beauty. Nothing will satisfy him but that she should become his wife. The youngest of the old sisters successfully conceals her identity until after the wedding. When she is discovered, in a rage the king throws her out of the window. By chance preserved from being dashed to pieces on the ground below, the old woman attracts the pity of some fairies, who transform her into a beautiful young woman. She is discovered by the king and taken back. Finally, the old sister comes visiting. She is envious of her sister's good fortune, particularly of her physical transformation, and asks how it came about. I had my old

55

skin taken off, is the reply. The old sister goes to the barber and despite his protestations that he can't, she insists that he must do the same for her. However, the first little scratch of the razor has her jumping up and running home to her house in the woods, there to remain.

Both stories contain extremes of behaviour towards women; on the one hand violence, on the other passion and worship. Beauty is a chimera in both, to be sought and sought and only rarely or perhaps never found except in the imagination or by enchantment. In both, beauty acts as a kind of poison, setting brothers at each other's throats, or sister against sister. The way in which folk narrative often contains juxtapositions of moral inequality is interestingly commented on by Katherine Briggs.

> The very tale whose main emphasis is on the kindness of the hero which secures for him helpers in all kinds of unlikely directions, is often contradicted by the ruthlessness by which he acts, or allows others to act. Otherwise it strikes me that this is probably the sign of a rather primitive tale when kindness is a new and almost unrecognized virtue and ruthlessness is taken as a matter of course.[30]

Be this as it may, I like to think a fruitful state of unease is likely to remain in the mind of the hearer or reader left to ponder the lessons of the tales.

What are the alternatives to rewriting? Firstly, I would suggest the selection of positive or challenging (possibly less well known) stories to go alongside more familiar ones. At the moment, such stories have to be hunted out from source books rather than selections. A list is appended to provide a starting point for such searches. Secondly, I would recommend the reconsideration of familiar tales. Too ready a dismissal of all of them can overlook neglected but positive elements. Thus Hansel and Gretel need not be construed as a tract on male protectiveness towards women; both the boy and the girl save each other at different points in the story, Hansel by planning to lead the way safely home and succeeding on two occasions, and Gretel by outwitting the witch and pushing her into the oven.

Finally, I would like to urge that to adopt the practice of telling is to become subject to the rules of the oral tradition and thereby to enjoy a storyteller's licence to embellish, to forget and to change, rather than to fix and to freeze in writing: 'telling some tale, old yet ever new . . . told in the sunrise of the world, and [to] be told in its sunset'.[31]

Notes

1 A list of recommended titles can be found in Bob Dixon's two-volume *Catching them Young: Sex Race and Class in Children's Ficton* Pluto Press 1977 London

2 BRIGGS, K. M. (1970) *A Dictionary of British Folktales*, Part A, Vol. 1 p. 1

3 *ibid.*, p. 1

4 *ibid.*, p. 2

5 *ibid.*, p. 3

6 *ibid.*, p. 2

7 TOLKIEN, J. R. R. (1975) *Tree and Leaf* p. 34

8 STONE, Kay 'Things Walt Disney Never Told Us' in *Journal of American Folklore*, Vol. 88, No. 347, January–March 1975

9 TOLKIEN *op. cit.* p. 53

10 STONE *op. cit.*

11 TOLKIEN *op. cit.* p. 33

12 STEEL, Flora Annie (1973) *Tales of the Punjab* p. 6

13 CAMPBELL, Marie (1972) *Tales of Cloud Walking Country*, Bloomington Indiana Woodland, are notable in that a careful sketch is provided of each narrator. I am indebted to Dr Briggs for this observation.

14 A good version of this Grimm tale can be found in Wanda Gag's *Gone is Gone* Puffin 1975

15 TOLKIEN *op. cit.* p. 32

16 JACOBS, Joseph (1968) *English Fairy Tales* p. 79. Also in Briggs *op. cit.* p. 400

17 LANG, A. (1973) *Fifty Favourite Fairy Tales* London: Bodley Head p. 220

18 *ibid.* p. 226

19 JACOBS *op. cit.* p. 224; also in Briggs *op. cit.* Part A, Vol. 2 p. 238

20 STEEL *op. cit.* p. 149

21 BRIGGS *op. cit.* Part A, Vol. 2 p. 238

22 BRIGGS *op. cit.* Part A, Vol. 2 pp. 1–364

23 Told to the author by Judy Keiner 18th December 1977

24 CRANE, T. F. (1885) *Italian Popular Tales*, pp. 1–7. Crane mentions the French Legend of 'Melusina' and the Sicilian story 'The Story of the Merchant's Son Peppino' as examples of the type of tale where the husband's curiosity is punished, and makes five other references to Italian versions.

25 The rhyme appears in Grimm as follows, in the Pomeranian dialect in which the story was first collected. For further details see *Bruder Grimm Werke*, 3 Volumes, Stauffacher Verlag A G, Zurich 1974, Vol. 1 p. 332
Manntje, Manntje, Timpe Te
Buttje, Buttje, in der See,
Myne Fru de Ilsebill
Will nich so as ik wol will.

26 The version of 'The Fisherman and his Wife' given here is Andrew Lang's, appearing in his *Green Fairy Book*. In common with many versions in English of the Grimm original, it becomes mealy mouthed when it comes to the denouement of the tale. The wife's wish to become 'de lewe Gott' ('der liebe Gott') appears as 'I will be a god', or in the

first version to appear in English under the title *German Popular Stories* as 'I want to be lord of the sun and moon'. Presumably this was out of an English horror of anything remotely construable as blasphemous. I have given here a more accurate rendering of the German.

27 *The Juniper Tree and Other Tales from Grimm* (1973) selected by L. Segal and M. Sendak, with illustrations by Maurice Sendak, Bodley Head p. 109

28 The version of the tale retold here can be found in Andrew Lang's *Green Fairy Book*

29 In HAMPDEN, John (1966) *The House of Cats* p. 18

30 BRIGGS, K. M., personal communication 27.1.78

31 Steel *op. cit.* p. 6

Bibliography

AARNE, A. (1961) *The Types of the Folktale* F.F. Communications, 74. 2nd revision Helsinki

AUSUBEL, N. (1948) *A Treasury of Jewish Folklore*

BASILE, Giambattista (1850) *The Pentamerone, or the Story of Stories* London.

BRIGGS, K. M. *A Dictionary of British Folktales* 4 vols.
  Part A Folk Narratives 1970
  Part B Folk Legends 1971
  London: Routledge & Kegan Paul

BRIGGS, K. M. and TONGUE, Ruth L. (1965) *The Folktales of England* London and Chicago: University of Chicago Press

CAMPBELL, J. F. *Popular Tales of the Western Highlands* 4 vols 1890–3, Paisley and London

CAMPBELL, M. (1972) *Tales of Cloud Walking Country* Bloomington Indiana, Woodland

CLOUSTON, W. A. (1888) *The Book of Noodles* London

CRANE, T. F. (1885) *Italian Popular Tales* London: Macmillan

GAG, W. (1975) *Gone is Gone* London: Puffin

GRIMM, J. L. and GRIMM, W. K. (1975) *Household Tales* (complete edition) Routledge & Kegan Paul, London *Household Tales* (selection) Picador, London 1977

GRIMM, J. L. and GRIMM, W. K. (1892) *German Popular Stories* London: Chatto and Windus; reprint of original 1823 English edition Scolar Press, Menston, Yorkshire 1971

GRIMM, J. L. and GRIMM, W. K. *The Juniper Tree and Other Tales* 2 vols, London: Bodley Head 1974

GRIMM, J. *Teutonic Mythology*, tr. J. S. Stalleybrass, 3 vols, London 1882–83

HAMPDEN, John (1966) *The House of Cats* London: André Deutsch

JACOBS, J. (1968) *English Fairy Tales* London, Bodley Head

LANG, Andrew (1892) *The Green Fairy Book* London

LANG, Andrew (1977) *The Blue Fairy Book* London: Kestrel Books

LANG, Andrew (1973) *Fifty Favourite Fairy Tales* London: Bodley Head

STEEL, Flora Annie (1973) *Tales from the Punjab*, London: Bodley Head

STONE, Kay 'What Walt Disney Never Told Us' in *Journal of American Folklore* Vol. 88 No. 347, January–March 1975

THOMPSON, Stith (1955) *Motif-Index of Folk Literature*, 6 vols, F.F. Communications, Helsinki

TOLKIEN, J. R. R. (1975) *Tree and Leaf* London: Allen & Unwin

Index of recommended story titles

Index of tale-types

In the scholarly study of folklore, tales are classified according to type. Recommended tales are listed here under their tale-types.

Other examples can thus be found by consulting type-index lists such as that given in Briggs (1970) vol. 1 p. 35–77. (Briggs lists other type- and tale-index catalogues on p. 11.)

Details of where to find the examples listed can be obtained by consulting the accompanying list of recommended story-titles.

Tale-type	Examples
311 Three sisters rescued by their sister	'Peerifool'
313 The girl as Helper in the Hero's Flight	'Nicht Nought Nothing'
326 The Youth who wanted to know what Fear was	'The Dauntless Girl' 'The Boy who wanted to know what Fear was'
328 The Boy Steals the Giant's Treasure	'Jack and the Beanstalk' 'Mollie Whuppie'
366 The Man from the Gallows	'Teeny-Tinie'
400 The Man on a quest for his Lost Wife	'The Princess of the Blue Mountain' 'Melusina' 'The story of the Merchant's Son Peppino'
425 The Search for the Lost Husband	'The Black Bull of Norroway' 'Brother and Sister' 'East of the Sun and West of the Moon' 'The Singing Soaring Lark'
451 The Maiden who seeks her Brothers	'The Seven Ravens'
480 The Spinning Women by the Spring	'The Three Spinning Women' 'The Gypsy Woman'
510 Cinderella	'Ashpultel' 'Catskin' 'Tattercoats' 'Cap o'Rushes' 'Mossycoat' 'The Princess on the Glass Hill'
514 The Shift of Sex	'Bellucia' 'The Twelve Huntsmen'
519 The Strong Woman as Bride	'Bellucia' 'Brunhilde'
555 The Fisher and his Wife	'The Fisherman and his Wife'
875 The Clever Peasant Girl or 910	'A Pottle o'Brains' 'Clever Gretel' 'The Barber's Clever Wife' 'The Close Alliance'
955 The Robber Bridegroom	'Mr Fox' 'Bopoluchi' 'The Robber Bridegroom'

Tale-type	*Examples*
956B The Clever Maiden at Home Kills the Robbers	'The Brave Maidservant' 'The Robbers and the Old Woman'
1200 Numskull Stories	'The Wise Men of Gotham' 'The Three Sillies' 'The Schildburgers' 'The Sages of Chelm' 'The Silence Wager' (the Jamming Pan) 'Clever Else'
1408 The Man Who Does His Wife's Work	'Gone is Gone' 'The Old Man in a Wood'
1600 The Fool as Murderer	'Silly Jimmy and the Factor'
1940 The Extraordinary Names (not ascribed to a tale-type)	'Master of All Masters' 'Kate Crackernuts'

Section Two
From Experience to Literature

Introduction

The writers in this section are all concerned that children's own life experience should be recognized as the starting-point for learning. Without taking that experience into account, the teacher has no context for introducing literature or, indeed, anything else.

Harold Rosen's chapter is a reminder that the school is just one part of the community, not an institution '. . . out there in the "social context" there is a culture which is alive and kicking. Just as we have discovered that children do not come to school to be given language but arrive with it as a going concern we need to discover that children come with this too. Indeed, their language, the despised vernacular of great cities and industrial towns, is part of it.'

To the writers of the next three chapters the stories within family and community and in well-remembered books are a fundamental part of learning and vital to the formation of experiences and values for life. Margaret Walden then offers a detailed account of a class of children who became deeply involved in the books they read, an experience which transformed their learning.

7 Out there or where the masons went

Harold Rosen

> Not knowing the people, they are like heroes without a battlefield . . .
> What do they not understand? The language.
>
> Mao-Tse-Tung[1]

So we are going to talk about the social context? And a good thing too. But strange. The tidy abstraction of it; a non-combative, dusted-down, orderly little phrase. What does it stand for? The little world we can look at through the window, go shopping in, take buses from, play truant in? The invisible hinterland of this morning's *Times* where I read of 'the magnification of state benefits as the major source of subsistence for unproductive members of society'? The portable 'construction of reality', the internal architecture we have built for ourselves out of our social encounters? It cannot be the ramshackle edifice of institutions, pronouncements, channels of communication, labelled strata, laws and doctrines cobbled together by history for us to scuttle about in. The social context, as we call it, is not an arena in which we perform our dramas. It is the dramas themselves; people in action with each other and against each other improvising the text as they proceed.

Thus it is not language which generates what people say. Language does not possess this magical power or possesses it only fitfully and dubiously. What people say derives from praxis from the performance of tasks, from the division of labour – arises out of real actions, real struggles in the world. What they actually do, however, enters consciousness only by way of language, by being said.[2]

Therefore, if I am a bit needled by the phrase, 'the social context', it is because, cropping up like this, it announces that we are moving on to our next interesting theme and in due course we shall proceed to others. But that isn't it at all. Essentially, *there is nothing else to talk about*.

And we have talked about it. When we have, it has turned out to be not a fastidious excursion into the streets, not an awestruck promenade round our minds, not a jolly linguistic field trip (though it often starts in

Source: ROSEN, H. (1975) 'Out there or where the masons went' *English in Education* Vol. 9 No. 1 pp. 202–11

these ways) but a battlefield on which the lines are being more and more clearly delineated. It is becoming increasingly difficult to refuse to take sides. We have to choose between descriptions of an impoverished restricted code and the unearthing of a living oral tradition, between visions of school as a civilized and well-ordered island in a sea of barbarism and anomie and the aspiration that they should be reincarnate through the nourishment of the neighbourhood and community, between reading 'schemes' and literacy through critical consciousness (Freire).[3] Indeed all the choices we make, minute, urgent, even trivial, are more and more seen as taking sides. English teaching has become overtly a political matter. Chris Searle can be heard demanding passionately 'reciprocity, comradeship, shared experience'[4] against the amplified phantasmagora of Sir Keith Joseph, making our flesh creep with the teeming illegitimates spawned by the plebs, calling for a return to the old orderly ways.

It is out of assumptions about the nature of our society that new ways of English teaching have grown and changed. One old new way is for the teacher to open the eyes of his gullible pupils to the seductions of mass media and advertising. Himself immune (by what process of innoculation?), he will give immunity to others. He assumes that all around him the most baleful cultural forces of our society work fully and effectively and that only his critically-trained perceptions pick up the nuances of the non-stop confidence trick. Yet Raymond Williams showed us years ago the great difference between what people *make* of television and what they are expected to make of it. The banner-bearers of the High Culture have been telling us for so long that 'mass' culture is debased and fraudulent and sterile. Nevertheless, the cankers have got at their own confidence.

> Our dried voices when
> We whisper together
> Are quiet and meaningless
> As wind in dry grass
> Or rats' feet over broken glass
> In our dry cellar.
>   T. S. Eliot[5]

Our voices? Take this one which Connie Rosen[6] collected from a school in Birmingham, an ordinary voice,

> This ordinary woman
> Works in the factory up the road
> Putting bolts in the drill
> She presses the pedal that starts the drill working
> The clashing and the grinding
> The clicking and the shuttling

Are soothing to her ears
Filling her arms with rhythm
Her head with day-dreams.
The siren sound
And my mother faces the world again.

The doleful litany chanted endlessly is that the children and young people in schools are totally submerged by powerful manipulative forces outside their control which brutalize and stupefy them. If that message strikes home then it is small wonder if teachers who step forward to expose, analyse and demolish, feel in their hearts that they are puny in the face of giants who can spend more on one advertisement than one of them will spend on school books in the whole of a teaching career. Of course it is right to see and understand how such things work but the mistake is to believe that all around us are nothing but sad and spiritless victims. There are other forces at work. The miracle is not that we are all deformed by the dominant culture of our society but how much grows in the teeth of it, how our humanity asserts itself, how it asserts itself in the world of our pupils. We should not see the tabloids and commercials as the only emblems of their world, just as we should refuse to let a sanctified canon of literary works be the only alternative voice.

For there is that other assumption about society which corrodes our thinking, that the great working class of this country with its largely unwritten history, its heroism, its self-transforming engagement with life, its stubborn refusal to be put down is nothing but a deprived inarticulate herd. Even the new radical teacher sensitive to the language of working-class pupils and armed with political theory can be corroded by the social assumptions which abound in current educational and sociological literature. We are told that working-class children cannot learn to read because they have no books in the home and their parents do not read. Transmitted deprivation I believe they call it now. Yet millions of people throughout Europe in the late nineteenth and early twentieth centuries won their way to literacy from homes which were totally illiterate. Theories about the cycle of deprivation, glibly cited by politicians, have lurking beneath their surface an unhistorical notion that generations passively reproduce cultural attitudes; long before the *1870 Act*, in 1844 Engels[7] showed that, from amidst conditions of appalling squalor and exploitation, workers were producing a literary culture of their own

> They have translated the French materialists, Helvetius, Holback, Diderot, etc. and disseminated them, with the best English works, in cheap editions. Strauss's *Life of Jesus* and Proudhon's *Property* circulate among working men only. Shelley, the genius, the prophet Shelley, and Byron, with his glowing sensuality and his bitter satire upon our existing society, find most of their readers in the proletariat; the bourgeoisie owns only castrated editions. . . .

67

Turn to David Craig's magnificent book *The Real Foundations: Literature and Social Change*[8] which is so much more than literary criticism, and you will find the careful documentation and interpretation of changes in working-class consciousness, imagination and culture over more than a century and-a-half.

Teachers who have peered over the school wall and are intensely aware of 'out there' find themselves caught in a tormenting paradox and heart-breaking decisions. They see that most of their pupils are bound for jobs which are destructive of the spirit, that they will be working in conditions which are a denial of initiative, imagination, and participation. And yet all their teaching has been designed to foster personal sensitivity, personal response and self-exploration. Thus there are only intolerable choices. Prepare them for boredom and docility (euphemized into 'preparing them for society') or have them jettison all the work of the school years as soon as they perceive its irrelevance to their situation. But there are several flaws in the picture. Our own location in society and our own formation lead us to see only three forces at work – the grinding and destructive power of brutalizing jobs, the downward pull of bookless homes and philistine communities ranged against our informed wisdom. Whatever we have gained from our education, what it is least likely to have given us is a confident belief that there is any nourishing resource and vigour in the pupils' homes and community and that we have much to learn from that community. Perhaps, in the necessary emphasis we have given to *personal* growth, language for *personal* development and literature as an intensely *personal* exploration we have made English sound like the greatest ego-trip ever invented and we have forgotten that when working-class children have responded to our teaching then it is either because we have lured them into a world of private experience and cushioned individualism or because we have seen them as socially constituted human beings who can draw sustenance for the imagination from their own world and its values, from parents, grandparents and neighbours. I believe the best of new English teaching has been of the second kind. Ken Worpole[9] has shown through the work of Centerprise and *A People's Autobiography of Hackney* what kinds of responses are nurtured and evoked in places which seem from the outside either silent and subdued or centres of degrading violence.

Few of us have seen English as a training in conducting inaccessible dialogues with the self. We have sensed the health in uninterrupted transactions between private experience and social experience but we have lacked a sufficient understanding of the social consciousness of our pupils. So much has already been achieved by pioneering English teaching, but if it is to take, to bite deep then we must engage with working-class life and learn to apply our educated ears to its voice, with the same respect, awareness of nuances and human warmth we have applied so readily elsewhere. This is really the next bold step for English teaching. And it takes a lot of courage: for it means shifting our centre of gravity away from the usual sources of confirmation and approval. This is the shift that Chris Searle[10] has made. He quotes Mazine, aged thirteen,

All living in one community
Thinking for each other
Helping each other
No betrayals . . .

and comments

The English teacher in the schools is probably in the best position to give back to the child his own world and identity in education, to re-affirm it, to share it himself, support it and strengthen it.

Chris Searle is concerned with working-class identity not with how to create an individual awareness so frail it will melt in the heat of the production line.

One of the most deeply rooted ideas among us is that working-class life is a miserable and squalid affair unredeemed by delicate joys and sorrow, devoid of deep understanding and bold aspirations. I am not speaking of that suburban squeamishness which fears and hates every form of working-class assertion from the bold, shameless voices and noisy laughter to the nasty tendency to act together in defiance of established power. Nor am I speaking of the way in which the ruling class knows its enemy and manages to despise it, fear it and attack it. What I am speaking of is that tendency in progressive opinion of all kinds, including all kinds of socialists, to see working-class life as a horrifying ulcer springing from the unwholesomeness of capitalist society, a deforming disease which a new and better society would purge and cleanse.

Ever since industrialism took over, writers in the vein of Ruskin and William Morris have either argued from the physical ugliness, the blight of spoiled ground and sprawl of unplanned jerry-building, to the feelings of the people themselves, not seeing that human beings have extraordinary powers of resistance and enjoyment; or else they have taken a disgusted line about modern human nature itself and supposed that our actual capacity for experience has been weakened since the good old days (whenever they were).

D. Craig[11]

The alternative view amounts to this, that out there in the 'social context' there is a culture which is alive and kicking. Just as we have discovered that children do not come to school to be given language but arrive with it as a going concern, we need to discover that children come with this too. Indeed, their language, the despised vernacular of great cities and industrial towns, is part of it.

69

I do not think this means a sentimental vicarious undiscriminating adoration of everything which takes root in working-class communities, any more than I believe that it means the rejection of everything our own education has taught us. But the disentangling and sorting has still to be done. This is one of the huge tasks ahead of us – a vast relearning and an application of responses refined in the study of poetry and novels to everyday speech.

I might have begun in another place. Let me spend a little time there. Suppose I tell you that there is a little-known story of D. H. Lawrence, which contains this,

Well, when my poor ole pot and pan were working, were working at Tickleton Main – ooh it were a deep pit you know. They used to come out wringing wet, their trammin' drawers you know. I've seen him slosh it on floor and it's sloshed down like a dirty old floor cloth. I've had to swill 'em out, swill 'em, swill coal dust off them and dry them before he went to work next day. His pocket which he brought his tramming drawers home in and his belt which used to fasten his trammin' drawers to 'im when he was trammin' – he weren't in good health and I know he was on nights – I had nightmares occasionally.

When aught depresses me I always have a nice little nightmare to myself and I know this night I didn't – I had Leonard's mother with me, you know, for twenty years – after dad died, after her husband died and she were in t'other room and she said,
'Amy, what couldn't you sleep through t'night?'
I says, 'Eh, why?'
She says, 'You did sing.'
I says, 'Did I?'
'I heard somebody singing,' she says, 'Well, you were singing.'
She said, 'A for what you're singing?'
'Well,' I says, 'It weren't me, Gran, it weren't me.'
'It were you what were singing.'
I tell you and I felt – and I said, 'were it this.'
(Sings)
   For he toils down that mine, down that dark dreary pit,
   So that folks like us round the fireside will cheer.
   And he toils down below far from heaven's glorious light
   And his face may be black but his big heart is white.
I says, 'Was that it?'
'Aye', she says, 'that were it.'
I says, 'Oh my God.' I said, 'No it's never come to that.
I'm singing in my sleep because I'm upset about his work.'
But it must have been me because she said, 'That were t'song.
That were it I heard you singing.'

How did you read that? What kind of careful, reverent attention did you give it? What can you say about its dialogue, its shaped utterance, its sense of felt life and so on? But now read it again but bear in mind that it is in fact not by D. H. Lawrence but is the spontaneous language of a Yorkshire miner's wife which appears in *Language and Class Workshop, No. 2*.[12] Charles Parker recorded it and it came *not* in response to a request for a story or autobiography but to his request for old songs. I might have chosen other items from the collection, West Indian children telling traditional stories, miners' jokes, political fables, working women from Manchester and Liverpool finding fluent and powerful language as they become involved in controlling their own lives, and working men and women giving their complex views about language. Give material like this the same loving attention you have lavished on literature and you will extend your humanity. It is not a matter of asserting that working-class culture is infinitely superior. (Who suggested that anyway? Where? When?) but rather of demonstrating that it is there at all, that it is pertinent to our concerns, that we build on it or build nothing.

> In the evening when the Chinese Wall was finished
> Where did the masons go?. . . .

Bertolt Brecht

Notes

1 MAO-TSE-TUNG (1950) *Problems of Art and Literature* International Publishers
2 LEFEBVRE, H. (1968) *The Sociology of Marx* Allen Lane
3 FREIRE, P. (1974) *Education for Critical Consciousness* Sheed and Ward, *Education: The Practice of Freedom* Writers and Readers Publishing Cooperative 1976
4 SEARLE, C. (1973) *This New Season* Calder and Bryars
5 ELIOT, T. S. (1936) *Collected Poems, 1909–1935* Faber and Faber
6 ROSEN, C. and ROSEN, H. (1973) *The Language of Primary School Children* Penguin
7 ENGELS, F. *Condition of the Working-Class in 1844*
8 CRAIG, D. (1972) *The Real Foundations: Literature and Social Change* Chatto and Windus
9 WORPOLE, K. (1974) 'The School and the community' in Holly, D. (ed) *Education or domination*, Arrow
10 SEARLE, C. *op. cit.*
11 CRAIG, D. *op. cit.*
12 Language and class workshop, No. 2 Nov. 1974 H. Rosen (ed) (41a Muswell Ave., N10 2EH)

8   Historical novels for children
Anna Davin

Historical fiction is a medium which should be taken seriously by historians, especially socialist ones. It serves and renews a widespread popular interest in the past which is not satisfied by learned books and articles; written or on film it creates people's view of the past; and yet it is not quite respectable as history, and its writers are seldom allowed the status of historian.

True, some of it is very inadequate as history. The 'period setting' of an adventure story or a romance can carry as little conviction as the costumes in a pantomime, and be as inessential to the story. Some books are set in the past as they might be set in foreign parts, to create a spurious excitement by evoking the exotic and faraway or to disguise the implausible turns of an over-dramatic plot, or to allow the author to play on the reader's nostalgic illusions about the past – the patriotism and courage and beauty and wit and integrity of our forebears. Baroness Orczy's *The Scarlet Pimpernel* (1905), is a classic example of all this; but plenty more are to be found on station bookstalls today.

Even books whose real historical content is minimal may still have an important historical function, that of stimulating the historical imagination. This is of particular importance where children are concerned, and the focus of this essay is historical fiction written for children in the last twenty-odd years. The effort to understand the past, or even just to make sense of and remember the random chunks of it served up at school, becomes much easier once the imagination is engaged. But stories also have great advantages as vehicles for information: they can convey a range of different knowledge (events, names, relationships, chronological sequence, material background, beliefs and opinions, and so on), and a framework for storing it, so even when complex they are likely to be understood and remembered.

In the past this was taken for granted: history and story were the same thing. Wherever history has been (or is) transmitted orally, stories have been the means, though serving other functions as well – political, for instance, and religious, and cultural. They might trace the origins of a

---

Source: DAVIN, A. (1976) 'Historical novels for children' *History Workshop Journal* Vol. 1 No. 1 pp. 154–65

people or a dynasty, affirming a cultural identity and justifying possession and rule by celebrating the conquests and feats of heroic ancestors, or identifying the generations and the alliances which marked the stages of their inheritance. Or they might lament defeats and wrongs, preserving the memory of lost power and possession and perhaps calling on the hearers to recover what had been lost. Or they might through the example of great figures of the past recommend particular virtues, or explain customs, or impart necessary knowledge of a whole range of social and economic activities. Sometimes such stories have survived the society which they served and recorded, as folk tales for instance, or taken up into an international repertory of storytellers' material. Sometimes too they survived to be written down, incorporated into early histories or perhaps recorded in their own right. So they are to be found in the chronicles of medieval Europe, or the comparable but much earlier Chinese Shu Jing ('History Classic') of the Zhou dynasty, or the old Irish cycle of Cú Chulainn (first written down in the early ninth century and recording such events as the Cattle Raid of Cooley), or the stories of the Iliad and the Old Testament. In an interesting historical novel, *The Eagles have Flown* (1954), Henry Treece uses material of this kind – the legends of the Arthurian cycle – along with more conventional sources, for his reconstruction (almost creation) of the shadowy historical figure Artos the Celt, alias Artorius Count of Britain, the last ruler to claim Roman authority.

But now history and stories have diverged, with the ignored exception of historical novels. History has the solemn dignity of an academic discipline, while the humble story is an indulgence, left to children, or for tired adults relaxing after a hard day. Formal history seems alien to most people, the province of specialists and experts; even those who are studying it often see it as ground to be conquered rather than explored or enjoyed. Stories are very different. They don't make anyone feel alarmed and inadequate: they invite interest, they are easy to remember and perhaps to pass on; they are common property, everyone's right.

The problem lies perhaps in the character of modern institutionalized history: the emphasis on facts, statistics, analysis, the scientific approach. Propagandists have always known the usefulness of stories. Heroic legends of the Samurai were revived to serve modern Japanese militarism and the Meiji state; Nazi nationalism called up the Teutonic Knights; and in Britain too 'Stories from History' less formally but no less effectively served to carry and to inculcate ruling class ideology concerning the present as well as the past. Generations of children until recently acquired their history through such chauvinist and imperialist collections as Henrietta Elizabeth Marshall's *Our Island Story*, backed up by the works of novelists like Henty. If such books are discredited it is not only because they proclaim too blatantly outmoded ideas, or ideas which are permitted only in more moderate and discreet versions. It is also because of their form. Stories have been replaced by textbooks. Stories are dangerous: they are fiction not fact; they engage the emotions where detachment is all; they are contaminated by imagination. But this is surely the essential quality and advantage of stories – they excite the imagination.

History for me was for many years just a school subject. I sat through classes, took notes from the blackboard, read textbook chapters for homework or learnt dates and events and names, or wrote a composition, and I passed exams painlessly because remembering and writing both came easily to me. My friends were not all so lucky: for them it was often a matter of chance whether they hit even the right century for a particular battle or a king's accession or a treaty or an Act, and their versions of events were often hopelessly confused. My good fortune lay in having grasped the difference between 'here and now' and 'there and then', in having a sense of the continuities and the differences between one time and place and another. Without particularly knowing it, certainly without having been taught it, I had a framework within which I could place and remember the various items of information fed to us at school so that they weren't random facts to be learnt parrot fashion, but sequences of connected information. The historical understanding which enabled me to make sense of school history had, I now think, two main sources, both taking the form of stories, neither connected with school. One was the oral tradition of my Irish-New Zealand family – the stories of other times and places that I heard from as early as I can remember, and asked for again and again. The other was the novels set in the past which from the age of eight or nine I avidly read. I did not think of either as history – they were far more enthralling – but they were the imaginative stimulus which made the past real.

Stories were part of the explanation of things: clothes, pictures, books, photographs, furniture, had stories attached, and so sometimes did habits. My mother's preference for unsweetened tea, for instance, had a story behind it which we loved to hear, an incident in the rural New Zealand childhood of her own mother, Winnie Crow. Winnie and two little friends walking home from school were caught by a storm, and the friends, who lived further on, were invited by her mother (Ellen Crow, my great-grandmother) to come in and wait out the squall before finishing their tramp. She poured them out tea and asked if they liked sugar in it. The younger one said 'Yes please', but on drinking it burst into tears, whereupon the elder explained that their mother had promised them each a new hat if they could go without sugar in their tea for a whole year, and the child was crying because she feared she had lost her right to the hat. Winnie's mother convinced the anxious child that sugar in someone else's house wouldn't count, and anyway it was an accident: she hadn't asked for sugar but truthfully answered the question as to whether she liked it. When they had set off again, consoled and warmed, her own child Winnie, impressed by the idea, asked whether she could make the same bargain, and gave up sugar for the year to win a hat. She

74

never regained the taste for it, and never in later life put it in her own children's tea, so her daughter, my mother, never expected or liked sweetened tea.

My sisters and I, listening to that story, would recognize some things – the shy child's anxiety, for instance, unable to explain that she did *like* sugar, but she didn't *want* it, or the older child speaking for her, or their scrupulousness about the undertaking they had made; but our appreciation of the story came also from the strangeness of its world, evoked by the details that were part of it, and indeed by the situation itself. Unlike us, those children had had a walk of several miles between school and home, and along country tracks not the pavements we knew. They wore hats and liked them – were prepared to make sacrifices for the promise of a new one – where we associated them with school and hated them accordingly. Their mothers bought sugar by the sack, and flour and oatmeal; they went shopping infrequently and with horse and cart, not daily with shopping bag and pram or bicycle; they baked their own bread and grew their own potatoes; and money was short enough for every spoonful of sugar to count. Our own mother provided a link between that world and ours, and we never tired of stories about it, every new detail building up our image and understanding of it.

The ramifying explanations which our endless questions evoked brought us in touch with each generation's world. The furthest back was always Ireland, with stories even beyond the family chronology, of English invasion and injustice. (Here there was the occasional overlap with school history: Oliver Cromwell, for instance, figured in lessons and in stories, though in one he was an august and principled, if misguided, leader, and in the other a ruthless invader and murderer.) In Ireland our great-grandmother had churned butter and sat at her spinning; there were matchmakers and travelling storytellers; women had smoked pipes; and people had spoken a language we didn't know. There were echoes of it in the names of the people in the stories (including our mother's: like her mother she was Winnie, but to her grandmother and while the family spoke Irish she had been Oonagh), and in their speech, as told by my mother, which was more elaborate than our own (and than her normal speech), with unfamiliar turns of phrase which were perhaps translations of their half-remembered words; sometimes she would tell us their actual words, strange soft phrases which meant nothing till she translated them but which attracted us, like 'Tabhuim póg, cailín óg' – 'Give me a kiss, little girl'. After crossing the world to join the young man to whom she was 'promised' our great-grandmother had worked with him to create farmland out of virgin bush, in the remote southern tip of New Zealand where even Maoris did not then live: that was another world of which we loved to hear, and through stories about her children and grandchildren we saw it change. The family chronology of all these stories must have helped us understand their basis in time: it was not just differences between England and New Zealand that we were learning, but differences between our now and a whole series of thens. And we could gauge the passage of time by analogy with the familiar gap between ourselves and our parents.

Through books, I entered historical worlds more complete in themselves, less part of a continuum. Each book stood alone, with its own set of characters and its own time and place; they were not interwoven like the family stories, the same figures rarely recurred, there was no tradition of relationship or acquaintance linking them and me, and I could not enlarge my knowledge of them by asking questions. But perhaps because of their more isolated character, and because there was no familiar storyteller between them and me, my involvement in them (at least for as long as I was reading) was also more complete. Absorbed in E. K. Seth-Smith's *When Shakespeare Lived in Southwark* (1944), or Geoffrey Trease's *Cue for Treason* (1940), or Rosemary Sutcliff's early books, *The Queen Elizabeth Story* (1950), *The Armourer's House* (1951), and *Brother Dustyfeet* (1952), I felt a familiarity with sixteenth-century England which I never knew in school lessons on the Tudors and Stuarts. I smelt its smells, tasted its foods, heard its sounds, saw its spectacles. It was peopled with characters I could watch and listen to, sometimes even identify with, not monarchs and prelates with stiff titles and stiffer robes, but moving living people, working and sleeping and eating, getting on with each other or quarrelling; not leaders of parties or advocates of policies, but apprentices and children and strolling players along with their parents, masters and mistresses, patrons and acquaintances. True, 'real' historical characters were often brought in, but again they were more real in the stories than in class: Shakespeare for instance appeared, now (in *Cue for Treason*) as a kindly friendly person, now (in *When Shakespeare Lived in Southwark*) more stern, but either way because he spoke and reacted he was a person and not just a famous name.

Returning now to some of my childhood books I see that their accounts of the past have limitations, set partly by the material available to their authors, partly by today's definitions of what is right for a children's book. The historical context is usually conveyed by reference to obvious differences in everyday matters such as clothes, transport, housing, perhaps work, and street or farm life. Sometimes too a political context is given which ties it firmly to a particular time and place, and famous names of the time (monarchs or politicians or writers or whatever) figure by name or in person. The plot may also be keyed to contemporary events: war and invasion, for instance, or technological invention, or a specific cultural context (like the Elizabethan theatre) which can serve as a constant reminder of the historical setting. And sometimes it is a question of language, the use of archaic words in descriptions or in dialogue which are intended to give a flavour of the past. Occasionally too there are author's interventions explaining and instructing, as when in Rosemary Sutcliff's *Brother Dustyfeet* the father's plan to send his son

76

to Oxford as someone's servitor when he is 'thirteen or so' is followed by a parenthesis: '(People went to the Universities much younger in the days of Queen Elizabeth than they do now)'.

Parenthetical explanations are a clumsy device: they interrupt the flow of the story and jolt the reader back into the present, sometimes even with an uncomfortable sense of being patronized. The use of archaic language is also, for different reasons, difficult to bring off. Too much of it emphasizes the inaccessibility of the past: continual thees and thous, prithees, quothas, and methinks make for stilted dialogue, and archaisms – by definition unfamiliar – may also be incomprehensible. (On the other hand I remember the attraction of words like posset, ague, wimple, pomander, coif, sarsenet, tansy, and so on, whose approximate sense could be guessed, and whose unfamiliarity was part of the spell of the past.) The use of modern language does not usually prick the historical bubble, though many writers seem to avoid turns of phrase with an exclusively twentieth-century ring. An exception, though he gest away with it, is Geoffrey Trease. In *Cue for Treason*, for example, which is set in late sixteenth-century England, the hero protests 'You must think me pretty mean'; his friend Kit warns him 'The Desmonds think you're cracked'; and Tom Boyd with whom they are unravelling a northern plot against the queen, warns that 'a whistle gives the show away'. Trease's books often consist mainly of dialogue, and it is exceptionally good: it offends neither by archaism nor by anachronism, is fast moving and natural, carries the plot efficiently and fits his characters.

Geoffrey Trease is also exceptional in his emphasis on the political context, choosing as the setting of many of his books some moment of political crisis which is expounded during the course of the story, as well as furnishing material for an exciting plot. In *Bows Against the Barons* (1934) for instance, a yeoman's son shoots a deer in defence of his family's young crops, and takes refuge with the outlaws in Sherwood Forest to escape the likely penalty of death. His adventures make a good read, but the political situation which has made outlaws of the others as of him is never forgotten: they are outlaws because of laws which they oppose and which support feudal privilege and depredation. *Follow My Black Plume* (1963) and *A Thousand for Sicily* (1964) are about a young Englishman's adventures with Garibaldi in 1849 and 1860; *Thunder of Valmy* (1960) engages the young reader's sympathy with the French Revolution; *The White Nights of St Petersburg* (1967) with the Russian, and so on. One of the major values of Trease's books for me and no doubt for other children was that they gave a version of the political past which was more easily understood and also more acceptable than what was taught at school: they were on the side of the people and enabled one to see and argue things in those terms, whereas in school history the ruling class was always doing its best. Trease's books still read well, and children are still gripped and convinced by them. They are adventure

stories with a good political line, and they are historical in that they describe and explain events in the past. But they give no more detail of
everyday life and the specific complexity of a particular society at a
particular time than is needed to carry through the plot.

Other writers often convey the historical context not by language nor
by more than passing reference to the contemporary political situation,
but primarily by detailed description of everyday actions and objects.
The material setting is given informed and often loving attention, and
sometimes carefully illustrated. Cynthia Harnett, for instance, in books
like *The Great House* (1949), *The Wool Pack* (1951), *Ring Out Bow Bells*
(1953), and *The Load of Unicorn* (1959), includes her own sketches of all
kinds of everyday objects which figure in the text, which I remember
made it much easier to visualize how things were different in medieval
England. Such emphasis on the material context of everyday life is a
good antidote to the tendency of exam-based history to concentrate on
high politics and a rather generalized account of social change. It can
give the child a clearer perception of the material implications of class
difference than orthodox history teaching is likely to do. (Barbara
Willard's *Priscilla Pentecost* (1970) for instance, presents a graphic contrast between the life of a parish orphan in a farming family, and the
spoilt child of rich parents, set in eighteenth-century England.) And
certainly it is an invaluable aid to the imagination. Unfortunately this
scrupulous attention to objects is rarely matched where subjects are
concerned. How people talked must always be largely speculative, and
even for attitudes, roles, and relationships the sources – particularly the
secondary sources on which the researching novelist is likely to depend –
are inadequate.

Children's books often centre on children, but we know little about the
children of the past; little about family life, its forms and the extent of its
importance to the various children of any given society, and very little
about the thoughts and feelings of children at any time, because even
more than women, and even more than the mass of labouring adults,
they left no account of themselves. And until recently historians ignored
the under and inner life of the societies they studied, so that not only was
there little information on such areas as childhood and the family, but
also people scarcely realized the complexity and variety of their history.
So historical novelists can hardly be blamed for having expected and
imagined patterns in the past which fitted today's, supplementing inadequate evidence by creating attitudes and relationships whose real
basis was modern, or even conjuring up a 'timeless' world of rosy care-
free childhood and fond, fair, unharassed adults. Books like Elizabeth
Goudge's *Towers in the Mist* (1938), are marred in this way, at least for
the adult rereading – I must admit that their saccharine did not offend
me as a child. So are Rosemary Sutcliff's first three novels, but the later
ones, from *Simon* (1953) and *The Eagle of the Ninth* (1954), are very
much stronger (and also historically more convincing) because the

characters are young adults, exposed to adult pains and difficulties, suffering and developing in a harsh world.

Another obstacle to realism in children's books is the writer's deference to the supposed needs of child readers. All storytellers have the problem of how to keep things exciting without killing off the main character, but child readers are more likely than most to be shielded from the worst possibilities and given happy endings, and this softening or trivializing particularly affects the everyday story: in battles and adventures death occurs (though honour and glory disguise it and it has little enough reality for the excited child in the armchair), but in more familiar settings death and bereavement are almost taboo. Yet until this century almost any child would have made their acquaintance, and historical novels by ignoring this omit a major element in the experience of children in the past. (The taboo is of course a recent one, and a function of the demographic and social developments which in real life have made death unfamiliar; earlier children's writers made deathbeds and orphans their stock-in-trade.) Poverty and illness and suffering are not totally barred, but they are not likely to be shown as a permanent part of most societies, nor as making possible the security and comfort of the few: they appear as temporary and individual, ended or modified by luck or personal effort, not by collective organization and struggle. Work scarcely figures, whether child or adult, drudgery or enjoyed. In *Brother Dustyfeet* the first few pages describe Hugh helping his bad-tempered aunt with work such as a great many children in sixteenth-century England would have done, and he runs away because of overwork and her cruelty, falling in with a happy-go-lucky band of actors whose life suits him better till finally he comes across his dead father's best friend, who adopts him into his family and will send him to college. The stories of heroism and war seldom mention the labour which supported them – who looked after crops and cattle while the Northmen were off raiding, who paid for feudal pageantry or made the armour or cooked the food. And women are almost totally absent from such books, to an extent which often exceeds any historical probability. Ronald Welch's *Knight Crusader*, for instance, which won the Carnegie Medal in 1954, has an entirely male cast, even when the crusader hero returns to England. Jill Paton Walsh, on the other hand, in her bleak and bloody *Hengest's Tale* (1966), shows (though very much in passing) something of women's place in Frisian and Jutish warrior society.

A useful device for enlarging the scope of a historical novel even when its characters are children (or all but children) is the journey. It enables the writer to keep things moving and to introduce new material and new characters without needing to explore any context too deeply or in unavailable detail: it evades for instance the problem of evidence on domestic life, and allows the writer to string together contexts and activities about which more is known. It also makes possible comparisons between different ways of life at a particular time, an important dimension of historical understanding. Most commonly this involves the difference between town (or often metropolis) and country, or perhaps between one country and another. Sometimes it is used to raise larger questions of social and economic organization: Rosemary Sutcliff for instance contrasts imperial Rome with Britain (*Outcast*, 1955), or Roman life in comfortable southern Britain and in frontier forts, and tribal life north of Hadrian's Wall (*The Eagle of the Ninth*, 1954); and in Henry Treece's *The Children's Crusade* (1958) Geoffrey and Alys find that Saracen and Frank are not so different – 'There is good, and evil, in all men, whatever the colours of their skin'. Some journeys provide incident for the plot at the expense of character development, but in the best journey books the travellers learn and develop as they go. In Peter Dickinson's splendid *The Dancing Bear* (1972) for instance, there are three improbable travelling companions, Bubba, the bear, Silvester, her slave keeper, now running away, and Holy John, the domestic saint from the same wealthy Byzantine household as Bubba and Silvester, forced down from his pillar after the house has been sacked by a band of Kutrigur raiders. They set off in pursuit of these returning Huns, the boy slave because he hopes to rescue the Lady Ariadne, daughter of the house but his foster sister and friend, whom they have carried off; and Holy John because he has discovered a vocation to take Christ to the Huns. The journey changes all the travellers. Bubba discovers how to fish and to find honey and to enjoy woods and hillsides and streams. Silvester also, more gradually, learns to relish freedom; he has to take initiatives and decisions, and gradually throws off the habits of the slave; and his assumptions about the superiority of 'civilized' Byzantium and the barbarity of all who live outside its sway are challenged by his experiences. When they reach their destination, the Kutrigur encampment far north beyond the Danube and the Dniester, he is also forced to realize that for Ariadne capture was liberation: she is happier herding cattle than she has ever been and does not want to return to her puppet life in Byzantium. ('In the City *she* had been a thing – the inadequate channel through which a great estate was to be passed from one owner to the next – but here in the camp she was a person.') Holy John has to relearn the importance of the body: in his years on the pillar he ignored discomfort so as to mortify the flesh for the glory of God and to impress luxury-loving Byzantines; but now ignoring sore feet only slows his progress and so delays his mission.

As *The Dancing Bear* might suggest, the range of setting and theme of children's books has widened since I was a child. My books had often something homely about them. Some of them even explored the past by transporting modern children back as historical tourists; and many of them were stressing what was common between past and present, even at the most superficial level, like the forced echo between the late sixteenth century and the 'new Elizabethan age' of the 1950s. Now, perhaps because fantasy worlds have become an established part of children's reading, the unfamiliar is altogether acceptable, and the child reader is offered tales from every possible place and time.

At the same time, since I suppose the early sixties, the taboos against a realistic portrayal of society seem to have lost some of their force. The definitions of 'what children want' are less protective and patronizing, and indeed it is often hard to tell where the boundaries between child and adult concerns now lie. The historical novels I read in the fifties were undoubtedly children's books; but their successors are often capable of holding adult readers as well. The best of them make a sustained attempt to explain as well as to evoke the past, and to show its complexity; work is given more place, and the viewpoint and experience of working people more often represented; the characters are more likely adolescent or adult than child, which makes possible a wider range of experience and relationships; and the intellectual content is altogether more substantial. Hester Burton for instance, in such books as *Castors Away!* (1962), *Time of Trial* (1963), and *No Beat of Drum* (1966), takes periods of intellectual and social ferment (the 1800s in the first two, 1830 in the third) and explores them through characters who themselves are trying to make sense of their world, to reconcile their own values and ideals with the injustice and oppression they experience or see around them. They talk and think and argue, about justice, about glory (*Castors Away!* has an excellent account of the disintegration of a boy's patriotic fervour and thirst for the glory of battle when he serves as a powder monkey at Trafalgar), about woman's role, about politics. Bob Leeson is another more recent writer who makes ideas and argument an integral part of his children's books, and he also tries to tie them in with economic and class structure. In *Maroon Boy* (1974) and *Bess* (1975) he explores the motives and effects of sixteenth-century voyages from Plymouth to the New World, and the workings of the port town as they affected merchant and sailor and their families. His characters argue out the conflicts between religion and profits based on privateering or the slave trade, or the contradiction of dreaming of a new world settlement in which people should be free and equal, and raising money to finance it by lending out money at high interest rates, or by speculating in corn. And Bess, in his second novel, is a fine intelligent independent girl. She rebels against expectations of domesticity and deference, lives as a man while she searches for her lost brother Matthew who is said to be 'on Darien shore', trades and prospers as a business woman back in Plymouth, suffers barbarous but legal treatment from her husband, and escapes eventually to join idealists who are going to found a new world settlement the hard way, with determination and faith in a new life rather than financial backing and the hope of profits.

So political discussion is now admissible in children's books to an extent which used to be rare even in historical novels written for adults. (Alexander Cordell's were the splendid exception, and interestingly his two books for children – *The White Cockade* and *Witches' Sabbath*, both

1970 – are almost straight adventure stories though set in Ireland in 1798: their political analysis is much less important or indeed complex than in his adult books, and he also omits the vigorous sexual relationships which characterize his other books.) And realism allows accounts of poverty and disaster, unemployment, strikes, evictions and even massacres. (Cf. the Highland clearances in Mollie Hunter's *A Pistol in Greenyards*, 1965, or her account of the Glencoe massacre in *The Ghosts of Glencoe*, 1966.) The combination of open political content (and commitment) with a realistic account of ordinary people's lives and their social context is producing books which are really exciting to the socialist historian, as well as to the child reader. There are stories which explore class conflict through the experience of working-class characters, and show the relationships between a social and economic situation, personal factors, and the various possible political standpoints. One such is Peter Carter's *The Black Lamp*, which gives a powerful and convincing view of the build-up to Peterloo through the eyes of a fifteen-year-old, a weaver's son who has the consciousness of an engineer (there is a very good sense of his growing mastery of and interest in his work), and yet identifies with his father and the weavers who march to Manchester to defend a status they have already lost to the mechanized future. And writers today are not ashamed or afraid to draw on local tradition rather than archives in order to re-create an undocumented past: Susan Price for instance in *Twopence a Tub* (1975) presents an account of a Black Country pit village in the 1850s which rings entirely true, especially in people's language and attitudes and experience, but which she says is based more on guesswork and invention (and certainly also on local tradition) than on research and cold facts.

There are problems of course in setting out to write the history of the oppressed, in fiction as in formal history. Inadequate evidence is one difficulty, the risk of idealization is another. These difficulties are particularly acute if one is concerned with women in the past. Orthodox history shows them (if at all) as secondary and subservient, and alternative versions are only gradually being rediscovered or built up. Anyone who presents women who contradict the stereotype will be accused (like Bob Leeson with his Bess) of creating an impossible ideal character in a twentieth-century image. But there are always rebel slaves, and in any case the slavery was far less complete and more varying than we have been taught.

Barbara Willard is a writer who succeeds particularly well in presenting strong independent women who are also clearly and convincingly of their time. They are rooted indeed as firmly in place as in time: their activities derive clearly from local and contemporary possibilities. The books in her Mantlemass series span the experience of a related sequence of families in the Sussex Weald in the manor house of Mantlemass, starting with *The Lark and the Laurel* (1970), which is set in the late fifteenth century, and continuing through to the mid-seventeenth century with

The Sprig of Broom (1971), *A Cold Wind Blowing* (1972), *The Iron Lily* (1973), and *Harrow and Harvest* (1974). In the first, there is Dame Elizabeth Fitgerald, who runs a warren where she breed rabbits for their skins; she is a widow and a business woman, and at the beginning of the book takes on the re-education of her court-bred niece Cecily. Comparing their hands when Cecily first arrives, Dame Elizabeth calls Cecily's the hand of a cosseted gentlewoman. It can only embroider and play the lute.

> 'Now take my hand,' said Dame Elizabeth. 'This hand, also, is the hand of a gentlewoman. But it has taught itself to grow strong. It has learnt many skills. This hand will bake, will brew, will write accounts fairly, will strike in anger, soothe in sickness, be silk or iron on a rein. It will cull herbs, bind up sores, carve meat, shear a fleece or gut a coney. Yes, indeed – you will tell me it has grown hard with all this service. But I shall answer that it has grown proud.'

Cecily, shocked and alarmed at first, comes to understand and share her aunt's values (the change is beautifully told and accounted for), and in the next two books figures as an equally strong character herself. The Iron Lily, in the fourth, is a woman ironmaster; while in *Harrow and Harvest*, interestingly, Cecilia, brought up in a wealthier generation of the family, has the same robust intelligence as her predecessors without their practical training, and feeling inadequate sets out to learn the skills her grandmother had. Her motive is practical: 'If the war go for Parliament they say there'll be none servant and none master, but all level. So ladies must learn to be women.'

I have been selecting points concerning women, to show Barbara Willard's recurrent concern with the question of women's identity and standing; but her books are admirable in other ways. The linking of national and local is nicely achieved, for instance in the impact of large economic or religious change. The local economy (apart from production for subsistence) is based now on horses now on iron, and national demand – the result for instance of wars – is shown to alter the local situation. Local speech and identity are strongly portrayed, and the gradual distancing from them of the manor people as their prosperity increases, till even loyalty to place and tenants and employees is so weakened that almost the whole family emigrates after the destruction of the house during the Civil War. By writing books which are more or less linked, like those of the Mantlemass series, Barbara Willard has the advantages both of the novel, whose length and complexity can enable the reader to gain a fairly close understanding of whatever society or part of society the writer fixes upon, and of family stories, like those of my childhood, which are enriched by internal overlaps and connections, and in which the names from each generation mark the passage of time and build up a structure within which it may be understood. But individually

D

too these novels stand as convincing evocations of time and place, focusing on a group of one class but not ignoring others, nicely balancing the demands of storytelling with the historian's recreation of a setting, providing the key to a political and economic understanding and at the same time engaging the reader's attention and sympathy through characters who are credible and interesting.

The historical writer's task is not easy. A good historian who is a bad storyteller will not be read, so the craft of writing, and of writing fiction, is essential; and writing for children has its particular requirements, even if they are less limiting than they have recently been considered. But a gripping writer may also be one who gives a partial or misleading picture, from ignorance or from prejudice, or from a desire to meet the needs of today's adolescent and adult escapists, for whom certain periods (the Regency for instance) and themes (Royalist intrigues or aristocratic love affairs) are supposed to be more suitable than others. The immensely popular writers of historical romances, however carefully they claim to research their backgrounds, never give a balanced view because it is illusions they want to evoke, not reality. Every detail in the descriptions of splendid costumes may be correct for the month and the year in which they are being worn, but there will be no hint of how they were made or paid for. Often too they falsify history by personalizing it. Everything is explained by stereotyped personal factors – love, jealousy, enmity, insecurity, friendship. Fourteenth-century England in Anya Seton's *Katherine* (1954), for instance, resembles an Edwardian 'mediaeval pageant', a celebration of the feudal aristocracy in which the only non-noble characters presented favourably are those who subordinate their own interests to personal or feudal loyalty to those above them. It is a chronicle of personal relationships (themselves dominated by sexual obsession – Katherine is the passionate but innocent temptress, her sexuality overpowering but fulfilled only in submission) in which John of Gaunt's political moves are time and again explained by the state of his love-life. It may be said in favour of such books that even a bad historical novel can awaken the historical imagination and provoke an appetite for history; but the reader whom they have so stimulated will have to go elsewhere for the real satisfaction of that historical appetite, for they provide a poor, unbalanced diet.

The personalizing of history is the potential strength of the historical novel, enabling it to impart a richer historical understanding than formal history books can usually give. Economics, social relationships, political experience and opinion, come alive because they are *lived*, by characters whom the child can envisage and hear. But the relationship between the particular and the general is crucial. It has to be understood by the writer; it has to inform the novel and be passed on to the reader. Otherwise the storyteller may succeed, but the historian fails.

9 Experience of literacy in working-class life
Peggy Temple

I want to be a bit more particular now and talk about my own experience of working-class life in two different contexts. The first one when I was a child in a Norfolk village forty years ago, and what literacy meant in our surroundings. I would say that we were working class, but perhaps we had a rather uneasy position in the village between the tradespeople, the vicar and our headmaster and the doctor and the farm labourers at the bottom of the scale who were regarded then as the lowest of the low – who went to the Co-op to do their shopping and you would never have been seen dead in the Co-op! But I still would say that we led a working-class life in general. My father was a railway porter at a village station and later on, a clerk, and later still a stationmaster but not 'til after I'd left home, and he left his village elementary school at the age of thirteen; boys from the country schools were not entered for the 11+ or expected to go any further, they were destined to be farm labourers or something similar, and anything they did beyond that had to be self-education. We lived in a small house in the village which was originally intended for farm labourers with one kitchen/living-room with a black grate, a small front room that was never used except at Christmas and christenings and funerals and so on, the front door was never opened, but we did have books in the house. We even had a bookcase in the kitchen and the book that I remember seeing there was *The Life of Maxim Gorky* in a red cover with the Heinemann windmill imprint on it. Whether my father had read it, I don't know. I never did, but that's one I remember, presumably because of the name – names of people fascinated me. I remember showing utter disbelief when my father told me there was a film star named Clark Gable; I could not believe it.

And there was a big box of books under the bed in the back bedroom, the forerunners of paperbacks and Penguins, the Everyman cheap edition novels, and a Marie Stopes which I discovered and read under the bedclothes with a torch (laughter). And in the front room we had a big bookcase that was remarkable because it had no screws in it, we just

Source: TEMPLE, P. (1977) 'Experience of literacy in working-class life' in Hoyles, M. *The Politics of Literacy* Writers and Readers Publishing Co-operative pp. 79–85. Transcript of a talk given to fellow education students at NELP, 1975

pulled the glass front out and slotted it back and that was full of my granny's books, in quotation marks, which she willed to me when she died; Arthur Mee's children's encyclopaedias, countries of the world, a set of Everyman encyclopaedias and a whole lot of religious books because she was a divinity student, all with leather gilt tooled bindings – none of which I ever opened, but which still sit in that bookcase in my mother's front room. And one enormous one – *The Life and Work of St Paul*, about that size, by Dean Farrar, and they are still there.

But of course, when my granny read, she read thrillers and books on Spiritualism and so on, and she introduced me to those when I was about ten and it got to the point where I was too frightened to go to bed. But what undermines our status rather as a working-class family was the fact that my granny was a teacher, but she came from Bethnal Green and she began her teaching life as a pupil/teacher at the age of fourteen with sixty children in a class, but she did do what many of them in those days didn't, she went to college, St Catherine's, Tottenham, and got her teacher's diploma in 1892. She went to Norfolk and became headmistress in various village schools, so I was familiar with school and books and things like that from an early age. When I stayed with granny the schoolhouse adjoined the school and I used to knock on the door and go into the classroom with the children as a baby.

Coming back to my own parents, my father was a great reader of magazines and newspapers; in those days *Titbits* and *Answers* with green and pink covers, *The Daily Mail*, *The Passing Show*, which gave coupons and you could get a set of Dickens from those. Our set of Dickens is in the bookcase in the front room. Some of them I read, but he read them all and he was reading *Bleak House* for the umpteenth time when he died. Now he liked non-fiction which I think would be true of many people of his age and generation in that situation. It was real to them, it described things that were actually in the world, experiences that they could have, and share, particularly he liked books about the war because he went to the First World War when he was seventeen, having added a year to his age, and while he was out in Mespot, as they called it then, he wrote a long diary of experiences. He wrote it in pencil and he rolled it up and we've never been able to decipher it to this day. Anyway, he wrote it. So I grew up with books. (I must mention one or two others, I expect some of you remember Collie Knox, of *The Daily Mail*. That was another name that stuck in my mind and my mother used to make me cut out his column and I had to make them up into a scrapbook for her. And then there was Hannen Swaffer – I couldn't really believe that people had these names (laughter). We did Bullets in John Bull, the competition where you add the ends to phrases and if you're lucky you get a voucher to go in again next week – free. And then, when *Picture Post* came out, we had that from the first issue, and these things were talked about as well; I remember hearing people talking and discussing, oh, Amy Johnson, Jim Morrison and the Lindberg kidnapping, the Abdication

and all those things.) The first really political thing I remember is the
Spanish Civil War and we had evacuees in our village and Franco was
burnt on our November 5th bonfire on the village green. That isn't
really so long ago, but I haven't been able to find anybody else who
knows anything about evacuees coming from that war to Britain, and I
definitely remember that we had them; I even remember the name of one
of the boys who came – he was a great footballer.

But anyway, from that childhood I became a reading addict, I read
everything, from Biggles to books on Spiritualism. Jeffrey Farnol, Ethel
M. Dell, Maria Correlli, and Limehouse Nights from the box under the
bed. And I'm sure that the friends whose houses I went into had the
same sort of reading habits, plenty of papers and magazines and comics
always lying about and always a bookcase, however small, with some
books in and other treasured possessions that may have been passed
down.

Well, when I left and after two years at college, I went to teach in
London, the war was still on and I was only nineteen, and it was a
foreign country to me to start with, which I liked because I'd listened to
my Gran's tales of Bethnal Green in the 1890s warning me against white
slavery and things like that (laughter), and I'd always been determined
to come. I began by lodging in Ilford in rather middle-class surroundings
and here I would define middle class as people who have dinner in the
evening and not in the middle of the day (laughter), and having not
much money – I think my first teacher's salary for part of the month of
August was £13 out of which I had to pay back the college loan, so I
used to go to bed early and read all the books in the public library.
Again, I wasn't unhappy to do so, I enjoyed the reading. Then we were
bombed out and I went to live with a girl from Old Canning Town,
what you might call yer genuine working class, where bugs fell out of the
roof at the old school in Bidder Street; I dare say she enlarged on some
of the stories to horrify me and I was duly horrified but also fascinated.
Our acquaintance developed from the book under her arm when she
came to the school where I was teaching – it was Engels' *Condition of the
Working Class in 1844* and I scoffed at it. Then from that I was introduced to Jack London, another great author which the working-class
people have always enjoyed reading, and we joined a small political
party and we sat about in basement kitchens in Hoxton, with slogans
such as 'all men are liars' on the wall (laughter) and various bits of
Marxist philosophy. We emptied the teapot out of the window, broke up
a few more boxes for the fire and sat up all night, which is not to say that
we all read these books, but there's a large number of the working-class
people who read them and read them well enough to discuss them. It
was a university of a kind, no doubt biased, but an education in itself.
On another occasion we sat in the back room in Upton Park, we were
very cold, with a gas ring alight under the table to keep our legs warm,
and amongst the things that we read and discussed – what was this –

thirteen, twenty, twenty-five years ago? – Karl Popper, Schumpeter, Marx, Engels, Kant, Spinoza, Hegel, Sidney Hook, Wilhelm Reich, then later, there was deCastro's – *The Geography of Hunger*, Galbraith, Vance Packard, the more modern ones, and this is still going on in plenty of places amongst working-class people, more and more I should say and more and more papers and magazines are being published by people themselves. Amongst the group that I knew there were many Jews and that ties in with another paper we had to read connected with literacy in the Jewish cultural tradition – and they certainly had a great respect for the written word and were great arguers, everything was a matter for contention and a good argument was worth sitting up three nights in a row for, and the many Jews in this group fitted in with a similar type of working-class subculture of non-Jews, the gentiles, with no class, race, man, woman or bias of any kind that I was aware of at that time, and looking back I still don't think that I can see there was any bias then – we all met on equal terms; if you were ignorant, you were going to be instructed, and helped along. If you had anything to say, you said it. You went to the home of somebody who had a decent home, a fire to sit by, or you went to somebody's attic, it made no difference.

And now, just to touch on one more thing in the East End of London which a lot of people have already heard about – the enterprise which seems to be centred on a place called 'Centerprise' in Hackney, where I live, and Ken Worpole in particular, who was a teacher, but there's a whole group of people and it's going on in other places in the area as well as in Centerprise where local people are being encouraged to write their life stories, their poems, their novels, stories, schoolchildren as well as adults. In some cases they're taping it first and it's being knocked into shape or they're being helped with it by the people who work for Centerprise, but it's being published and it's being sold, people are buying it. It's not great literature – it's not meant to be, but it's enthralling and more and more people, having read other people's reminiscences are coming forward, the whole thing that Ken Worpole is doing is called *The People's Autobiography of Hackney*. He has also written books about the children's lives to be read in school; I found when I took 'The Hackney Half-Term Holiday' to my classes, it wasn't local enough for them, that it would have had to have been a Newham half-term holiday to really have appealed to them, because it was Hackney – another place, it might as well have been Timbuctoo or somewhere else – but the idea is good and there seems some purpose in all the covering of sheets with writing when it is to be published and read by other people, and not just handed round in school in duplicated form either. I feel that the working-class culture is much more acceptable these days, but that even though it's tolerated in schools we're building on it rather than jumping on it, it's still much stronger in the oral traditions than in the written and the old wives' tales, the weather lore, the family saws, are still things which children are told. We sometimes regret they don't know nursery rhymes and so on, but I think it's surprising how many they do still remember in the face of so much that's poured out of television, radio and in comics which doesn't relate to this sort of undercurrent of culture.

And my conclusion is that the working class now, this vast generalization covering the lot, compared with a hundred years ago, is literate, often highly literate and creatively so – most still choose only to use it for instrumental purposes, job, for information on their hobbies, to pull their motor cycles apart and so on and therefore they often prefer the typewriter and the telephone to the pen, but I still think there are far more children who take pleasure in writing than there were when I started to teach thirty-two years ago.

10 Oral history in the primary school

Sallie Purkis

It's likely that those of us who can still remember the history we 'did' in the Junior School will have similar recollections. The Romans almost certainly featured, and possibly the 'olden days', when ladies wore crinoline dresses and were carried about in sedan chairs, watched by ʒentlemen with deformed legs suffering from gout. I remember the Ancient Greeks, and most of all, those gods – only I was never quite sure about them. Were they people or weren't they? They lived, so I believed, up there in the mist on Mount Olympus, just where we lesser mortals – less than half their size – couldn't quite see what they were up to. But yes, they were real alright – because of those human activities which always interested me more than their supernatural powers.

In this article you will read about children in Primary School, aged seven and eight, whose first encounter with history in school was finding out about real people, *from* people; collecting and using their own source material like the professional historian. Family History has been tried successfully in Berkshire schools for many years under the guidance of D. J. Steel and L. Taylor; Oral History is well established in at least two Universities, and adult historians who practise history as a leisure activity have produced several valuable monographs as a result of interviewing old people; but I know of no previous work which has been done with children so young, several of whom had minimal language skills.

Our project began with a photograph which was produced by the Librarian of the Cambridgeshire Collection, when I mentioned one day the school I was working in. It had been built in 1908, and in the old photo, builder's rubble could still be seen in the background. Better than this, however, was the row of girls, dressed in their outdoor clothes – black stockings, lace-up boots and hats. They were gardening. A check on the School Log Book revealed that gardening had indeed been on the curriculum – a girls' subject – while the boys did woodwork.

My children recognized the spot where the photo had been taken immediately, and could line up in front of the same drainpipe. Alas, the garden was no longer there; and though a tiny patch of grass has been

Source: PURKIS, S. (1977) 'Oral history in the primary school' *History Workshop Journal* Vol. 2 No. 1 pp. 113–17

retained, the area is largely asphalted for car parking. But their curiosity was aroused by those strangely dressed pupils from another time, and their reaction was similar to the time they had seen Polynesian dancers on a film – 'funny'.

A concept of time is something most children come to late in maturation, and we used a number line, as in mathematics, going backwards. Fortunately, in the Primary School, you can blur lines a little, unlike the graduate historian writing a thesis; and we arrived at the conclusion that when the pupils at school had looked like those in the photo, the children's grandmothers would have been the same age as the children were now. Did their grandmothers wear clothes like that when they went to school? Well, there was only one way to find out.

There is often a refreshing ease of communication between the young and the elderly, and a special relationship between children and their grandparents. Half-term was the time they were likely to meet each other, so I duplicated a simple questionnaire for the grandmothers, asking if they could help us and let us know what they could remember about their lives when they were seven or eight. There was nothing very specialized in the questions and nothing that could be construed as inquisitive. They were all concerned with everyday topics like clothes, work, food, shopping, school, travel and entertainments. They were deliberately phrased in an informal conversational way, and although it was necessary with such young children for the replies to be written down, I hoped that grandparents and grandchildren would in fact talk to each other. In a short note to 'grandma', I asked her to recall her childhood and promised that however little she could remember it would help us, and that if she did have any photographs to lend we would take great care of them.

Not all the children had grandmothers, and there was an American boy and an Italian boy in the class; so to avoid any stress I began to build up 'grandma' as a symbolic figure, explaining that any elderly person who was prepared to talk to the children would have valuable information to give. This made one enthusiast feel free to interview three people.

When the material was returned, I made certain that all the information became part of a central pool rather than the property of the questioner. I began to read it out during the last five or ten minutes of the morning or afternoon sessions, like a story time, and never once did the children get bored. Gradually I transcribed the replies into a clear script that the children could read, and collected extracts together on sheets of sugar paper under subject headings. Never at any time was it necessary to alter the actual words used by the grandmas in their replies, as they had unconsciously phrased their answers in exactly the best way for their audience.

As will be seen from the extracts which follow, the replies we received from the grandmas were of a richness and quality I do not believe we could have had in our classroom by any other method. There is very little published for children on the period between 1900 and 1914, and what can be picked up from topic books about homes, shops, transport, etc., does tend to give the impression that our Edwardian ancestors were more wealthy and important than in fact they were.

Since the starting point for our investigation had been the clothes of the schoolgirls in the photograph, it seemed logical to analyse first what the grandmas remembered about the clothes they wore as children. The first thing that registered with the children from the replies was the discomfort of the clothes. This conclusion was reinforced both by the original photograph and the photographs sent by the grandmas, by now pinned up on the wall, protected by plastic bags:

'In school, I used to wear dark dresses as a rule, often of serge and always a frilly white pinafore on top.'
'Girls wore a vest, bodice, drawers, three petticoats, a frock and a pinafore.'
'Girls wore knee socks or woollen stockings and leather lace-up boots.'
'Tacky boots, with tacks in heel and toe – very heavy.'

Nor were boys any luckier:

'Breeches and leggings with hob nail boots.'
'Knickerbocker suits, with a stiff white collar.'
'Eton collars . . . but up to the age of two or three boys wore dresses like girls, only slightly less frilly.'

As first seen in the school photograph, hats were the rule even in summer.

'Our best hat in summer was a large brim straw with a floral wreath and ribbons. In winter it would be a large furry felt, trimmed with cherries.'

The children used this oral evidence to make drawings and a class scrapbook was compiled of the drawings captioned by the grandmothers' replies. Had a traditional book on costume been available, it could not have been so complete and accurate as ours.

For the second stage of their investigation, the children had even less visual material and had to bring their imagination into full play. We moved on to Washday – and it is not a subject that photographers of the past thought worth recording. Yet it is a topic that undoubtedly dominated a great many lives in the past and memories of it remain vivid and alive. The young Laurie Lee remembered 'Mondays, edgy with starch and panting Mother rowing her red arms like oars in the steaming waves.'[1] And Helen Bradley, who painted her childhood memories for her grandchildren, has a delightful picture of washday. Our grandmothers' memories, though perhaps not so poetically expressed, were concise and gave the children the opportunity to produce their own pictures.

'When I was a little girl, I hated washdays. I was one of a family of seven, so you can imagine what washdays meant to my mother.'

The children could indeed, when they read through the replies. Here is a sample of them in sequence order:

'All the water required had to be carried from the pump to our house.'
'My mother would rise early and light a coal fire under the copper.'
'The hot water was baled out with a dipper.'
'The clothes were put in a tub full of hot water, called a Dolly tub in which they were beaten up and down with a Dolly.'
'My mother did the washing in a galvanized bath on the kitchen table with a washboard made of wood.'
'After rinsing, it was put through a mangle with wooden rollers and turned by hand.'
'She dried on the line with gypsy pegs or hung the clothes on the hedge.'
'Ironing was done by placing the iron on the kitchen range and using it when hot. Ironing took ages, because one had to wait for the irons to get hot each time.'

With evidence like this to read, the children had no difficulty in producing sequential pictures with written comment, using their own words. Drawing on their previously acquired knowledge about clothes, they were able to dress their picture characters in the correct dress. Not, however, that they regarded the people in the drawings as characters. 'That's my Nanna, helping her Mum doing the washing,' wrote one girl who usually found written communication difficult.

'Great-grandma getting water out of the clothes with a mangle.'
'My great-grandma's got a fire built in her kitchen.'

There was rich evidence like that quoted above in answer to all our questions, and for six weeks the children went on writing, reading, making models and painting pictures about life sixty to seventy years ago. Some childhood memories, obviously the pleasant ones, had remained longer than others. The muffin man with his bell, the milkman with his horse and cart, featured frequently. Had going out with the jug to the milkman perhaps been one of the children's jobs? One grandmother, who had lived in the country, remembered the milkman with his yoke on his shoulders. Treats unknown to children today were recalled – tiger nuts, stewed eel, playing marbles in the street, home-made whips and tops, catapults. In the shops you had watched your own tea and sugar being weighed out for you and the paper bag made before your eyes. 'A square of paper would be twisted into a cone by the grocer.'

93

School dinners were unheard of; 'Granny took bread and cheese and a bottle of cold tea.'

It is true to say that after a time the project literally took us over. All the space on the walls and cupboard tops soon became covered with pictures, writing and objects. Old bottles, coins, weights, many items of clothing, flat irons, toffee hammers, button hooks – we had them all and a 'museum' was set up, only it was better than a museum because we could handle the objects.

In the last week of term, we invited the grandmothers to visit the school, have a cup of tea, and look at all the work the children had produced as a result of the questionnaire. Grandparents do not usually get a direct invitation to school and many accepted, some travelling from outside the town for the occasion. Three generations mixed happily that afternoon and were united by the common interests of past and present. Even the shyest boy in the class, whose grandmother neither replied to the questions nor came to the exhibition, enjoyed himself, as he wrote in his book next day, 'The day the grandmas came was the best day at school I ever had.'

Black Paper supporters, and others who seek to control the curriculum, will argue that history in school should be a series of 'facts' to be learnt in sequential order, and that there exists some body of knowledge that teachers have a responsibility to impart. They turn their backs on the idea that facts can be distorted or manipulated, particularly if they are over-simplified, and discount evidence brought by scientists that learning materials for young children should be related to their experience. What will undoubtedly be lost under a controlled curriculum is the possibility that 'by looking from the bottom upwards, we might get a more accurate picture of the whole of society and the state, than if we look at Society from on high'.[2] In the climate of a controlled curriculum, no study of Washday sixty years ago would be valid, and one fears for the continuation of collecting and studying evidence in school at all.

My objectives were simple with this scheme of work – to find out about the past from evidence the children could collect themselves. The way the evidence was collected and used was determined by the age and abilities of the children. With older children, many other avenues could be opened up.

By using a questionnaire, we restricted our replies; skilful use of a tape recorder would release evidence which if put in written form might have appeared too inquisitive. With a tape recorder there would be more possibilities for comparison and judgment-making about the past, especially with older children. Broad topics like change, work, cleanliness could be explored. The reliability of memory as evidence at all, might be questioned; but if it teaches the pupil to treat all evidence cautiously, then a valuable lesson will have been learnt.

I would be the last to remove story telling from the teaching of history at all levels. In the Primary School, many good historical studies emanate from stories or poetry and they are the starting point for creative writing, art, drama and music which nurture the imagination. But I believe it would be wrong to cut children off from what propels the professional historian forward: direct contact with source material, whether in the form of tangible objects, which can be brought into the classroom, relevant documentary material, the environment around them or, as in this project, oral evidence collected from their grandmas.

Notes

1   LEE, Laurie (1962) *Cider with Rosie* Penguin edition, London p 15
2   HILTON, R. H. (1967) *A Mediaeval Society* London p. 4

This is an extended version of an article which appeared in *Teaching History* in May 1976. Anyone attempting work similar to this would find the following books useful:

STEEL, D. J. and TAYLOR, L. (1973) *Family History in Schools,* Philimore & Co. Ltd
BRADLEY, Helen (1971) *And Miss Carter wore Pink* London
BRADLEY, Helen (1973) *Miss Carter came with us* London
LEE, Laurie (1962) *Cider with Rosie* Penguin edition London
JARVIS, Stan (1973) *Victorian and Edwardian Essex from Old Photographs* Batsford
REEVE, F. A. (1971) *Victorian and Edwardian Cambridge from Old Photographs* Batsford

Comment

So what has this to do with literature? The teacher has the responsibility of encouraging all children to read and to want to expand their reading to cover as wide a field and to encounter as many experiences as possible. Some children only need to acquire the basic reading skills and no one will be able to stop them from thirstily soaking up all they can lay their hands on. For others, literature will enter their lives more gradually and with more difficulty.

Introducing them to the most exciting story of all, the story of man, will often provide the incentive to start the search. The child who is excited by discovering history from primary sources will want to seek further and will inevitably find his way to literature.

This poem, written by Tonia, aged eleven, illustrates the progress from talking about history to experiencing it for oneself. It is an extension of finding out about history through conversation: a piece of writing like this can only be achieved by opening all the doors into both history and literature.

The Find

Up in the attic, alone at night,
Hunting through trunks and boxes,
All that comes tumbling out are photographs.
But what is this? It's a letter
To my Great Great Grandma.
And pressed between its leaves are flowers,
Faded with texture of tissue.
All I could imagine was my Great Aunt picking
Flowers of delicacy. Walking in a field of sunlight,
And honeysuckle blowing in the breeze.
Walking back to her picturesque cottage, snatching
Her hat as if the wind was playing a game.
She entered the house and wrote the letter, putting
The flowers inside.
And history now lies in my hands.

Tonia Scrivenor

The chapter on the work of a middle-school class illustrates the way in which a child's total experience of learning is developed through literature.

11 One class and its reading

Margaret Walden

In 1963, at the end of my PGCE year of training as a Secondary History teacher, I had no knowledge of children's books apart from the traditional stories which had formed part of the rigid diet of my grammar school. As I was preparing to launch myself into a girls' Secondary School in South-East London my younger sister was packing her trunk ready for a three year course at St Hild's College in Durham.

Among the items that went into the trunk were the books on her compulsory reading list: a variety of books, heavily weighted on health education, and one children's novel – *The Woolpack*, by Cynthia Harnett. I enjoyed reading it, bought myself a copy, and, when I started teaching, rejected the unattractive selection of class readers in favour of reading it aloud to the children. It was not an outstanding success, but I ventured to try one or two more children's books and during my four years at that school I continued to read to every class I had. I never mentioned what I was doing in the staffroom as I knew it would meet with disapproval amongst the other English teachers, who spent half-an-hour or so every week reading round the class.

Some years later, in 1969, my husband attended the first of the Children's Literature conferences at St Luke's College, Exeter. I read all the books that he took with him and was excited by his accounts of the writers he had met and the exhibition he had seen.

From that time onwards, we became compulsive collectors of children's books. Having three young children of our own we felt the expense was justified and we even went on an expedition to Heffers' Bookshop to spend money our eldest child had been given for a savings account. We felt not a shred of guilt, being fully convinced that the returns were far greater than any building society could give on our investment. We were particularly delighted at the early publications in the Picture Puffins series and spoilt ourselves on special occasions by buying beautifully illustrated hardbacks.

In 1975, after various part-time and supply jobs all over the county, I found myself as a third-year class teacher in a newly organized nine to thirteen middle school. The classes in the school are of mixed ability and the children from a wide range of backgrounds, including a number from West Indian, Asian and Italian families. The first class I had benefited from my avid reading during my years away from full-time teaching and

I was able to choose books that they really enjoyed listening to. My energy in that first year was expended on finding out how to teach across the curriculum instead of just within my own specialist field. The complexities of modern mathematics took much of my time. I was surprised at the end of the year how much I had enjoyed myself and determined to give my all to the class I was due to have in September.

In our school, the development of higher order reading skills features high in our list of priorities. During the first term I paid lip-service to such activities as cloze procedure and prediction exercises, and again read to the class at some length. We had some amusing and interesting discussions and I would not hesitate to acknowledge their value: children were beginning to engage with their reading. But I still felt at the end of that first term that the spark was lacking that would set light to our shared experience of literature and produce a full commitment to learning through it.

During the Christmas holidays I was looking through some educational publications to find something impressive to put in my forecast book (produced on a regular basis for my Head of Year) and I came across the assertion in the Schools Council Working Paper No. 52, *Children's Reading Interests*, that the most important factor at work is that primary school children borrow more library books than older children since 'primary schools almost invariably provide a class library for their pupils'.

Well, I thought, this is it. We did have a class library – thirty-three books between thirty-one children. I had told the class how important I thought reading was and I had certainly encouraged them to read but I had failed to convince them that becoming fully absorbed and involved in a book is a great experience in itself.

I gathered together every book in our house that I thought they might be interested in, from *Paddington* to *Wuthering Heights*. This amounted to a collection of about one hundred. I took them to school and told the children that the class library was going to feature as the most important activity that we shared. We spent the next fortnight preparing for an extended visit to the Cotswolds, where we were to be studying the Romans, features of medieval life, and the Civil War as it had affected the Cotswolds. I fed them with all the literature I could find to give them a taste of the periods they were to study. Where there was not time to read a whole book I duplicated relevant passages. We had a particularly heated discussion about the chapter in Rosemary Sutcliff's *The Eagle of the Ninth* on the basic differences between Celtic and Roman culture. I was amazed and delighted that they could feel so strongly about a period so far removed from their own.

We had covered a considerable amount of work on the Civil War as part of the History syllabus and they fell upon books such as *The Moated Manor* like locusts. I have always turned to literature wherever possible to enlighten History or bring it to life, but never before have I had such a rewarding response.

We spent an unforgettable week in the country. The children's relationships with each other – and with me – blossomed. We felt like real historians rummaging around for original detail, sharing knowledge and findings. We worked long hours each day and the children were recording their findings far into the evenings. There is no doubt in my mind that the quality and freshness of their writing was brought about not only by what they saw but also by the stories they had read, which brought to life so many of the places they visited. It is true that they were a perceptive enough group of children to admire and appreciate Chastleton House, a Tudor/Jacobean Manor House built on land owned by Robert Catesby, but the literature they had read put real people scuttling up the stairs, pacing the long gallery or hiding in the secret room.

The two poems which follow are by no means perfect. By the strictest standards, the first has only one really good line and the second tends to pay too much attention to the conventions of poetry, but the feeling and delight and understanding with which they were written makes them completely worthwhile.

Chastleton House

1   The main hall
With its table long and thick
The armour hanging up
Pictures hanging from the wall
The fire jumping high up in the air
The maid rushing by
With plates of pewter and cups of glass

The stair case is high and old
The wooden carvings strong and bold
A rustle of skirts and a soft pat of feet
The picture faces look down
With eyes bright and heads held high
A creek of the staircase
As some one passes by

The books lining the shelves
Are turning yellow with age now
But then they were crisp and white
And the clock when you pulled the string
Always gave the right time
Books of famous authors and
Of poets well known looked down
On a shadow of the master writing alone

Elaine

2   Dust and decay now shroud these panelled walls,
    Where generations of proud Jacobites,
    Whose tales of Worcester, Naseby now enthrall,
    Gaze down in solemn and censorious state
    As we invade their guarded privacy

    The threadbare tapestries which once were bright
    Hang limp and rotting on the dank dark wall,
    The rich embroidered bed awaits no bride
    Its colours dim, and faded by the light
    Of years, the glare of centuries of sun.

    Silence now reigns alone in the long gallery,
    Where ladies once took exercise
    And laughed and talked on rainy days.
    Perhaps they gazed out on the same green fields
    Where pole and pylon reign supreme today.

    March on relentless time, creep on decay
    And when the limestone crumbles into dust
    The lives hopes loves that in you lay
    Will live as long as we, in memory
    And in the lasting pages of biography.

Debbie

The boys particularly enjoyed the Roman section of the work. I think they were attracted more than anything by the amorality of the Romans. We had plenty of stories to bring to life the excellent models in the Corineum Museum. We could only spend half a day there, though they would have happily returned day after day. There were so many exciting pieces of writing to choose from that it is difficult to find one that is representative, but perhaps the story written by Steven shows how a combination of story with actual remains and models can give a child a real feeling for an event or a period.

We had marched for days on end from Londinium to Isca. We stopped for a few days at Corineum to rest our tired feet and while we were there we took advantage of the public baths. When we arrived at this miserable outpost of the Empire everything seemed to be peaceful. We had come to relieve the Eleventh Legion who had been on duty for a year.

    We made ourselves as comfortable as possible in the cramped quarters of the forts and some of us made a few expeditions out of camp to sample the local talent. This tribe the Dumnonori had been quiet for almost a year and we expected no trouble. Rumour had it however that there had been a gathering of the Druids although we had banned their activities. I mean what would civilized people be doing cavorting around and chanting with all this nonsense about mistletoe.

Our first suspicions were aroused when we saw new heron's feathers on one of the native's throw-spears. It could have been coincidence but with a new moon due we could not afford to take chances.

We doubled the lookout on the night of the full moon and hoped the rumblings we heard in the village were our imagination.

When the attack came we were prepared. The alert was given and the whole cohort tumbled out of their bunks and into their protective leather tunics and bronze helmets. Swords at the ready we crouched waiting for the attack. Nevertheless we were amazed at the reckless daring of these savages.

The most worrying thing was our scouting party due to return at any moment. We caught a glimpse of them marching over the hill and the order was given to march out in Testudo to bring them in.

We met up with them and had almost reached the safety of the fort when we heard the thunder of horses' hooves and saw the racing chariots which were all the tribesmen had since the war chariots had been banned, but fixed to the wheels of the chariots were vicious scythes that would tear a man (even a Roman) to pieces.

We were saved only by the bravery of our cohort commander who threw himself on the leading charioteer.

Fortunately we subdued the rising with little loss of life but we will be more wary in future.

Steven

On returning to a more formal classroom situation I was anxious not to lose the enthusiasm, the willingness to write and talk, and the ability to listen, observe and record which the shared experiences of a week away had made so rewarding and enjoyable.

As the leader in this experience I set about attempting to formulate ideas into a policy of using literature as a springboard to all the activities in the classroom. The school's policy of keeping a reading record for each child – I now reviewed the records weekly – was the first tool to help me keep in close touch with the children's reading. The children were used to writing reviews on completion of a book, but I was more anxious that they should have as wide an experience of literature as possible than that they should spend a lot of time on a detailed analysis of a particular book. During the Autumn term we had been issued with group readers. Sessions with these resulted in some lively discussions but the tremendous variety in speed of reading and the limited number of books available led to a breakdown in the circulation of the books. The children filled in their record sheets at the completion of a book and added a brief comment.

From now on, one lesson each week was passed in informal chat about books currently being read. The enthusiasm of the readers coupled with comments from those who had read the book under discussion already proved to be better advertisement than formal reviews had been.

Having contributed so many of the books myself I had the advantage of having read most of them and I tried to read those of the original thirty-odd that I did not already know. This was particularly valuable with the section of reading books on loan from the reading workshop for the less able children. It was very important to them that I had found the books which they were able to enjoy worth reading myself.

It soon became obvious that with the rapidity of circulation the number of books we had available was inadequate. We considered ways of raising money to acquire more books and hit upon the idea of a coffee evening at my home. The children sold tickets and collected items for a 'bring and buy' sale. The evening was a success in two ways. Approximately forty people came and we raised over £20; a parent who was able to get a considerable discount on books purchased over fifty additional paperbacks for the library. The evening also gave the parents a chance to talk to each other and to me about the books which their children were reading. It was very encouraging to find that both parents often read the book which a child took home for his weekend reading. Many parents commented on the general improvement of work as a result of the increased reading – a marked advance; normally, few parents are aware in any detail of the content of their children's school work.

Not satisfied with the boost to the class library that the evening had given, children hunted down books in jumble sales and charity shops, and at the end of the year we had a library of over 350 books.

With so many additional titles to choose from, I was able to recommend books according to children's individual interests, although there were two or three children in the class who proved very difficult to inspire. I noticed on looking through the reading records that many of the children were becoming more discriminating and more ambitious in their choice of books. I decided to try to develop their powers of discrimination through their own writing. I took in a collection of books for small children including *The Owl and the Woodpecker*, *Joseph's Yard*, *A Snowy Day*, *A Baby Sister for Frances*, a couple of 'Topsy and Tim' books and some Enid Blytons. We discussed what we thought small children wanted from their stories, the main categories of stories for small children, the place of illustrations and which stories we thought were the most successful.

They then set about writing and illustrating their own children's stories. We found a group of young children on whom we could try them out and we were fortunate to get a local Upper School to reproduce some of them, although the story that follows was typed, illustrated and published by its author.

Sam and the Seagull

Sam had just moved to a new house by the sea. Sam goes down to the beach every day, because he has not got any friends and he gets very lonely. When he is on the beach he listens to the seagulls, and the crashing of the waves. Sam is very sad, no matter how hard he tries, he can't find any friends.

One day when he was playing on the rocks he found a seagull. At first he thought the seagull would fly off, but as he got nearer he saw that there was a little bit of blood on its wing. Sam then knew that the seagull had hurt its wing, and could not fly. Very carefully he picked the seagull up, and took it home where he nursed the seagull back to health. The bird could not fly so Sam had to give food and water to it every day. At last Sam had found a friend.

The seagull had by now made a nest in the rocks. Sam went down there every day to give the seagull its food. Sometimes they played games. They enjoyed it.

Then one day something terrible happened. Sam had to move house! Sam's parents would not let him take the seagull even though they were moving to the seaside again.

So, sadly Sam had to part with the seagull. Sam was very sad because he knew the seagull could not fly, and the seagull would not be able to catch food so he would die.

Meanwhile the seagull was getting ready to see if he could fly. The seagull counted to three and jumped off the cliffedge. His heart began to beat furiously. Frantically he flapped his wings. Then suddenly he started to slow up. He was going up. He could fly! Now he could fly he went and got some food. Then he decided to see if he could find Sam.

After a few days of travelling the seagull thought that he would never find Sam. Then a storm blew up. The wind howled, the rain fell, thunder crashed, lightning flashed. The wind blew him off course. He could not control himself. Then in a clearing he saw a beach with some rocks. Quickly he flew down to the rocks and found a shelter where he fell asleep. Next morning the sun was shining. It was a beautiful day. He had landed in a big city by the sea. There were big funfairs and other lively stalls.

Then he thought he saw a figure he knew. Yes, it became even more clear as he scrambled over the rocks. At first the figure jumped past him. The seagull knew now for sure it was Sam. He flew up onto Sam's shoulder. Sam was overjoyed at seeing his friend again. This time Sam was definitely staying at this town, and whenever storms came the seagull came into Sam's house. So they became the best of friends and lived happy ever after.

Alan

The End

My next effort was to collect together my ideas for integrating literature with the rest of the curriculum. We were not always aware whether we were reading a story for the sake of the work in history or geography or science that it enlightened or vice-versa.

One of the topics on the Environmental Studies syllabus was 'Anglo Saxon and Norman England'. It was easy to find plenty of novels and poems dealing with the Vikings, and the Henry Treece books were successful with both boys and girls. The pace of the following poem about the Vikings illustrates the sense of atmosphere which infiltrated the children's own writing.

The Vikings Attack

They're coming, they're coming!
Hear the boys cry.
How do you know?
We saw from up high.
Quick run for your lives
Grab your children and wives
They'll murder and plunder
Till we're all trodden under.
We saw on the shore
With a mighty great roar
The warriors fierce
Their swords raised to pierce.
We saw them pillage
And steal and take
From our own dear village
And from fear we did quake.
Then they were gone
And we all carried on
Living our lives
With our children and wives.
Living in fear
Should we once again hear
With a mighty great roar
The men on the shore.

Sarah

The Battle of Hastings must be the most widely-taught historical event in our schools, but there is still a delightful freshness about Alun's account of the battle, written after he had listened to an extract from *Harold Was My King*:

The Battle of Hastings

My name is Alfred Siward and I was a captain in the army of King Harold during the year of 1066 when he made his courageous attempt to unite England and defend our country against its many foes.

I had served him in his battles against the Welsh at Hereford and against the Norsemen at Stamford Bridge outside the City of York. We were weary after these fierce battles and it was with a sinking heart that I heard King Harold tell us that we had to march south immediately from Stamford Bridge to London to meet a Norman army from France.

When we reached London we were exhausted and battle weary, and at a meeting, we captains begged King Harold to let our men rest before meeting the Normans. The King did not take our advice and after conscripting a few poor quality levies led us through Sussex into Kent.

King Harold was a great soldier and chose his battle station against Duke William with care. We were positioned on a hill outside Hastings. We were protected at the sides and rear, by sharp falling ground. If our shield wall held firm we could go on killing the enemy and still survive. The great Norman soldier called Taillifer the minstrel, singing the Latin sounds of Charlemagne and Roland, throwing his sword in the air and catching it as he rode, perished with the first charge.

'Holy cross,' 'out, out,' we cried as our house carls wielded their two handed axes.

We had few archers and fought entirely on foot, and it was the Norman archers and cavalry, together with better discipline, which wore our defences away.

It was impossible for King Harold to control the soldiers and twice we were deceived by Normans pretending to flee. Our soldiers broke ranks and chased them, only to be cut to death by the Norman horsemen. It was the terrible arrows though that wore us down. Man after man was killed under that hail of death until our line of shields was very thin.

As darkness came King Harold was hit by an arrow and a final charge of the Norman horsemen broke our thin line of shields. I fled into the woods with only a few other survivors.

Alun

Finding myself in a non-specialist situation in a middle school, having spent my initial years of teaching as a specialist in a secondary school, I was, as I mentioned earlier, apprehensive about my ability to teach in the curriculum areas which were unfamiliar to me.

After a week of teaching mathematics for the first time I invited a friend who is a mathematician into the school to introduce my class to the section on integers at the beginning of Fletcher Book 8. I was surprised at how interesting the lesson was for me as well as for the children. He took the mathematical topic of integers and translated it into concrete terms by telling four different stories, all with the same ending. It would be difficult to think of many children's stories that would have a direct bearing on maths teaching, but since that lesson I have tried to be particularly aware of the need to relate maths to concrete situations and to think carefully about the language I am using in explaining mathematical concepts.

I had similar misgivings about the time I was to spend with my class in the Science Laboratory. The children follow the Nuffield Combined Science Course with a specialist teacher but we have a double period each week which is used for science related to the Environmental Studies syllabus. To begin with, I felt very uneasy in the Science Laboratory. Just before our first lesson I had been reading some poems about school and had chanced on one about a science lesson, the last line of which reads: 'What I lacked was faith.' I too felt like an atheist at a prayer meeting.

Many of the children in the class were far more interested in Science than in arts subjects. Their desks were cluttered up with batteries, bulbs and lengths of wire which they made into electrical circuits. On the whole, they were the children who read for information rather than for pleasure. It seemed a pity that one section of the class was missing out on the experience of literature and the other part, including the teacher, was failing to enjoy the experience of science.

It occurred to me that had my own Science lessons at school been less technical I might have been less afraid of them. With the help of the class I tried to find common ground for two of the topics we were studying in science: wood and trees, and insects. We decided that the key factor, whether we were writing scientifically or creatively, was observation. As an extension to a 'monsters' topic we looked at insects from a biological point of view and when the children started their story and poetry writing those who were most interested in science were able to make valuable contributions.

ANTS! (Magnified)

They came. They were big. They were strong. They terrorised. They tortured. They stole. They killed. They were ants. They destroyed all in their path. They had big long legs divided into three sections. They had bodies. They had claws. They had fangs. They were ants.

They had antennae, 12 feet long like a telegraph pole. They had a triangular head. They had eyes, big as footballs. They had jaws bigger than anything. Their legs covered in bristle moved them fast. They had strength ten times that of an elephant. They could carry fifty times their own weight. Their weight heavier than that of the heaviest elephant.

They came. They were big. They were strong. They terrorised. They tortured. They stole. They killed. They were ants!

Alan

Alan made use of observation for this story, but Anne returned to a more traditional source for her writing on monsters. She had read the story of

Beowulf in the accounts of Rosemary Sutcliff and Ian Serraillier, and she brought her own vigour to an extension of the story.

The Wet Battle

Beowulf not satisfied with an army was out to search and kill Grendel. He had arrived at a lake which he believed Grendel to be in. He called for Grendel to come out and fight, but instead of an answer he heard a magnificent roar, then slowly Grendel's body appeared from the sea-bed. Beowulf entered the water and walked towards Grendel. Immediately Grendel swung his arm to hit Beowulf. Instead Beowulf ducked and swam nearer to Grendel. Grendel now very worried was searching and fumbling around him to find Beowulf. As Beowulf had now reached Grendel's feet he began to tug at them.

Grendel feeling this clumsily reached down towards his feet. Finding nothing down there he had turned a half somersault and had landed on the lake bed. He had come down with a thud and had sent an earthquake travelling throughout the surrounding land.

Beowulf had acted quickly and was now swimming towards Grendel's head. With his great strength and stamina, Beowulf just managed to heave Grendel's head down and crash it against the nearest rock. Blood now filled the lake and Grendel lay at the bottom still and motionless. Beowulf had achieved his aim. His lungs now filled with water meant that he would have to find the surface. It seemed a long time until he reached the top of that wet battle field. But the whole journey there had been worth it.

Anne

One of our best finds was a large wasps' nest. One group of children went to the Resource Centre to find out all they could about how it was made, while another group discussed the perfection of its shape and the delicacy of its texture and colour. We all saw the connection with our tree topic when we discovered the pines which had provided raw material for the nest.

Considering for a moment the wider significance of this work, I hope that by endeavouring to break down some of the traditional barriers between arts and science subjects it has been possible for the children to share their abilities and inclinations, to have a greater understanding of other people's interests, and also to leave their options open. The opportunities for achieving these objectives are excellent in a Middle School and it is the particular responsibility of those who teach this age range to see that sufficient breadth and cohesion is established in the curriculum.

The last book I read to the class was *The Witch of Blackbird Pond*. It was after the Summer examinations and Sports Day when things are always apt to fall a bit flat and I was looking for a complete topic which would make the last fortnight of the year as useful and enjoyable as any other.

I read the book fairly intensively as I wanted the children to hear the whole story before any other work was attempted. We studied the geography of the area, we talked about the reasons for settlement in the new world, about religious toleration, and, above all, witchcraft. I told them about the Salem Witch Hunt, and a boy brought in a copy of *The Crucible* the next day. They were eager for other stories about witches and St Joan obviously sprang to mind. First they found out her story and demanded that I should read her trial in Shaw's *St Joan*. Some of the girls acted an extract from Anouilh's *The Lark*. Surprisingly, one of the most sensitive pieces of writing on the topic came in the form of a book review from Anna, a lively girl from an Italian family. She is good at languages but would be classed as of no more than average ability. She is a great talker; her father is very politically aware and she will launch into an involved discussion about any controversial topic. She is emotionally mature, a fact reflected in the choice of books on her reading record. The thought she has given to the issues involved in *The Witch of Blackbird Pond* made the study of the book for her at least very worthwhile.

The Witch of Blackbird Pond

Is set in seventeenth century New England. It tells the story of Kit Tyler, brought up to a life of luxury and freedom, by her grandfather in Barbados. After her grandfather's death she sets sail from Barbados to live with the family of her aunt. She arrives unannounced and does not feel very welcomed by her stern puritan uncle. While she is living in Wethersfield Kit befriends a child who is regarded by her parents as being stupid. She also makes friends with the witch of Blackbird Pond, a branded quaker woman, who does not attend the Sunday meetings and who is treated as an outcast. Eventually Kit herself is tried as a witch and it is only after she is acquitted that she begins to settle to her new life, and eventually finds love and happiness. This is one of the best books I have read this year, the story moves quickly and the writer gives a very clear picture of the hardships of life in the New World. Through most of the book I thought that no one could bear to work so hard, live in such discomfort, wear such coarse home-spun clothes, have hardly any outings or pleasures to look forward to, and above all to have to sit for dreary hour after hour in the meeting house. But just occasionally I understood the urge for religious freedom and the desire to be ones own master which gave the early settlers the courage to carry on. It is this which makes Matthew Wood, Kit's uncle, not quite so hateful as he would otherwise seem. Perhaps he was made hard by the rigours of life in seventeenth century Connecticut. Sometimes we see a glimpse of the other side of his nature in the treatment of his crippled daughter Mercy.

Even the minor characters in this book are written as very clear people – Hannah the poor confused quaker woman provides a haven for Kit in her misery and a refuge for the unloved Prudence. I thought that if the people of Wethersfield had looked on Hannah as a friend the town would have been a happier place.

The witch trial does not play a very large part in this book, only one chapter, but Mrs Walden read us an account of the Salem witch trials and parts of The Crucible and the trial from St Joan, so it was easy to see how terrifying it must have been to have been accused of witch-craft and how willing people were to make up evidence against an innocent person. Perhaps it was because life was so dull and they needed something to liven it up a bit to stop them going mad.

The best thing of all about this book is the character of Kit because she was such a fighter and she would not let herself be squashed by puritan narrow-mindedness.

I wondered as the book finished whether the America of today is built on the descendants of people like Kit and Nat or those of the miserable narrow-minded mealy mouthed goodwife Cruff. I suppose it's a mixture of both!

Anna

We had few formal poetry lessons during the year, preferring to read a remembered poem that augmented an area of study from the section on the shelf, or to search for a relevant poem. There were two small sets from the school stockroom, the English Project *Creatures Moving* and *Family and School*. In addition to these, my own collections became well thumbed. Charles Causley's *Figgie Hobbin* and his collected poems were undeniable favourites, and his work was a source of inspiration for much of the children's writing. We compared 'My Mother Saw a Dancing Bear' to James Stephens' 'The Snare', and although the children liked the rhythm and metre of the latter, Causley's poem gave rise to a fuller discussion which opened out into consideration of the changing nature of cruelty to animals, and the writing then produced by the children in-cluded sensitive responses to such widely different subjects as cock-fighting and vivisection. Nichola wrote:

The Lions

In the circus ring, one summer's day,
When all was hot and dry,
The gate was opened slowly –
And the lions rushed quickly by.
Into the cage where the trainer stood,
They galloped on velvet paws,
And when the trainer cracked his whip
They yawned and stretched their jaws,
They stood on tubs and pawed the air,
They leaped on painted stools,
Their coats were hot and ragged,

But their eyes shone like jewels,
And when the act was over,
Clapping echoed round the ring,
While the lions crouched in the corner,
Brooding with restless longing,
As they dreamed of their far-off homeland,
So many miles away,
The luscious, life-filled forests,
And the Kings of the Jungle, stalking prey.

Nichola

It was surprising how easy it was for some children to use as a model the style and metre of a poem they had read, as in this first stanza from a long poem called 'The Annunciation' written by Elaine after reading *The Ballad of the Bread Man:*

Mary went to find Joseph,
She looked him straight in the eye,
'Joseph, I've news for you,' she said,
'An angel came from on high,'

Elaine

The first promising poem that Alun wrote during the year was also on a theme from the RE syllabus:

The Massacre of the Innocents
A soldier marches up the street,
Behind him all the people weep.
Screams and wails and sobs are heard
But no one utters any word,
Why are these people all so quiet?
There should be revolution, riot.
The soldier barges through a door,
He leaves behind bloodshed, uproar.

It's death for children under two.
Think soldier next it might be you,
Who finds your sons and daughters dead,
And through your door the tears run red.

Alun

The most rewarding result of poetry writing is that less able children, who often struggle with the formalities of punctuation and correct usage in a piece of prose can contribute a few lines, or even a single thought in a poem that stands alone as a fine piece of writing. By way of comparison, the following three extracts were by children of widely varying abilities:

1   Twisting and turning, writhing and churning
    The peace of the sea holds no peace for me.
    Only I can see the ripples spread
    And surging forth a monstrous head.

2   Old is the age of these roots
    Tangled by Seasons, the Shape
    Of the Universe's forms: Winter,
    Spring, Summer and Autumn.

3   They twisted and turned
    Gripping on to each other
    For endless time they had been
    Not living not breathing
    They had come from nowhere
    They had just been.

I have always had a conviction of the potential for poetry in all of us, ever since at the age of nine I was taken to an amateur production of *The Corn is Green*. The children in this class confirmed that feeling.

The children's work as a whole at the end of the year showed that they had all developed significantly in competence and maturity. I can only believe that this was a result of their enthusiasm for literature and of the thoughtfulness and sensitivity which they achieved through sharing their experiences of literature in discussion.

For me, the most exciting and rewarding feature of the year's work was that by the end of the year most of the children wanted to write. They considered themselves to be writers and they wanted to read their efforts to their fellow pupils. They all felt confident enough to talk about what they were doing in the knowledge that they would have a sympathetic if critical audience. The less able children were producing stories and poems that were as refreshing and readable as those of the most gifted: each day had something exciting to offer.

References

HARNETT, Cynthia (1951) *The Wool Pack* (1961) Puffin

BOND, Michael (1958) *A Bear Called Paddington* (1971) Armada Lions

BRONTË, Emily (1970) *Wuthering Heights* Penguin

SUTCLIFF, Rosemary (1970) *The Eagle of the Ninth* Oxford University Press

WHITTLE, Norah (1963) *The Moated Manor* Arnold

WILDSMITH, Brian (1971) *The Owl and the Woodpecker* Oxford University Press

KEEPING, Charles (1969) *Joseph's Yard* Oxford University Press

KEATS, Ezra Jack (1967) *A Snowy Day* Bodley Head (1969) Puffin

HOBAN, Russell (1970) *A Baby Sister for Frances* Faber

LEWIS, Hilda (1968) *Harold was my King* Oxford University Press

SPEARE, Elizabeth George (1960) *The Witch of Blackbird Pond* Gollancz

MILLER, Arthur (1966) *The Crucible* Secker and Warburg (1970) Penguin

SHAW, George Bernard (1969) *St Joan* Penguin

ANOUILH, Jean (1971) *The Lark* (translated by C. Fry) Eyre Methuen

SUMMERFIELD, G. (ed.) (1970) *Creatures Moving* Stage 1: English Project Ward Lock Educational

JACKSON, D. (ed.) (1970) *Family and School* Stage 1: English Project Ward Lock Educational

CAUSLEY, Charles (1971) *Figgie Hobbin* Poems for Children Macmillan

WILLIAMS, Emlyn (1956) *The Corn is Green* Heinemann

Comment: a reminder

It is Thursday, 8 September 1977, and a nine-year-old girl, just starting in a middle school, writes in a brand new 'English' exercise book. 'A Noun is the name of someone or something. A common noun is the name of an ordinary or common object such as a pen, field, money, girl, boy. A proper noun names a special person or thing and must always begin with a capital letter such as Bedford, Mary, Peter, Londen, Queen Victoriea.' Queen Victoria, no doubt, would have approved of all this, apart from occasionally creative spelling, and applauded the following pages of neatly numbered exercises. On 26 September, a page headed *Plurals* has a lot of red on it. Carol commented, 'Miss makes an awful mess of my book – this is my *worst* page.' There are big red crosses by 'chimneies', 'gooses', 'pianoes' and 'skys', and by the sentence 'funny means cheerful very happy' – Miss has written *See Me*. Carol's English comprehension book – modestly entitled *Complete English* Book Two (*Complete English, Books 1–5* E. G. Thorpe (1962) Heinemann Educational reprinted in 1975), states in the preface that, 'it is intended for the consideration of teachers who believe that children come to school to work to the limit of their ability, that they should enjoy so doing through the provision of interesting work and that they should be encouraged to find out for themselves as far as possible by confident use of dictionary, atlas, reference books, etc.'

The formula for comprehension and related work is an extract from a novel or short story of two to three hundred words followed by a set of questions to make sure that it has been understood. (Carol rarely writes in sentences; 'fell down flat means fell on your tummy', is typical of the kind of answer she gives.)

By the end of January 1978, Carol is on to apostrophes and *Complete English* throws up a poem. It is Robert Frost's *Stopping by Woods on a Snowy Evening* and the comprehension questions are either banal or impossible: 'What is the weather like?' 'What is the meaning of a snowy evening?' 'What is the meaning of the sweep of easy wind, downy flake, dark and deep, fill up with snow?' Related exercises invite Carol to 'Think of interesting adjectives (describing words) to go in the spaces' – 'The mother sparrow was . . . when she found her . . . nestlings.' By the time Carol has struggled through *thirty* questions, all moving away from the poem, it is unlikely that she will have any memory of the way she felt when she first read it or even that she has ever read it at all.

Section Three
Talking about Poetry

Comment

Articles thus far in the Reader have mainly assumed or explicitly re-inforced the general theory that literature can be strongly bound into the inner processes of thinking and feeling in the child growing towards adulthood; both the experience offered in story and the language through which it is offered are of common importance as a kind of integration of inner and external experience.

So far, we have concentrated largely on narrative story. What about poetry? Margaret Walden 'always had a conviction of the potential for poetry in all of us'. This potential can be seen in children as they write their own poems and as they read and listen to other people's poems. However, for most children as they get older, and for many of their teachers, the prospect of poetry in the classroom is likely to summon up images of boredom and embarrassment. If Carol's experience is anything to go by, an approach to poetry via comprehension questions in a text-book is likely to consolidate these images.

What is it that young readers and listeners find difficult in looking at poems in the classroom? Is it, as the textbooks so often assume, a simple matter of unravelling the meaning of words by paraphrasing with the aid of a dictionary? Or is it more a matter of recognizing the 'voice' of the poet who has found these particular words appropriate when shaped in this particular way to say this particular thing?

It seems to us that much of the literary critical apparatus that is acquired by English graduates during higher education is of little help in the school classroom. However, by working hard to come to terms with children's own interests, problems with and approaches to literature, we may be able to assist them towards sensitive understanding and ap-preciation. How far *should* the teacher go in the classroom in introducing a poem? The following example is from a tape-recording of one teacher, Peter Medway. It is worth asking, after reading, if anything more is necessary, as a lead in to the poem. Would the majority of children (of, say, thirteen years old) be helped to a closer appreciation of the poem? Or does it intrude too far?

12 Introducing the poem 'Frustrated Virtuoso' by Norman MacCaig

Peter Medway

You know the noise a donkey makes. It's sometimes called braying. Suppose you have to listen to a donkey braying his head off as he gets himself into a state about something. It goes on and on.

I listen to him braying.

The donkey's notes come in pairs, don't they – one high, one low.

I listen to him braying – up and down.

He's getting more and more worked up. You can't help listening to him he's making so much noise – up and down, up and down.

As you listen and listen, you imagine something about the donkey and his noise.

You know when you listen to a noise going on a long time, your imagination gets to work on it. You hear a kettle whistling and imagine it's trying to take off. You hear a pneumatic drill and imagine it's digging out decay in some gigantic tooth. Don't you.

O.K. – you hear this donkey going on. What do you imagine?

Go back a bit. Here's how Norman MacCaig has got it so far in his poem.

>   I listen
> to his heehawing

So, he's made a word up. Hang on, though, he hasn't finished. The donkey's voice goes up and down. So, next line:

> seesawing

He hears it seesawing.

>   I listen
> to his heehawing
> seesawing

Jokey, eh? Better than

>   I listen to his heehawing seesawing

Right. Here's how he goes on:

> I listen
> to his heehawing
> seesawing and imagine

So now we're back to what you imagine when this donkey's racket is going on and on.

Suppose you imagine that what the donkey's trying to do is get a really nice sound out. (He can't – that's why he's getting in a state – frustrated.)

This good, satisfying sound would be the opposite of his normal voice, wouldn't it?

What's his braying like, his heehawing? Hoarse? Strained? Switching from high to low in an undignified, out-of-control way?

He's going to produce *one* note that's exactly how he wants it. Describe this note. It's:

> . . . .
> . . . .
> . . . .
> . . . . etc.

What about the way he gets it out? Instead of coming out in that forced way, half-strangled, how's it going to come out?

Pouring out generously like Guinness from a bottle? Spreading in waves like the boom from a gong?

How?

Change the subject. What's a satellite do round the earth?

Orbit.

Sometimes you can look up and see them. Men stare with faces turned upwards, spellbound. Right?

Suppose this beautiful sound the donkey wants to produce is so perfect it's like an object that goes up in the air, a bubble or capsule. Sailing away free. You could imagine it going up overhead and into orbit.

Back to MacCaig's poem:

> I listen
> to his heehawing
> seesawing and imagine

That's where we got to last time. Now we're going on.

> I listen
> to his heehawing
> seesawing and imagine
> the round rich note

Hey up. Round and rich. How's that compare with your description?

> the round rich note
> he wants to –

wants to what? What's he going to say here? make? produce? sing? give out? let out? boom? Here it is:

> the round rich note
> he wants to propel into space

Propel. Fine. He's on to a good idea now – propelling into space – it gets up there – then what? Now his imagination goes to town:

> a golden planet of sound orbiting

How about that?

> a golden planet of sound orbiting
> to the wonder of the world.

A planet orbiting to the wonder of the world. That's where we've got to at the end of the first part of the poem. But where did we start? What's the poem about? A donkey, making his ungraceful, frustrated noises. Bit of a contrast between a tatty donkey and golden planets.

I didn't tell you the start of the poem. Now I will. It makes still more of a contrast with golden planets orbiting.

> In the corner of Crombie's field
> the donkey gets madder every minute.

Not outer space – Crombie's field.

Here's the whole of the first part. While you're at it, notice how the two things the poet says he does come at the end of lines:

> I listen
> ... and imagine⌝

> In the corner of Crombie's field
> the donkey gets madder every minute. I listen
> to his heehawing
> seesawing and imagine
> the rich round note
> he wants to propel into space,
> a golden planet of sound orbiting
> to the wonder of the world.

The corner of that field probably isn't a very luxurious spot. Poor grass. Maybe it isn't even grass that the donkey has to eat.

Anyway, the poet imagines the reason the donkey's getting worked up is that he'd like to produce this rich round note and he can't. The only noise he can make is this strangulated heehaw.

> that whooping-cough trombone

No wonder he gives up in the end. What does he do then? Goes back to eating.

> His head drops to eat the plants.

119

That's not what MacCaig says. He describes the donkey's head. He makes it sound as awkward and unbeautiful as the donkey's voice.

> His box head drops

Good, eh? You wouldn't have thought of that, would you?
And what is there for him to eat? And how does he eat it?

> his box head drops
> to lip the leaves of thistles

Lip, know what he means? Donkey's leathery lips.

> No wonder
> when he hears what comes out of
> that whooping-cough trombone
> his eyes fill with tears
> and his box head drops
> to lip the leaves of thistles

How do you like those two lines when you say them together –

> his eyes fill with tears
> and his box head drops

Say them again.
'To lip the leaves of thistles.' That could be the end of the poem, but it isn't. When he gives up the idea of producing the beautiful note and goes back to his lousy thistles, what's his attitude? Furious? Exhausted? What does he think about himself now he's failed once again?

He'd better face it, he's no good. Golden planets? That's not his scene. Thistles – that's about right for a donkey with a whooping-cough voice and a box head.

I think the last line and a half are the saddest.

> and his box head drops
> to lip the leaves of thistles – accepting that
> they're all he deserves.

I find this sad because it reminds me of people. Perhaps Norman MacCaig was really thinking of people when he wrote it. People start off convinced they've got something pretty good inside them. Then they find themselves trapped in ordinary, unexceptional lives, the same as everyone else, doing boring, unbeautiful things. Their lives are hard, a constant grind, never letting up. What's sad then is when people tell themselves that's all they're good for. They never produce that round rich note to the wonder of the world, they end up with a rough deal and thinking that's all they deserve.

But you also see people who haven't given up – still trying to produce that note. Maybe getting mad with themselves as they struggle – and disturbing the neighbours. Awkward customers.

If this is something you've noticed in people, try writing a poem yourself – or some other sort of writing. About a person, not a donkey.

Can you say the poem by heart now? Cover it up and try it, uncovering
a line at a time.

There are more poems by Norman MacCaig in *Worlds* and in a paperback in T2.

Frustrated Virtuoso

In the corner of Crombie's field
the donkey gets madder every minute. I listen
to his heehawing
seesawing and imagine
the round rich note
he wants to propel into space.
a golden planet of sound orbiting
to the wonder of the world.

No wonder
when he hears what comes out of
that whooping-cough trombone
his eyes fill with tears
and his box head drops
to lip the leaves of thistles – accepting that
they're all he deserves.

Norman MacCaig

Introduction

The next three chapters are taken from an unpublished report *Children as Readers: The Roles of Literature in the Primary and Secondary School* (a NATE project sponsored by the Schools Council 1968–73). During the lifetime of this project, some of the most fruitful evidence about the nature of children's engagement with and capacity for making sense of compressed and self-contained literary expression, such as poems and short stories, began to emerge. The three chapters here are concerned with the same material: transcripts of ten-year-olds discussing two poems.

The first chapter looks at the way the groups generate their own pattern of discussion as they explore the poems together, the second briefly demonstrates the possibility that a close study of recorded material can enable us to isolate and analyse moments when learning seems to be taking place.

The third chapter deals with wider issues, discussing the implications of this kind of material in the present context of the teaching of literature.

Before reading the three chapters in this section it is important to read the poems and the transcripts. Understanding of the ideas presented here depends on familiarity with these texts.

The Small Dust-Coloured Beetle

The small dust-coloured beetle climbs with pain
O'er the smooth plantain leaf, a spacious plain!
Thence, higher still, by countless steps convey'd
He gains the summit of a shivering blade,
And flirts his filmy wings, and looks around,
Exulting in his distance from the ground.

Robert Bloomfield

The Snare

I hear a sudden cry of pain.
There is a rabbit in a snare:
Now I hear the cry again,
But I cannot tell from where.

But I cannot tell from where
He is calling out for aid
Crying on the frightened air,
Making everything afraid.

Making everything afraid,
Wrinkling up his little face,
As he cries again for aid;
And I cannot find the place.

And I cannot find the place
Where his paw is in the snare:
Little one, oh little one.
I am searching everywhere.

James Stephens
from *Collected Poems of James Stephens* published by MacMillan

Transcript 1

Kenneth, John, Mark and Clive discussing 'The Small Dust-Coloured Beetle' by Robert Bloomfield.

Mark: How does she know it's in pain? When it, where it says 'The small dust-coloured beetle climbs with pain'. Does she know it's in pain?

Kenneth: Ah, come on, Simmy, if something's small, really s, really er, climbing, something small to us, is very big to him, it must be tired. You've got to admit it, you're going to be tired, ain't yer?

John: Yeah, you can see what it means, this poem, because it would be hard for a beetle to climb up a leaf, wouldn't it?

Mark: It must be breathless, because the, I mean, you know, it's kind of growing

John: Mm

Clive: A leaf, if it is a leaf, isn't, er, very big though, compared with a beetle

John: No, that's true, it depends what kind of beetle it is

Kenneth: 'Spacious plain'

John: No. It says a 'spacious plain' so it must be quite big

Kenneth: It is, big to a beetle

Clive: I think the beetle must be small because not many leaves

John: Because there's lots of different kinds of beetles and it's probably small

Clive: Unless it's a dock leaf, that can be pretty big

John: Or rhubarb

Mark: That must really, that must be hard work for a little beetle, mustn't it? Specially that colour

Kenneth: It is

Clive: And beetles' legs aren't exactly the biggest

John: Not very long

Kenneth: Ah look, they're not very thick to us but surely they're quite thick to a beetle

John: Yeah, you see, because, if you look at, say if a beetle's

Mark: They'd think this is a leaf, they could easily just fly on to it, couldn't they?

John: Yeah, it all depends whether they're winged beetles or not

Kenneth: Yeah, why would it climb it, if it could fly to it the top

John: Yeah, so it must be, it can't really be able to fly, can it?

Mark: It must be, because look, um, 'flirts his filmy wings'

Kenneth: Yeah, but some of these have small sort of wings, but don't fly

John: Yeah, you look at ostrich or a penguin

Mark: I wonder what kind of beetle this is. It could be a ladybird, it could be any kind of beetle, for all we know

John: Mm

Kenneth: But there again, it could be a [   ] thing that could fly
          down but not up

John: Yeah, perhaps it has to have a high point to start off flying,
          you know, so it doesn't fall, it can't take off

Mark: Has to have a wind

John: I doubt if it could fly against wind

Mark: He's got, Robert Bloomfield or whatever his name is, he's got
          it very well, hasn't he?

John: Yeah, he's captured the things

Kenneth: I like . . . the way he writes it

Mark: I think he's wrote this one well. I like this one, I think . . .
          must have took quite a long time

John: He must have had one, studied and watched it all the time,
          he must have watched it climbing . . . You can't, you can't
          really write about something unless you see it, can you?

Mark: He must have been in a quiet place

John: Like you were told to write about the moon, what it's like,
          it'd have to be imaginary, wouldn't it? A long way out

Clive: He also knows all the insects that you often find on wood,
          on furniture, in books. I'm thinking of 'dust-coloured' –
          they're usually that colour . . . it isn't a ladybird

John: Could it be up a bit of wood – they're, they're greyish, ain't they?
          And they're small, kind of like half an egg

Kenneth: It says a 'small dust-coloured beetle'

John: It's probably a wood-beetle

Clive: Wood-louse

John: Yeah, wood-louse, that's right . . . And – another thing that
          proves it's big, it says, um . . .

Mark: 'By countless steps'

John: 'Thence, higher still, by countless steps convey'd'

Kenneth: And 'exulting in his distance from the ground'

John: So, not only must the, um, the leaf be big, but the plant he's
          on must be quite

Kenneth: You know – [inaudible comment]. This is interesting, isn't it?

John: Yeah, I think this is the best one, really. I know it's short, but
          it catches the way it moves and the way it acts

Mark: And it's descriptive

Clive: And it rhymes . . . when you're doing a very descriptive poem
          to get it to rhyme

John: Yeah, it all rhymes, but the first part, I think, where he tries to
          make it rhyme there that sounds too much alike, dunnit? Pain
          and plain?

Kenneth: Ah, when you look at it, yeah, but 'The small dust-coloured
          beetle climbs with pain/O'er the small plantain leaf a spacious
          plain'

Mark: Yeah, it is a kind of a plain to the insect, isn't it?

Kenneth: When you're reading it in lines, that doesn't sound alike but when you're reading it down, 'pain' 'plain', 'convey'd' 'blade', you realize that there is real, real likeness

John: Mm, I see what you mean, like if you look at buffalo on a er, er um plain it's big to them same as a beetle is on a leaf

Kenneth: Yeah

Mark: We think leaves are small and that, but it must, I reckon it's huge to them, if you went down to the smallest beetle, I bet you, I bet there'd be

John: Well it says a 'spacious plain', dunnit?

Clive: And a quarter of an inch high, on most beetles, I suppose it could be pretty big [Inaudible mumbles and rustling]

Mark: What colour is dust, Jumbo?

Kenneth: 'He gains the summit' – I like that bit

John: Yeah, that makes, this is this is the best one, not the last one, not 'Glasses', this is the best one, 'Small Dust-Coloured Beetle'. It's small, but it's descriptive

Kenneth: Yeah, look, I get the descriptive bit, let's look *in* to it

John: Cor, I can *see* it

Kenneth: Small, dust-coloured beetle, in other words that's his colour

John: In other words it's grey

Kenneth: 'Climbs with pain'

Clive: What it's doing

Mark: Look, let somebody read it all now, and then we'll talk about it

John   No

Clive: What it feels like, what its colour

John: Yeah, I wonder what it thinks when it's climbing up a leaf

Clive: Well mostly I'd think beetles can't think because they're so small. I don't suppose any

Kenneth: What do you do when come to planning

John: Think – if you're going to reach, if you're going to reach the top

Clive: You're going to think about the next step

Kenneth: What's ahead, what's going to happen, it's so cold

John: I think, I don't think they're scared because if they fall they aren't really going to kill themselves, are they?

Mark: They could easily glide down with their wings, couldn't they, really?

Clive: There's just one good thing about beetles, I mean, when you consider how long they are, imagine that was our height they fall off a leaf, I mean you could imagine that was about a hundred feet high . . .

John: It wouldn't kill them, it would just stun them

Clive: they don't die, but if that was in a mountain

John: Yeah, they'd die, wouldn't they?

Kenneth: What've they done

John: Because they're so small, you see, ain't they? And when they

Clive: And when they're so light, the air just holds them

Kenneth: Yeah, they always fall on their back, don't they, and just lie there with their

John: Feet in the air. Well, their backs probably protected, eh, like you know

Kenneth: Yeah, it is hard, isn't it?

John: An armadillo, you know, them big scales they have on their backs. It's probably tough

Kenneth: Yes, that's where he got the idea

John: Yeah, and that's why he falls on its er, he probably . . .

Mark: I reckon

John: makes sure he falls on his back so he doesn't hurt himself

Kenneth: That's what he could've done, he could've done a bit more

Clive: The trouble is

Mark: I reckon he knows that it's a long fall. I bet you he must be, it's a kind of a, he must be like a life of a beetle 'cos he says

Kenneth: Yeah

Mark: In his distance from the ground, that, that must be quite a long way to a beetle really – like climbing up a tree and getting to the top and falling down

Kenneth: Yeah, how long does a beetle live?

Clive: I dunno

John: Oh, we don't want to know that

Kenneth: If he lived a very short time, that would be quite a major part of its life

John: Yeah, it would he'd probably go boasting 'I've climbed the biggest tree'

Clive: Um, er, a butterfly only lives about one or two days . . .

Mark: I bet you he must have

Clive: or three, so I mean a beetle, which isn't the same family, is it, sort of, would only live about two, three or four days

Kenneth: Yeah

Mark: It must be nerve, it must be nerve-wracking for the beetle

Kenneth: People do things to try, people climb mountains . . .

John: So why don't beetles

Kenneth: because they want to accomplish something, so why do beetles climb things

John: Because they probably want to accomplish something themselves

Kenneth: Yeah

John: They're probably just the same as us but we don't know, they probably think I'm going to be the next expedition trying to climb up that tree, so I'll set out today whereas they set out tomorrow and I'll beat him up the top

Mark: It must be . . . I reckon it's

Clive: [   ] don't do that, they don't go about with bows and arrows shooting other things, do they?

John: No

Mark: I reckon it's nerve-wracking for a

John: They must kill other little insects

Mark: I reckon it must be nerve-wracking for the beetle, 'cos you know, the grass shivers, you know, and so does the leaf shiver, you know

John: It says 'shivering blade'

Mark: Yeah, that's what I mean

John: It must be wobbling, kind of. It wouldn't be wobbling with his weight so it must be quite

Kenneth: 'He gains the summit'

John: Now that's a nice bit

Mark: Yeah, that reminds, no, it makes you think of a, kind of like us, you know, climbing up to the summit of a mountain

John: Mm

Kenneth: Mm. Lucky for us, Mount Everest doesn't shiver

John: Yes, that's a good point

Mark: Yeah, but it has rock falls, though, doesn't it?

Clive: Imagine how long it's going to take a beetle to cross the wall, with its size and it takes us just a matter of seconds

John: I wonder how long it would

Kenneth: Yes, but that's how long does it take us to get across the Sahara Desert?

Mark: Fifteen years

Kenneth: Generations

John: I know how long it would take to get across, um, a desert for a beetle if it was in a plane – about twenty minutes. [laughter] Well, it doesn't live very long so it wouldn't, er, dare cross the other side, would it?

Kenneth: About a million a day go across the lawn, like us going across the Sahara Desert

Clive: They've got the blades of grass in the way

Kenneth: Ah, well okay us going through the jungle then, isn't it?

John: Mm, yes

Clive: [   ] and you get big machine . . . sucked down

Kenneth: We might get back to the actual poem

John: We're not supposed to be on about crossing the Sahara Desert in a plane

Kenneth: Ah yeah, but

John: Okay, okay, okay

Mark: We've made it

John: 'Filmy wings'. Does filmy mean thin?

All: Yes

Kenneth: You can see by this curtain here, can't you?

John: That's filmy

Kenneth: That's filmy, innit?

Mark: Yeah, but the wings

Clive: That's where the film is when, if you hold it up to the light you can see the [   ] through and you get a film

Mark: I reckon the, I reckon the wings, you know, they're very thin

John: They might be kind of like a little net

Clive: They remind me of water

Kenneth: 'And flirts his filmy wings'

John: Lets it blow – flirts

Kenneth: 'Looks around'

John: Its filmy wings, exulting in his distance from the ground. He must be quite high up, or it wouldn't say distance from the ground

Kenneth: Yeah. 'By countless steps convey'd'

John: Mm, mm. 'A spacious plain.' It's not a thing describing how high it is, what it's like, er

Mark: Do you reckon he could have done a little bit more than that?

John: No. I think he's put it just right in

Clive: I don't like very long poems, they get so boring

John: Six lines do it just nicely. In the first two lines he describes the climb, you know, he's in pain, and it describes the, the smooth leaf and how big it is

Clive: And also his colour

Mark: Jumbo

John: Yes, yes

Mark: Here's a question. Why do you think he's in pain? I reckon I know

John: Well, climbing so high really

Clive: Yes, I mean . . .

Mark: Well, you've got to be brave, be not to be all

Clive: people get tired, he's only a beetle. I suppose he'd get

John: Tired. I suppose he'd get even more tired

Mark: The wind, the wind kind of blows the breath out of him, you know

John: No, I don't know

Clive: I think so, yes. If you're ever [   ] in a situation, like if you lean out of the window, you sometimes find it a job to breathe

Mark: Yes, that's what I mean

Clive: So when he's in a gale, he'll get blown backwards a lot

John: It's hard, though, walking or running against, er, a wind, so it must be, it says shimmer, er, shivering, that must be moving a bit so he must be having difficulty getting up

Clive: When one comes to a thing and walks up to it, obviously its got very good suction of feet or something. We can't go up to a thing and just walk up straight, can we? We need ropes and

Kenneth: Okay, so he's got better climbing ability than us. We probably got a better swimming ability than him

Clive: Yes, I mean if he went in a pool, he would probably drown, even in a little puddle

John: He can swim

Kenneth: Yeah, some animals are faster at running than we are. Cheetah

John: You cheater Trim!

Clive: Jaguar

Kenneth: Yes, well that's how it comes, innit?

John: It does. I see what you mean. In other words, people are good at things, animals are good at things

Transcript 2

Kenneth, John, Mark and Raymond discussing 'The Snare' by James Stephens.

John:	Let's go on to the next one, shall we?
Kenneth:	Yeah. 'The Snare'.
John:	Well, in this one, I don't really think you'd hear a sudden cry of pain, because
Raymond:	Yeah, it might be
Kenneth:	You look at it, in nearly every other line, mostly, it rhymes
John:	Yeah, it does rhyme
Raymond:	But just a minute though
Kenneth:	Every other line
Raymond:	One thing, I have heard er a rabbit squeal, one time our cat was chasing a
John:	Yeah, but I wouldn't
Mark:	I don't think it's fair, I don't think it's fair to put those snares down
John:	No, but rabbits are a pest, aren't they?
Raymond:	He was a poacher and there's a pest-destroyer up on the LSA which was killing them off, and you could see them
Kenneth:	Honestly, I don't think this poem is terribly realistic
John:	No, it wasn't um quite right, you'd know really by experience who it was, wouldn't you?
Mark:	You'd know really by a mysterious scuttling, you hear a kind of little scuttling in the bush
Kenneth:	It must be pretty close for you to hear a rabbit squeal
John:	Well, they do make quite a lot of noise sometimes
Kenneth:	Look, 'oh little one, oh little one'
John:	Yes, and there's a bit here, if she didn't know where it was, how did she know it was little?
Raymond:	It might have been a he
Kenneth:	Yes, well, that's just the way you describe it, don't you?
John:	Yes, it's daft though, isn't it?
Mark:	How did she know, 'wrinkling up its little face'?
John:	Yeah, that's a point
Kenneth:	Where its paw is in the snare. It might have had its head stuck in the snare
All:	Yes
John:	It might have its body stuck in the snare
Kenneth:	It's not terribly likely, but it's possible
Raymond:	It might have its tail stuck
Mark:	How does she know it's stuck in a snare?
John:	It might have been caught in brambles, mightn't it?
Kenneth:	'Making everything afraid'

Mark:	Might have something in its paw, couldn't it? It's easy
Raymond:	When it says 'Making everything afraid' it means that everything's stopping to listen and wondering what the noise is, little bit scared like ordinary people stopping
John:	Yeah, um, making everything afraid, would make things afraid
Raymond:	It would, because if a rook came along, that'd soon scarper, wouldn't it?
John:	For the noise, you see
Kenneth:	That don't mean humans afraid, surely, only means
John:	No, animals. It means other animals
John:	This one is really a bit nuts
Kenneth:	I should say this one is about
John:	Isn't very descriptive
Kenneth:	I reckon 'Rock the Dog's' best, then '1939', but this one is bad
John:	Snares . . . not very good
Kenneth:	No
Raymond:	No. They're more imaginative
John:	I bet it's somebody
Kenneth:	He's gone a bit wild on it. He's over-exaggerated
John:	What has gone wrong in here, he's trying to make it rhyme, isn't he? You notice the way that he has to put the bottom line of the first verse . . .
Mark:	Yeah. Like the
John:	on to the top of the second one. Well, that spoils it.
Mark:	Like this, like this. 'But I cannot tell from where/But I cannot tell from where'
Kenneth:	'But I cannot tell from where/But I cannot tell from where'. He's repeating himself
John:	He just does that to give it a rhyme, doesn't he?
Mark:	He just does that really to get more in
Raymond:	Then went from second verse on to the third verse. 'Making everything afraid/Making everything afraid', and then in the third verse
Kenneth:	'And I cannot find the place/And I cannot find the place.' He's just rubbing it in, he's pushing it in
John:	This is quite descriptive, but there are some bits in here that's not true
Raymond:	I reckon I know why he didn't do another verse to this, because he couldn't get 'I am searching everywhere' on to the next one
Mark:	Surely, if it was caught, if it had a thorn in its paw and it saw you coming, surely that would try to get away before you could come and kill it?
Raymond:	Yes, but that's the best way to get rid of it
Mark:	I'd shoot it

Raymond: If you could find it, you could get . . .
John: Shoot it with a water pistol
Raymond: You could get a large stick and club it over the head
Kenneth: Put it out of its pain
Raymond: That soon kills them
Kenneth: Ah, but if it was held down by its paw, that's not going to kill it, is it?
John: Ah it would, because it wouldn't be able to move, would it? It's caught, can't move and sometimes if they do get free, their leg comes off and they'll still die because they get dirt and that in the cut and then that gets in the
Kenneth: Yeah
Raymond: They sometimes get it out and no one ever finds it, it's going to die of starvation, isn't it?
John: Unless he's in some kind of paradise
Kenneth: Well, yes, I really change my mind about that. I agree with you there because, look, if he did have his leg, bad legs and that, surely the people who hunted him down could be too too easy to get him
Raymond: Yes, that is a point
Mark: Yes, he should hide it in . . . covered area
John: They're not very good, are they, snares? They're cruel. Pity they couldn't suddenly, soon as they get caught, it just kills them suddenly, a shock or something
Mark: A 'lectric shock
John: A 'lectric shock goes through it and, pity it couldn't just kill it straightaway
Kenneth: I don't think it's good to kill them. Okay, they cause trouble but why don't you just catch them up and put them in a place?
John: You can't. You can't get a rabbit unless you kill it
Mark: You want to put it in a reserve or something like that
Raymond: Oh yes. I can imagine . . . running around after a rabbit with his butterfly net
Mark: Yes, well
John: No, no. Don't be silly
Kenneth: Yes, well he's just making
Mark: A safety thing. Why can't they make a safety thing?
Raymond: Yes
John: It's quite an idea about having a reserve because if they could get them, get some, that'd take down the population of rabbits. If they could get, ooh, a few thousand and put them in a reserve and get rid of most of the others, then that'd be better for everybody, wouldn't it?
Raymond: Because people go round killing these rabbits and when they get too rare

Kenneth: Yeah, they start crying over them, 'Look, they're practically extinct' and everything

Raymond: They're not now

John: In '56, when they produced myxamatosis, that, I reckon that's the worst thing that can happen to a rabbit is getting myxamatosis

Kenneth: Yeah

John: You know that, when their eyes all pop out and that

Raymond: You know what that's for, don't you?

John: Yeah. They were going to take it over to Australia but a rabbit got out over here . . . and it got into this country

Mark: If they can make something, if they can make a safety thingummy on a snare, then it won't cause so much pain and that would be all right, wouldn't it?

Raymond: No, but that would be easy for it to get out, wouldn't it?

Mark: No, it would still hold it firmly, but safely

John: It says here, um, 'I cannot find the place', yet up here it says um, um, I can't find what I'm looking for, you know, about, um, what's it say, something about its face

Mark: Wrinkled up its face

John: Yeah. How does he know that he's like that if he couldn't find it. That's daft. Stupid, daft and crazy

Mark: He must have seen it if it's wrinkled up its face

Kenneth: 'Now I hear the cry again/But I cannot tell from where'. Usually, me and my brother try a game like that, when somebody calls out, you turn, look, instead of me counting to get you ready, you call out when you're ready, when I've got to find you hiding. You do that because you know you're going to tell them where they come from

Mark: It could be a person

Kenneth: The sounds, you can do that with sounds

John: This, this is quite good really, isn't it? Because, um, it starts off

Kenneth: Ah, it's better than a lot

John: It starts off good but it finishes off funny, just gone weird at the end, isn't it? Um, where does it say that

Mark: For all we know, it could be somebody with a tape-recorder playing a trick on somebody. You know, pretending it's in pain and he's taking it from a cry of one and put it there and keeps playing it at heaps of different places

Raymond: You know you said that when you play hide and seek you say ready when you are?

Kenneth: And you don't know where they are

Raymond: No you can't, but you know it's that direction, so that's how you check that place

John: You would know

Kenneth: You know roughly the direction though
John: Yeah, because ears are kind of like radars, you can pick up where they're coming from and you can almost pinpoint down where the sound is coming from, can't you? Like someone was hiding over there by them trees and you heard them cry out, you'd know where they were coming from, wouldn't you?
Raymond: You'd straightaway go over to them trees, wouldn't you?
Kenneth: Very roughly, yes
John: For a start, if it comes from this ear you'd know it come round from that direction, wouldn't you? If it come in your left ear you know it was on the left half of you. If it come in the right you'd know it was on the right
Mark: Listen to a car . . . it's over there
Kenneth: Sounds like over there, don't it? You can pinpoint
John: 'I hear a sudden cry . . ./There is a rabbit in a snare./Now I hear the cry again/But I cannot tell from where.' That's mad
Kenneth: Now look, surely, a rabbit's cry isn't very loud
Raymond: That is
John: That is
Mark: It can make a lot of noise
John: If you got a rabbit and you hold it up by its back legs, that squeals all the time
Raymond: That makes a high-pitched squeal
John: It's a heck of a noise
Raymond: It makes a high-pitched squeal, don't it?
Kenneth: Yeah. Okay, it's a heck of a noise when you're close, but can you hear it twenty yards away?
John: Yes, easily, easily
Raymond: Yes, because I was up the bus stop and the rabbit was right over the other side
John: You can hear them about a hundred yards away
Kenneth: Yes, that's the way to get them, to be cruel to them, isn't it?
John: No, it was our cat
Raymond: It was a little baby one and she just kept on saying it was just playing with it
John: Yes, it was killing it at the same time
Kenneth: Yes
Mark: Nasty old thing
John: Come on, get back to the poem, for goodness sake. We're off the subject. And there it says 'As he cries again for aid'. That's not true. How does she know it wanted aid? How does she know it wanted aid? Perhaps it wanted some lettuce sandwiches or something
Mark: How does he know it's for aid?

Kenneth: How does he know it is a snare, maybe it's just starvation
John: Yes. If he don't know where it is, how come he knows it's a snare? Well, he can't see it, can he?
Kenneth: Some animal could have grabbed hold of it, really hurt it, but not killed it properly, so it's just lying there, can't move and screaming
John: Yes, a fox could have got it. Well, that would have killed it, wouldn't it?
Raymond: Not necessarily, because that may just be, you know, chasing it, may be chasing it
John: Someone might have shot it or something
Kenneth: Not properly
All: Yes
John: In the leg. You look at a 22-slug gun. If that got it in the thigh somewhere, er, it says, um
Kenneth: In its paw
John: In its paw. How does it know that for a start? It might be in its leg. If a slug got it and then it would be crying out even because that would be
Raymond: Yeah, but a cat might be chasing it
John: Anything might happen, we don't know what
[Various inaudible suggestions]
John: There is a point about this because, um, it says they would probably find the rabbit later if they didn't find it then. If they'd found the rabbit they'd have probably found the snare. They might have found the snare by itself and gathered that's where it come from
Raymond: Yeah, but I reckon . . .
Mark: See, it could have been the other
Raymond: That they might have found it afterwards
Kenneth: Yeah
Raymond: And that would make the poem of before
John: Yeah. I know, I know, the bloke might have come and got his rabbit and they might have found it and an old bloke called James Stephenson probably thought 'Oh, this is a good thing for a poem. I can write about what happened'
Mark: James Stephens
John: That's what I said
Mark: You said Stephensons
Kenneth: That doesn't matter about his name
John: No, no, that's silly, you old twit
Raymond: But the old poacher man come along
John: He, he'd have come along, he'd have got his rabbit and he might have found the snare
Kenneth: But are these poems true?
John: I don't know. Might be

13   Sharing responses to literature
Pat D'Arcy

This paper draws on work done by the author and other members of
two residential workshops organized, as part of the 'Children as Readers'
project, to study children's responses to poetry. It is concerned with
two tapes which were made by Elizabeth Grugeon, a member of the
panel, at a primary school in East Anglia. It was a village school (140–50
children in all) and the boys on these tapes were between nine and eleven
years old. Many of the children in the school came from a cooperative
settlement for market gardening just outside the village, where each
family had its own smallholding and each contributed to a common pool –
growing lettuces, cucumbers, celery, tomatoes, etc. The boys' teacher
commented: 'It's a tough way of life, and the children, who are members
of their family team, reflect this in their maturity and independence.'
Of their primary school she adds: 'The school is privileged, with extensive playing-fields, a swimming-pool, a good large airy hall – and an
active fund-raising PTA. The teaching tends to be formal with an emphasis on the acquisition of "skills". This means that in the top class of nine-
to eleven-year-olds, every child can read fluently and most can write
tolerably well, but they tend to find group work difficult. There is an
element of competition which makes talking to each other in class
discussion seem difficult.'

The two groups on these tapes were self-chosen; the boys all knew
each other well. (In the first instance, the group comprised Mark, John,
Kenneth and Raymond; in the second, Ray, who was ill, was replaced
by Clive.) Undoubtedly this helped them to find ways of talking about
the poems which the teacher had given them, which were not competitive so much as exploratory. In their discussion of 'The Small Dust-
Coloured Beetle' particularly, there seems to be a common concern to
discover what they have each seen and felt about the poem which involves a genuine sharing of response rather than an evaluative comparison of one comment against another.

These tapes were interesting for several reasons; the poems under

Source: D'ARCY, Pat (1975) 'Sharing responses to literature' in an unpublished report *Children as Readers: The Roles of Literature in the Primary and
Secondary Schools*, co-sponsored by The National Association for the Teaching of English and the Schools Council 1968–73

discussion elicited such different responses, not just from individuals, but each time from the group as a whole; the fact that they were operating without a teacher in the room seemed to facilitate discussion in so far as considerably more time was spent talking about each poem than would normally be the case in a class situation. Because there was no 'expert' present who could be looked to to take the leading role, the group had to generate its own patterns of discussion. On each occasion the question and answer approach is replaced by a much more flexible yet at the same time more complex pattern in which many balls are kept in the air simultaneously instead of a single ball being thrown in turn to each member of the group by a central figure.

Our pattern in this paper is to look first at what exactly the groups are sharing together, then at why and, more specifically, at how they are sharing their individual responses to the poems. We then touch briefly on two further questions which in our view are highly relevant to the study of how children may be able to arrive together at an understanding and appreciation of literature: how far the nature of the group affects the talk, and how far the discussion is affected by the nature of the poem or the story that is the focus of the group's attention.

First of all then, what is being shared by the group? To start with the most obvious factors, they share the same sex and the same class; they also share an ability to express themselves in speech. For both these discussions they share a common context – they have been given a task in a school situation. They also share the poems which they have been asked to discuss: three poems on each occasion, including 'The Small Dust-Coloured Beetle' by Robert Bloomfield on the first occasion, and 'The Snare' by James Stephens on the second. They all had copies of each poem which they could refer to.

These are all factors which they undeniably shared as a group. They may also share personal friendships or animosities which can sometimes be glimpsed in their talk. We have listened to groups on other occasions in which these personal factors coloured the discussion very noticeably, although in these two tapes this kind of dominant shift from poems to personalities does not occur. These two groups' central concern is to share their responses on each occasion to the poem: their own interpretation of its meaning, their feelings about the experience the poet is presenting, personal anecdotes which the poem may trigger off and factual knowledge (in these instances about rabbits and snares and beetles and different kinds of leaves) which they may need to call upon in order to clear up misunderstandings or clarify meanings.

If we ask why these children sit down together to talk about these poems, the answer must chiefly be because they are in school and they have been asked to talk about what they have read. It would be unlikely that a group of ten-year-old boys would spontaneously settle down either to read a poem together or to talk about one. But having said that, once the poem has been read, it may be sufficiently powerful – or sufficiently confusing – to provoke ready discussion. In the case of 'The Snare' and 'The Small Dust-Coloured Beetle', the former provoked a negative reaction so that the discussion became increasingly sceptical and irritated; the latter evoked a positive response which moved almost immediately into an imaginative exploration of how the world would look to a beetle. In their talk the boys prompt each other to project themselves sympathetically into such a world:

John: Yeah, you can see what it means, this poem, because it would be hard for a beetle to climb up a leaf, wouldn't it?

Mark: It must be breathless, because the, I mean, you know, it's kind of growing

There are moments in the discussion of each poem when they are puzzled and depend on suggestions from someone in the group to solve their difficulty or at any rate to have a go:

Clive: A leaf, if it is a leaf, isn't, er, very big though, compared with a beetle

John: No, that's true, it depends what kind of beetle it is

Kenneth: 'Spacious plain'

John: No. It says a 'spacious plain' so it must be quite big

Kenneth: It is, big to a beetle

Clive: I think the beetle must be small because not many leaves

John: Because there's lots of different kinds of beetles and it's probably small

Clive: Unless it's a dock leaf, that can be pretty big

John: Or rhubarb

We can see how the group work together to puzzle out and make clear for themselves the concept of comparative size which is implicit in the poem. They all offer suggestions and arrive (often by implication themselves) at a satisfactory solution to Clive's original query – that compared to a beetle, a leaf isn't very big anyway. They remember between them that there are different sizes of leaves as well as different sizes of beetle – so that if you put a small beetle on a large leaf, a dock for instance or a rhubarb leaf, then there would be sufficient difference between them for the leaf to appear a 'spacious plain'.

In their discussion of 'The Snare', the boys' attempt to answer each other's questions is more fragmented, partly because they do not experience the same sympathetic reaction to this poem as to the other. Their initial attitude to 'The Snare' is one of disbelief:

John: Well, in this one, I don't really think you'd hear a sudden cry of pain, because

Raymond: Yeah, it might be

Kenneth: You look at it, in nearly every other line, mostly, it rhymes
John: Yeah, it does rhyme
Raymond: But just a minute though
Kenneth: Every other line
Raymond: One thing, I have heard er a rabbit squeal, one time our cat was chasing a
John: Yeah, but I wouldn't
Mark: I don't think it's fair, I don't think it's fair to put those snares down
John: No, but rabbits are a pest, aren't they?
Raymond: He was a poacher and there's a pest-destroyer up on the LSA which was killing them off, and you could see them
Kenneth: Honestly, I don't think this poem is terribly realistic
John: No, it wasn't um quite right, you'd know really by experience who it was, wouldn't you?
Mark: You'd know really by a mysterious scuttling, you hear a kind of little scuttling in the bush
Kenneth: It must be pretty close for you to hear a rabbit squeal
John: Well, they do make quite a lot of noise sometimes
Kenneth: Look, 'Oh little one, oh little one'
John: Yes, and there's a bit here, if she didn't know where it was, how did she know it was little?
Raymond: It might have been a he
Kenneth: Yes, well, that's just the way you describe it, don't you?
John: Yes, it's daft though, isn't it?
Mark: How did she know, 'wrinkling up its little face'?

On this occasion the group are not uniting forces to reach a solution to the problem of whether or not it is possible (a) for a rabbit to give 'a sudden cry of pain' and (b) to discover its whereabouts as a result. Instead they proceed to scatter onto different themes, never really focusing on a common centre. Ken is preoccupied with the fact that the poem rhymes; Ray starts an anecdote about his cat chasing a rabbit; Mark comes out strongly with a dislike of snares; John counters this by putting up the point of view that rabbits are pests anyway. It seems that because they share a general feeling of dissatisfaction with the poem, they are less prepared than in the 'Beetle' discussion to pay careful attention to each other's remarks, so that although the poem provokes plenty of comment very little of it moves them on to common ground.

We have already begun to move from why a group share individual responses to how this process of sharing takes place. From our study of these tapes we would like to suggest four ways, which are all taken up by these boys in both discussions:

(i) *Brief acknowledgements* of common agreement or satisfaction (yeah, no, mm).

(ii) *Linked anecdotes* in which the group tell stories from their own experience which start from something in the poem but once in train may move away from the poem's centre.

(iii) *Problem solving* – the kind of puzzling out that we have already illustrated briefly, which may or may not reach a satisfactory solution. Success may depend on whether someone can produce relevant additional information or it may depend on how the group or members of it take the writer's tone and intention.

(iv) The group may join together *in the common pursuit of a single idea* which may lead them further into the poem (as when they grasp the idea of the beetle's relative smallness) – or further away (as when they doubt the poet's inability to find the trapped rabbit). This fourth kind of sharing may sometimes depend on the ability of someone in the group to formulate hypotheses (what if . . . supposing that . . .) which can then be discussed jointly.

The kind of brief murmurs and grunts that signify our first way that a group has of sharing their responses is common in all small group discussions, though it does not seem to occur so frequently when the group is class size. 'No' signals agreement as often as disagreement when it is used as a linking device with a remark by a previous speaker or with a previous train of thought:

Kenneth: Honestly, I don't think this poem is terribly realistic
John: No, it wasn't um quite right, you'd know really by experience who it was, wouldn't you?

Sometimes the group will use such sharing noises as useful fillers to give them time to think: 'Yeah . . . mm'.

Telling stories, sometimes brief and sometimes lengthy, may lead the group away from their concentration on the original piece of writing but often, given time, they will feed back into it. Anecdotal sharing is an 'adding-on-to' process; it does not demand close concentration and is therefore an enjoyable and relaxed kind of activity. Neither 'The Snare' nor 'The Small Dust-Coloured Beetle' as it happens produces as much anecdotal comment as other poems which the boys discussed. John does have one story in 'The Snare' discussion, about his cat playing with a rabbit which he tries to come in with fairly early on, but his efforts to tell it are ignored and he has to wait until the group come back to the poem (after turning their attention to one of the others that they had to choose from) before he can have another go, backed up this time by Ray who sounds as though he must have been present when the incident happened:

John: If you got a rabbit and you hold it up by its back legs, that squeals all the time

Raymond: That makes a high-pitched squeal
John: It's a heck of a noise
Raymond: It makes a high-pitched squeal, don't it?
Kenneth: Yeah. Okay, it's a heck of a noise when you're close, but can
        you hear it twenty yards away?
John: Yes, easily, easily
Raymond: Yes, because I was up the bus stop and the rabbit was right
        over the other side
John: You can hear them about a hundred yards away
Kenneth: Yes, that's the way to get them, to be cruel to them, isn't it?
John: No, it was our cat
Raymond: It was a little baby one and she just kept on saying it was just
        playing with it
John: Yes, it was killing it at the same time
Kenneth: Yes
Mark: Nasty old thing
John: Come on, get back to the poem, for goodness sake. We're
        off the subject . . .

We want to speculate here that, although he introduced the story, John becomes anxious for the group to stop talking about it not because it is irrelevant, but because remembering the incident upsets him. Whether or not a rabbit *can* squeal loudly when it is in pain, and over what distances the squeal can be heard, is in fact entirely relevant to the poem – and particularly to their doubts about the poem's reality.

The kind of sharing which we have called puzzling-out or problem-solving demands fairly sustained attention from all members of the group if common insights are to be gained and if any agreement is to be reached about possible meanings. At one level, puzzling-out is concerned with the appropriate meaning of specific words. The language in 'The Snare' is too simple to demand this kind of word teasing, but the eighteenth-century flavour of Bloomfield's language is slightly more obscure. In this excerpt the group is tackling the line, 'And flirts his filmy wings and looks around':

John: 'Filmy wings'. Does filmy mean thin?
All: Yes
Kenneth: You can see by this curtain here, can't you?
John: That's filmy
Kenneth: That's filmy, innit?
Mark: Yeah, but the wings
Clive: That's where the film is when, if you hold it up to the light
        you can see the [   ] through and you get a film
Mark: I reckon the, I reckon the wings, you know, they're very
        thin
John: They might be kind of like a little net

Clive: They remind me of water
Kenneth: 'And flirts his filmy wings'
John: Let's it blow – flirts
Kenneth: 'Looks around'
John: 'Its filmy wings, exulting in his distance from the ground' . . .

Here the group is engaged in making a combined imaginative effort.
They are searching for ways of expressing what 'flirts his filmy wings'
makes them feel and see. They start off by giving a very basic definition
for filmy: thin. Then they compare 'filmy' to the curtain hanging at the
staffroom window which presumably is light and fine, made of nylon or
some similar transparent material, so that although they do not specifically mention these qualities, they are there by implication in the comparison: 'You can see by this curtain here, can't you?' Sheer repetition
of the word 'filmy' – the sound and feel of it – seems to be another way
of offering its meaning to the group, as does quoting what follows:

John: 'Its filmy wings, exulting in his distance from the ground'

By moving to the final line like this, John succeeds in catching the
feeling of exultation which is also present in the notion of the beetle
'flirting' its wings. Clive and John also explore some of the meanings of
filmy by suggesting possible analogies. Clive suggests holding something
transparent up to the light; he seems to be struggling to capture that
what you can see, although very faint and delicate, is the 'film' which
prevents the transparency from becoming completely invisible. John
suggests 'kind of like a little net', a comparison which has something of
the same air of fragility about it, and Clive then comes back with 'They
remind me of water', which again suggests another form of light-
catching transparency. Certainly at this point in the discussion it would
appear that the group is puzzling out the meaning with an imaginative
and sensitive feel for possible connotations which a direct question from
a teacher might have crushed or precluded.

The discussions of both poems provide interesting examples of our
fourth kind of sharing: when the group join together in the common
pursuit of a single attitude or idea. In this excerpt they are expressing
their common dissatisfaction with the poet's assumptions about the
rabbit's plight when he hasn't even got the gumption to find it. (It is
intriguing that John, like Mark earlier, refers here to this inept poet as
she!)

John: . . . it says 'As he cries again for aid'. That's not true. How
            does she know it wanted aid? How does she know it wanted
            aid? Perhaps it wanted some lettuce sandwiches or something
Mark: How does he know it's for aid?
Kenneth: How does he know it is a snare, maybe it's just starvation

John: Yes. If he don't know where it is, how comes he knows it's a snare? Well, he can't see it, can he?

Kenneth: Some animal could have grabbed hold of it, really hurt it, but not killed it properly, so it's just lying there, can't move and screaming

Here, the group seem to be resenting the fact that the poet has made them suffer vicariously for an experience that was not even a reality for him, because he only heard – he did not actually see. The idea of the snare, of deliberately setting a trap to catch an animal which will keep it alive in great pain, clearly worries them, although they can't altogether escape into John's fantasy of the rabbit wanting lettuce sandwiches, and have to come back to possibilities of real suffering – starvation, or facing the hostility of other animals.

But setting traps is inhuman, and at one point in their discussion they arrive with great relief at the idea of a reservation for rabbits where they would not be a pest to anybody and could live in peace:

Kenneth: I don't think it's a good idea to kill them. Okay, they cause trouble, but why don't you just catch them up and put them in a place?

John: You can't. You can't get a rabbit unless you kill it

Mark: You want to put it in a reserve or something like that

Raymond: Oh yes. I can imagine . . . running around after a rabbit with his butterfly net

Mark: Yes, well

John: No, no. Don't be silly

Kenneth: Yes, well he's just making

Mark: A safety thing. Why can't they make a safety thing?

Raymond: Yes

John: It's quite an idea about having a reserve because if they could get them, get some, that'd take down the population of rabbits. If they could get, ooh, a few thousand and put them in a reserve and get rid of most of the others, then that'd be better for everybody, wouldn't it?

Another example of single-minded concentration on the exploration of one idea is from the discussion of 'The Small Dust-Coloured Beetle'. They reach a point where their previous emphasizing with the beetle leads them to consider the effect on the insect of the height to which it has climbed:

Mark: I reckon it must be nerve-wracking for the beetle, 'cos you know, the grass shivers, you know, and so does the leaf shiver, you know

John: It says 'shivering blade'

Mark: Yeah, that's what I mean
John: It must be wobbling, kind of. It wouldn't be wobbling with
           his weight so it must be quite
Kenneth: 'He gains the summit'
John: Now that's a nice bit
Mark: Yeah, that reminds, no, it makes you think of a, kind of like
           us, you know, climbing up to the summit of a mountain
John: Mm
Kenneth: Mm. Lucky for us, Mount Everest doesn't shiver
John: Yes, that's a good point
Mark: Yeah, but it has rock falls, though, doesn't it?
Clive: Imagine how long it's going to take a beetle to cross the wall,
           with its size and it takes us just a matter of seconds
John: I wonder how long it would
Kenneth: Yes, but that's how long does it take us to get across the
           Sahara Desert?

At this point, the group have between them come very near to the
poet's own sense that it is an enormous task for a beetle to scale a plantain leaf. In the passage that we have just quoted, each remark (and everyone in the group takes part) is closely related to the previous one. There
is a sense of excitement and discovery about their remarks *in relation to
each other* which illustrates well how generative shared responses can be
when one suggestion leads in to another. It is also interesting to notice
here how, when Mark talks about grass and leaves shivering, and John
quotes 'shivering blade' from the poem, Mark's thoughts are so concentrated on the beetle's precarious position that he acknowledges the
poet's expression *as though it were his own*: 'Yeah, that's what I mean.'
It would be difficult to come closer to a genuine appreciation of someone else's writing than that!

We noticed in both tapes how the kind of speculation that is half a
question is often taken by the group as an invitation for joint exploration.
For example:

Mark: I wonder what kind of beetle this is. It could be a ladybird,
           it could be any kind of beetle, for all we know
John: Mm
Kenneth: But there again, it could be a [   ] thing that could fly
           down but not up
John: Yeah, perhaps it has to have a high point to start off flying,
           you know, so it doesn't fall, it can't take off
Mark: Has to have a wind
John: I doubt if it could fly against wind

Notice how thoughtful and tentative this talk is: 'I wonder . . .', 'it could
be . . .' 'for all we know . . .', 'But there again . . .', 'I doubt if . . .'. This

145

willingness to accept an element of uncertainty would seem to offer the maximum opportunity for collaboration.

But now let us look briefly at which factors in the sharing process are most closely related to the nature of the groups, and which to the piece of literature under consideration. If we take the nature of the groups first, the extent to which the members know each other, and have chosen to come together, almost certainly affects the confidence with which they express their responses. It is easier to admit doubts to friends than to acquaintances; the degree to which each member is also willing to listen and respond to another speaker may also depend on how far they are friends in the first place.

When, for instance, Mark opens the discussion on 'The Small Dust-Coloured Beetle' by using a questioning technique that he is already familiar with from the earlier discussion of 'The Snare' and no doubt other discussions as well – 'How does she know it's in pain?' – Ken, who has already responded to the centre of the poem in a way that none of the group did to 'The Snare', is able to say, 'Ah, come on, Simmy, if something's small, really s, really, er, climbing, something small to us, is very big to him, it must be tired. You've got to admit it, you're going to be tired, ain't yer?' By making this friendly appeal, it looks as though Ken manages to change the whole approach of the group from criticism to sympathy and appreciation, without making Mark feel stupid or on the defensive; he knows Mark well enough to call him by his in-group name and so is able to persuade him to think again without losing face.

It would also seem from listening to the tapes that all the boys can express their ideas in speech without too much difficulty. There are the hesitations and unfinished sentences common to any discussion, but the talk flows easily, there is no sense that any individual is really having to struggle with language in order to say what is in his mind. Our impression is that individual comments are relatively brief because they are regarded by the speakers as contributions to a joint undertaking rather than as a series of monologues which set out each speaker's independent and 'total' response. We have listened to other tapes in which each member of the group was allowed a 'turn' to say what he had to say without interruption. With these boys there is a much closer intermingling of comments, even when they are following different lines of thought.

Two more factors worth mentioning perhaps, which depend on the speakers and their influence on the quality and depth of the sharing process when literature is the subject under discussion, are the extent to which the group possesses a precise critical vocabulary and the extent to which their literary assumptions are sophisticated or immature. This group of ten-year-olds, for instance, can express their interpretational responses more fully (and therefore more meaningfully) than their evaluative responses which are restricted to such comments as 'this one is bad', 'he's over-exaggerated', 'not terribly realistic', 'it's daft', or more positively 'you can see what it means this poem', 'I think this one is the best one really', 'you can't really write about something unless you see it can you?', 'it's small but it's descriptive'. All the evaluative comments are short and assertive like this; they don't invite discussion as some of the interpretational ones do. This would strongly suggest to us that as teachers we should encourage children to *interpret* what they read, in preference to judging it.

Finally, what about the literature that is put forward for discussion – how can that affect the nature of the group's responses and the quality of the sharing that takes place? In the case of these two poems, the suspect nature of the poet's feelings in 'The Snare' – as perceived by the readers, that is – seems to colour the whole of the discussion; as we have already noted, it tends to be fragmentary and disjointed, dotting about rather querulously from one point to another. By contrast, Bloomfield's perception of the beetle's world is taken up more sympathetically and at the same time more cohesively by the group. It is tempting to make an evaluation of our own here and to suggest that Bloomfield's poem is more finely conceived than Stephens' – and has influenced the group's responses more positively for that reason. But we have also listened to a tape of a girls' group talking about 'The Snare', where the responses were as sympathetic to the rabbit's plight as the boys' responses to the beetle; in consequence, the discussion seemed to have the same quality of shared satisfaction as the beetle discussion here. We can only conclude, tentatively, that for immature readers at any rate (and possibly for more mature ones too), the extent to which their own experience *chimes in with* the experience presented by the writer will be a powerful influence on both the interpretational and the evaluative responses of the group.

Literature may not ultimately be dependent on the personal experiences of the reader, but in terms of how far he is able to appreciate it 'from where he stands' it looks as though there must be sufficient common ground for him to gain at least a foothold, if he is to glimpse the poet's or the novelist's vision – what inspired him in fact to take up his pen in the first place. If readers are able to draw upon their own past knowledge and past memories so that *a two-way process* is made possible, of comparing or aligning their own feelings and ideas with those of the writer, the degree to which they can share their perceptions not just with the poet or novelist *but with each other* is bound to be increased.

The literary skill with which the writer has handled his presentation seems to be of secondary importance, although once a way in has been found to the poem or story, such an appreciation may then follow – as it did with the boys' exploration of the images involved in the line 'And flirts his filmy wings'. Thus, although in some respects Bloomfield's language is more difficult than the language of 'The Snare', the group is willing to work at it appreciatively, whereas they dismiss Stephens' use of language as artificial:

F

John: What has gone wrong in here, he's trying to make it rhyme, isn't he? . . .

Kenneth: . . . He's repeating himself . . .

Kenneth: . . . He's just rubbing it in, he's pushing it in

John: This is quite descriptive, but there are some bits in here that's not true

Raymond: I reckon I know why he didn't do another verse to this, because he couldn't get 'I am searching everywhere' on to the next one

There are still a great many features of shared responses that we are either unfamiliar with or unsure about, when it comes to deciding how far they can help the growth of a single reader's insight into a piece of literature. We don't know how clear individual comments have to be or how complete, for them to be seminal for other members of the group. As yet we can only conjecture how far a joint exploration of a poem or story depends upon the extent to which it is 'recognizable' to the reader or upon the kind of feelings it sets up in their initial responses. It is interesting to speculate, for instance, how far the opening half-dozen or so comments may influence the nature of the whole discussion that follows. If Ken had not been able to persuade Mark to drop his sceptical tone about the beetle poem so quickly, the group might never have explored the significant changes in perspective that an appreciation of the beetle's smallness involved. It seems to be important that members of a group have sufficient confidence or trust in each other to feel free to express their honest opinions without fear of ridicule or hostility; perhaps the size of the group is important – five or six boys or girls can be real friends and know each other very well, but more than that inevitably means that although each individual may have some friends within the group, others will be less well known. Whether the group is all one sex is another factor – frequently self-chosen groups like this one tend to be single sex; in our experience it is not common for boys and girls to choose to work together, even when they mix perfectly easily in breaks and lunch hours.

We have picked out from the tape studies which we have made of children talking about poems a variety of strategies that they may choose to adopt – some of which are outlined in this paper. What seems to be crucial is that the talk situation should be sufficiently flexible to cater for whatever comments they are able to make *as and when these occur to them.* Traditionally, this has not been the approach that reading poetry on a class basis has either encouraged or even allowed for. When the whole class and the teacher tackle a poem together, what tends to happen is more like an oral comprehension test than a genuine discussion. The teacher asks what he or she considers to be the relevant questions and the class search with varying degrees of interest and willingness for the appropriate answers.

When small groups like these two talk about a poem without a teacher, there are no 'answers', but we have tried to show how their less structured discussion may also be of value – especially when they like the poem and can find their own motivations for exploring it together. Does it matter how far the group reaches general agreement with each other – and is the stage at which they terminate their discussion important? Again, we don't really know, but what we are certain of is the value of encouraging small groups to share their responses to literature together in the reasonable hope that sometimes they will achieve insights through this kind of discussion which they might not be able to do either on their own or as a whole class.

14 An approach to analysis
Elizabeth Grugeon and Liz Cartland

In this investigation, we looked particularly at the way in which each child's contribution affected the range of possible responses, both to the poem and to the other members of the group, at the beginning of their discussion. Each new contribution has a new number and each continuous speaker has his contribution broken down into sections lettered (a), (b), (c), (d). In these ten utterances, there seem to be two distinct cycles of discovery or understanding. Looking at a small piece of transcript in detail seems to enable an outsider (the teacher in this instance) to isolate points at which group interaction and talk can enable individual discovery to take place. The analysis of this extract is an entirely speculative attempt to interpret or discover a learning process which might be taking place.

1 Mark: How does she know it's in pain? When it, where it says 'The small dust-coloured beetle climbs with pain'. Does she know it's in pain?

2 Kenneth: (a) Ah, come on, Simmy, (b) if something's small, really s, really, er, climbing, something small to us, is very big to him, (c) it must be tired. You've got to admit it, you're going to be tired, (d) aint yer?

3 John: (a) Yeah, (b) you can see what it means, this poem, (c) because it would be hard for a beetle to climb up a leaf, (d) wouldn't it?

4 Mark: (a) It must be breathless, (b) because the, I mean, you know it's kind of growing

5 John: Mm
(End of 1st cycle)

6 Clive: (a) A leaf, (b) if it is a leaf, isn't, er, very big though, compared with a beetle

7 John: (a) No, that's true, (b) it depends what kind of beetle it is

8 Kenneth: 'Spacious plain'

Source: GRUGEON, E. and CARTLAND, L. (1975) 'An approach to analysis', in an unpublished report *Children as Readers: The Roles of Literature in the Primary and Secondary Schools*, cosponsored by The National Association for the Teaching of English and the Schools Council 1968–73

9 John: No. It says a 'spacious plain' so it must be quite big
10 Kenneth: It is, big to a beetle
          (End of 2nd cycle)

1 Mark

As an opening remark this is one of two kinds of comment; either a simple request for information or a pointer to the possibility of rejecting the poem as unreal. Listening to his tone, it seems to be the latter, but his possible rejection is not aggressive or even strongly assertive. It is the questioning and tentative quality of his intonation which prevents his opening remarks determining the direction of the discussion.

2 Kenneth

This reply determines the effect of Mark's opening remark on the discussion. It is both an acceptance of Mark himself but a rejection of Mark's strategy. It functions in four ways:

(a) *Ah, come on, Simmy.* This rejects his idea, but insists on his inclusion, as a person, in the group. (Simmy is his nick-name.)

(b) *if something's small, really s . . . its very big to him.* He has grasped the idea of pain and related it to the idea of scale. He already seems to have touched on the central meaning of the poem.

(c) *it must be tired.*
You've got to [allow?] it . . .
These two assertions imply the presence of reasonable available evidence to support his view, but although assertive, are still tentative, as in (d).

(d) *aint yer?* He turns to the group for confirmation.

3 John

(a) *Yeah.* This suggests that what he is about to say will be supportive both of Kenneth and his point.

(b) *you can see what it means, this poem.* This defines the status of what he is about to say, i.e. the validity of it can be tested against experience.

(c) *because it would be . . . a leaf.* This restates Kenneth's remark (b) and at the same time replies to Mark's implied chaos in 1. It also supplies some of the evidence behind (b) *you can see what it means.*

(d) *wouldn't it?* This stresses what he has said and at the same time asks for support. This kind of combination of assertion and appeal is an invitation for further discussion. Straight assertion at this point might have closed such an opportunity.

4 Mark

(a) *It must be breathless.* This is interesting, as it now seems that Mark is capable of making a synthesis of 2 and 3. His use of the word 'must' implies that he is going to put forward a reason, make a firm assertion, but he seems to be struggling to find the evidence to substantiate it.

(b) *because, the, I mean, you know.* He struggles and loses his way. It is impossible for the group to reply to the content of what he has said, but they are able to tolerate his effort to express himself.

5 John

Mm. This is a supportive social acknowledgement of what Mark has just said. Mark has not contributed much to the context of the discussion, but he is not to be dismissed. At this stage we felt that we could isolate a *process of discovery* taking place through the enmeshing of individual understandings with group commitment:

(1) Mark has identified the problem.

(2) Kenneth has found a way of solving it.

(3) John confirms Kenneth's hypothesis by restating and substantiating it.

(4) Mark's 'breathless' is a personal discovery and a restatement of the implications of 1–3. He has realized for himself the meaning of 'with pain'. He is now *in* the group instead of being a potential destroyer. The group, however, now has to make a fresh start.

6 Clive

Like Mark's opening remark, Clive's entry into the discussion raises an area of doubt, this time about the synthesis which the other three appear to have agreed to. The idea (a) *A leaf . . . isn't, er, very big though, compared with a beetle* is one contention. It is confused by his qualification (b) *if it is a leaf.* His objection to the validity of the poem, however, leaves the discussion open because of its genuinely questioning tone.

7 John

(a) *No, that's true.* This accepts the force of Clive's arguments, but in

(b) *it depends what kind of beetle it is* he has found a way of refuting it.

8 Kenneth

'*Spacious plain*'. He does not expand this, but it is a crucial reference to the poem which will validate his next logical step, i.e. a lot depends on what the poet means by the image 'spacious plain' as well as what kind of beetle it is.

9 John

(a) *No.* This is not a negative but agreeing with Kenneth.

(b) *It says . . . so it must be quite big.* This fills in the context for

Kenneth's previous comment and affirms John's grasp of the point Kenneth has made.

10 Kenneth
It is, big to a beetle. The strength of this affirmation seems to draw on the group's thinking and seems to mark the end of another cycle of group discovery and understanding that we noted in the first five utterances.

15 Comments on traditions of literature teaching

Jeremy Mulford

What it comes to in our day is this: Who are the most usefully habitual people? Who are the most vivid members of any given people? It is all back in the street, even in small towns. There the distinction is clear in the East as well as the West. An Indian family crossing the inter-section of some dusty main street in a 1952 Ford. Or a Negro just released from a Utah prison trying for the life of him to find out, with all the dangerous sense of nuance a delicately experienced man has, how to get from this corner to the restaurant in the next block without becoming too precise in the eyes and noses of the indigenous loafer – whether he be businessman or town bully or cop, and the prisoner never has to sort the differences. Or a white bum wondering if, as he passes through Pocatello, he can get a job in Cheyenne as a dishwasher. If he gets to Cheyenne. Of course he can't. They can't. Nobody should have to.

Edward Dorn, *The Shoshoneans*

When I first read James Stephens' poem, 'The Snare', a few years ago, I thought, What a trite little item – I wouldn't give that to kids. Now, having heard lots of different children talking about it (some hostile; others not) I don't feel that. Not that I now think it's a fine poem. If pressed for my own judgment in a word, I might still call it trite. But I'm not as interested in that sort of judgment as I once was.

Thinking about literature and its readers commonly assumes that there is a correspondence – an identity, indeed – between *works*, con-ceived of as a hierarchy in terms of their intelligence, sensitivity, pro-fundity, formal achievement, etc., on the one hand, and *readers*, conceived of as a hierarchy in terms of their intelligence, sensitivity, capacity for profound response, selfconscious articulateness, etc. on the other. Literary pedagogy is imbued with this assumption, even though the implications of its élitism are spelt out only occasionally.[1]

The assumption takes two main forms. Firstly, that only those people

Source: MULFORD, J. (1975) 'Comments on traditions of literature teaching' a shortened version of 'Afterword' in an unpublished report *Children as Readers: The Roles of Literature in the Primary and Secondary Schools*, co-sponsored by The National Association for the Teaching of English and the Schools Council 1968–73

towards the top of the hierarchy of readers can appreciate the quality of the works located near the top of the hierarchy of works. Secondly, that only works of intelligence, sensitivity, profundity, etc. (i.e. those towards the top of the hierarchy) can occasion responses of intelligence, sensitivity, profundity, etc. The two are complentary obverses of each other. The élitist appropriation of literature and the effective denial of the value both of most people's experience and of their apprehension of it (the literary reference extends inevitably into the non-literary) are in fact one. And the process is simply reinforced by the accompanying notion – implicit at least, and occasionally explicit – that 'the literary student [should not forget that] the one right total meaning . . . should commonly control his analysis'.[2]

This ideological cluster can, without undue crudity, be personalized as: only someone with my degree of intelligence and sensitivity can properly appreciate . . . [insert appropriate works], and since you don't appreciate these works, for the time being at least you are denied occasions for the exercise of intelligence and sensitivity. If you are potentially one of that minority of readers of intelligence and sensitivity, then you are going to have to rely upon me as one of those with custodial access to the 'one right total meaning[s]'; but if you can't appreciate what I'm talking about, then not only will you permanently be denied occasions for exercising intelligence and sensitivity, but that denial will be essentially a function of your own inadequacy – and if this seems to be an indictment of more than merely your literary capacities, that is not my fault.

In so far as there is caricature in this characterization, it is almost entirely in the degree of its summary explicitness. The potency of such ideological attitudes derives largely from the extent to which, usually, they are covert, only implicit or semi-*ex*plicit.

It was a section from the East Anglian girls' discussion of 'The Snare' which first induced me to represent these attitudes summarily and over-explicitly, in order to see better what they amount to. I'm referring particularly to the section where, having established an emotional ambience for the poem, they go on to engage with it directly:

Judy: I like this second verse 'But I cannot tell from where/He is calling out for aid/Crying on the frightened air,/Making everything afraid'

Others: Yeah

Judy: I like 'Crying on the frightened air'. You get the feeling don't you?

Suzanne: 'Making everything afraid'. I suppose that's all the other animals

Sally: I like 'Wrinkling up his little face'. They do wrinkle up their face

Suzanne: Like dogs. Well, I think that 'Little one, oh little one/I am searching everywhere', I like that

Sally: I like the last verse. That's nice
Suzanne: Yeah
Sally: You know, you go 'Little one, *oh* little one', kind of thing. You feel as if you're going to, you know, as if the person who wrote this was just about to start crying
Suzanne: I should think the poet was watching with the rabbit, when it was in the snare
Judy: The last verse really gets the feeling of, um, something, you're just watching it
Suzanne: It's really got the point of it
Judy: 'And I cannot find the place/Where his paw is in the snare/ Little one, oh little one/I am searching everywhere' kind of gets the feeling you are in a field and you can hear it
Sally: You really *are*
Judy: Echoing in your head and everything
Sally: If you closed your eyes, you could probably imagine that you're in there
Mandy: You can see it, but you don't know where
Sally: Yeah, you were in that field and that was you who was saying this poem and looking for the [   ] thing
Suzanne: I wonder how old the poet was
Mandy: But sometimes if you get there, the rabbit's kind of too frightened to let you do anything for it and makes it worse
Suzanne: The poet, the poet is James Stephens, but it doesn't say how old he is
Sally: He's probably quite old, he is probably a grown-up – cos I think it would be too
Judy: I think he's got ever such a good imagination if he wasn't there. He's experienced what it's like, what a person would feel like
Suzanne: I've never heard of him before
Sally: I've never heard of half of these famous ones but
Suzanne: Sally
Judy: You get the feeling, you know, funny, you know, I've just gotta cry, I've just gotta find it, I have really, I mustn't let it die cos anyone
Mandy: Yeah
Judy: It's a horrible feeling
Sally: [Reads first verse again]

Clearly the response of these girls to the poem is different from mine; but I have no inclination to suggest that mine is better. For these girls are deploying a sensitivity and empathy, engaging in a ready commerce between the experience of reading the poem and other relevant experience. To suggest that what they're doing is spurious because the material they're engaged with is spurious – that would seem to me impertinent, in both senses of the word. What is significant is what the girls have brought *to* the poem *and made of it*.

I am not arguing towards claiming that an equivalence, or anything approaching it, runs through everybody's talk about everything. Nor am I denying the criteria that I myself bring to 'The Snare', or their possible relevance to the East Anglian girls at some time in their lives. My only concern here is to undermine the élitist, exclusivist position. Given the nature of that position – the very coherence of whose internal logic makes it especially vulnerable – one example is enough to do that.

One example is enough; but another pushes itself in at this point. Andrew is one of four members of a remedial class who are discussing 'The Snare', 'Rock, Our Dog' and a piece of prose from *The Excitement of Writing* about a swan trapped in ice. His voice is slow and halting but the imaginative understanding which the halting rhythms carry is quite beautiful:

> I feel I feel really sorry for for *all* animals during winter as they've got no no food, and they 'ave to fly so far. And and some of these animals do not survive. They 'ave to they 'ave to stop and rest on the boats, and the boats take them back to Eng, bring 'em back to England, and then when they fly over, over to to there the next day, they die in the waves, lashing waves catch catch them, and they're dead.

The creativity and sureness of this, culminating in the finality with which he utters 'and they're dead', are of someone who *knows* what he is talking about – and, for me at least, are of a different order from any of the material that occasioned what he says.

Examples such as these indirectly illuminate the conventional notion of 'the test of time' for literary and other works – a notion that has to be reactionary in influence and which buttresses the élitist position. The strength of the notion in these respects is made greater by virtue of the fact that it can seem to be working in a quite different way. Thus, it seems to be working, simply, *against* the merely fashionable (for example, that which might appeal temporarily to an élitist coterie) and *for* what is more comprehensively human. But this tends to make the 'comprehensively human' conditional on having been tested by time; and what is 'most truly human' is thereby put into the past.

If, on the other hand, you are influenced by examples such as those above to give more consideration to what people *bring to*, and *make of*, literature (literature in particular only because that is what is particularly at issue at the moment), then you are theoretically relieved, in some measure, from the tyranny of the past. For this enables you to look at the responses of people to works that are contemporary with them in a different light; to recognize more readily that it would be odd indeed if people did not commonly make more, in certain respects, of products of their own society than of products from other times and places. To reduce this inevitable human disposition to a matter of fashion – mere fashion – is to deny human experience in a way that links up with the élitist, exclusivist stance that I characterized earlier. And if this reductionism finds its readiest expression in the face of 'popular culture' or 'mass culture', then that link is doubly strong. This is perhaps the place to note that, although there are approving references in Leavis's work (and that of associated writers) to people with unlettered, intuitive intelligence drawing strength from their common, folk culture; these people always belong to the distant past or to distant lands. Such references are characteristically, in fact, sticks with which to beat twentieth-century 'mass civilization' at moments of recoil from it.

In a review, entitled 'A power to fight', in the *Guardian* some years ago (12 November, 1970) Raymond Williams wrote:

> . . . Imagination can be something that has happened: 'the best that *has been*', as in Arnold's definition of culture; 'the tradition', as in university departments of literature. Active creative power, which might transform an existing reality, is thus subtly made pre-existent; often in practice passive. And if real society, the total body of humanity, is revealed *only* by the arts and sciences, and thence not at all by direct contemporary experience and relationships, it is 'the tradition' against 'contemporary vulgarity', 'quest myths' against real propaganda, and our most evident liberating faculty is hypostasized to scholarship . . .

One classic form of this hypostasization – this transformation of 'active creative power' into sediment – is exemplified by the young teacher, fresh from a distinguished university career, who began her first lesson on the 'Metaphysical Poets' by drawing a diagram of the 'Line of Wit' on the blackboard. Maybe she didn't actually have an examination in mind; but this particular kind of sediment, 'Knowledge about' literature, is a very useful medium for the grading of people, down as well as up, which is so necessary to our society. As such, it is attacked by a certain kind of radical conservative – notably Leavis himself, who dismisses the 'end-of-course stand-and-deliver against the clock', the 'usual ready and confident superficiality of the "good student"', the 'canny amassing of inert material for the examination room', in favour of the encouragement of 'that conscious and intelligent incompleteness which carries with it the principle of growth . . . the organization that represents a measure of real understanding, and seeks of its very nature to extend and complete itself.'[3] But complementary to this view is the following one, which is specifically to do with the reading of literature:

> You cannot point to the poem; it is 'there' only in the re-creative response of individual minds to the black marks on the page. . . . A judgment is personal or it is nothing; you cannot take over someone else's.[4]

In the context of a preoccupation with 'tradition', however defined – with a view of culture as 'the best that *has been*' – this works for a form of hypostasization that is much more potent in its ideological influence than 'knowledge about'. For the emphasis on active – 're-creative' – response, in avoiding the 'passivity' to which Williams refers, diverts attention from the fact that the present is being appropriated on behalf of the past, from the way in which – to requote Williams – 'active creative power [defined as including liberating action in the larger political sense], which might transform an existing reality, is . . . made pre-existent'.

'The tradition of all the dead generations weighs like a nightmare on the brain of the living.'[5] A central strand of that 'tradition' is the one that, in its literary orientation, I caricatured earlier. It is important to recognize the extent to which the Leavisian sort of emphasis on personal response belongs to that strand. The passage about 'judgment', quoted just now, continues:

> The implicit form of judgment is: This is so, isn't it? The question is an appeal for confirmation that the thing *is* so; implicitly that, though expecting, characteristically, an answer in the form, 'yes, but—', the 'but' standing for qualifications, reserves, corrections. Here we have a diagram of the collaborative-creative process in which the poem comes to be established as something 'out there', of common access in what is in some sense a public world.[6]

Leavis does not explore the 'sense(s)' in which this 'world' is 'public' but the *extent* to which it is public (the point is a matter of logic) is necessarily limited, for the kind of 'collaborative-creative process' he describes must be a function of a *homogeneous* readership: otherwise there would be more 'Noes' than 'Yes, buts'. (Either that, or it would have to involve a repressive relationship – of one reader over another.) And, of course, Leavis himself would not balk at the élitist implications of this.

The influence – at least as much indirect as direct – of Leavis has been greater than it might have been because many teachers have, paradoxically, used some of his ideas for what they see as egalitarian purposes. They have cut into the élitist logic and – rightly believing that a small minority of people does not have a monopoly of intelligence and sensitivity, and that literature should belong meaningfully to everyone – have done surgery on the obviously exclusivist parts. But in doing this they have usually failed to recognize the élitist base of the Leavisian model of the 'collaborative-creative process'. In fact, the very self-image of a teacher who sets out to eschew being a transmitter of culture in the crude sense, or who is not interested in fighting a rearguard action on behalf of traditional 'standards' or 'civilization', can obscure the extent to which, in trying to develop his pupils' sensitivity to a work or a body of works, he is merely trying to induce in them an approximation to his own 'sensitivity', an imitation of his own responses. In that case, he is assuming an élitist position because the space he allows his pupils cannot but be too little to enable them to make what *they* can of what they have read.

I have used Leavis's work for examples of what I am opposing not only because of his great influence, but also because his work has a thoroughness, an explicitness and a distinction which are rare, yet which also make him classically representative. At this point, however, it is necessary to expand very considerably the framework of the discussion. The issues are very much more than a matter of characterizing and assessing the influence of this or that thinker. For every teacher of literature who recognizes, whether readily or grudgingly, a debt to F. R. Leavis, there must be half a dozen – or a dozen maybe – who would deny the suggestion, or who have never heard of him; but that does not make the issues I have been raising less relevant to the six out of every seven, or the twelve out of every thirteen. Teachers dealing in 'right responses' (of whatever kind) to literature merely represent a particular example of the general, habitual adult exercising of power over children. This exercising of power is *so* habitual as to be at once compulsive and commonly submerged – submerged just enough and no more, in that way which gives a vague sense of 'the nature of things' its greatest potency.

On an occasion when I played parts of the East Anglia tapes at a meeting of teachers, one member of the group – a college of education lecturer – said that although of course he already encouraged the idea of group talk without an adult present, he was impressed, in particular by the four boys' discussion of the beetle poem. But yet, he went on to say, pleasing though that exploratory talk was, he still felt the need for a teacher. And he cited three pieces of evidence. First, the children had not understood that – in the line, 'The small dust-coloured beetle climbs with pain' – 'with pain' had a different meaning from 'in pain'. Secondly, the meaning of 'flirts' ('And flirts his filmy wings, and looks around') had not been resolved. And thirdly, the children had drawn out and dwelt upon the anthropomorphism of the poem, and this could only reinforce their existing ignorance about the differences between humans and beetles.

Familiar though this sort of comment is, in the face of a discussion so remarkable for its concentration and richness and penetration and length, actually, I can't imagine any group of adults entering into the beetle poem as fully as those four boys. This is a reflection on the limitations of adults, not of the poem. The poem takes on the status of a classic case: the compulsive need to exercise power over children, in the texture of everything available, is revealed in all its impertinence. The *only* other explanation would have to be in terms of a view of education which sought, putatively at least, to teach everybody everything. For otherwise, it really does not *matter* that those children did not do what the tutor said they did not do; it does not *matter*, but it does provide an occasion for intrusion – luckily only notional in this example. The extent and the (except as an exercise of power) gratuitousness and absurdity of that intrusion is especially clear in the tutor's third complaint. Those boys are, it seems fair to assume, unlikely to go on anthropomorphizing about beetles into adult life, at least to the extent that they appear to be doing on the tape, even if they never have any specific instruction on the subject. But if, by a bizarre chance, they *did* enter adulthood with some misconceptions about beetles still unchecked, would that matter?

Notes

1 For example most notably and very influentially in F. R. Leavis's *Education and the University*
2 LEAVIS *op. cit.* p. 72
3 MILL *On Bentham and Coleridge* Introduction pp. 3, 4, 5
4 *Two Cultures? The Significance of C. P. Snow* p. 28
5 KARL MARX *The Eighteenth Brumaire of Louis Bonaparte* chapter 1
6 *Two Cultures? The Significance of C. P. Snow* p. 28

Section Four
Reading and Response

Introduction

The final part of the Reader deals with the experience of reading in education from Middle School through to College. The activities described should be seen in the context of the rest of the book; in particular, knowledge of the sections entitled **From Experience to Literature** and **Talking about Poetry** will inform these chapters.

Peter Dean sees the possibility that misplaced concentration on the skills of reading may be diverting attention from a full reading experience. He suggests that all efforts should be made in the middle years to encourage the enjoyment of reading: if children do not become committed readers at this point, then there is little chance that they ever will. His chapter is followed by a short account of the introduction of the story of *The Odyssey* to a class of fourteen-year-old boys. Like small children reading fairy tales (cf. Bettelheim and Lyons), these boys meet, through narrative, an expression of human experience which does not avoid the disturbing aspects of life.

The following three chapters are all based on transcripts of adolescents talking about literature, and should be read as further support for the findings of the 'Children as Readers' project. There is a gulf between the experience of the teacher as a mature reader of literature and that of the students – the students' perceptions being deeply affected both by the partial understanding of a first reading and by the preoccupations of their own lives. When they are allowed time to express their feelings about the nine books and poems, they develop a fuller awareness of what they are reading.

The transcript from James Squire was an early and important account of one person's reading. 'Like many other adolescent readers, she tends to test the actions of characters against her own experience, and the degree of her selfinvolvement rises perceptibly when experiences in literature (as in the following example) suggest problems and events of real life.' In addition, she is able, as the transcript shows, to adjust her reading of the narrative in the light of new evidence and without losing the spontaneity of her initial response to it.

When Penny Blackie's students are asked to formulate their own questions about a poem they reveal barriers to understanding which the teacher is not aware of, and a need to study the text at a straightforward level before moving on to the abstractions of evaluative judgments.

Jean Blunt, taking individual students for her study, shows that adolescents can talk about their reading, that they have different levels of awareness of literature, and that the teacher requires a sensitivity to these levels. 'One has to bear in mind the individuality of the reading response. It is a personal affair developing hesitantly and requiring the very gentlest of encouragement if a mature, worthwhile engagement with fiction is to result. The direct response can hardly be transmitted from teacher to pupil.'

In case it should be thought that the processes described in this book may be developed only with children, we include at the end Mike Torbe's account of a group of students in a College of Education who are accomplished readers in that they have a mastery of skills, but are still in great need of encouragement as they begin to develop their own responses to literature – it takes time for them to sort out their ideas.

16 Time to get hooked: reading in the middle years

Peter Dean

It is five years now since 'The Trend of Reading Standards' (K. B. Start and B. K. Wells NFER 1972) added what looked like real substance to all those Black Paper charges about educational decline. Since then we have had – amongst other things – the Bullock Report, the Schools Council Research into children's reading, and, of course, the Great Debate, to which the Prime Minister returns 'unrepentantly', he says, at the time of writing, 'obsessed with the basics of literacy and numeracy'. I do not draw in this latter remark out of mere up-to-the-minute appositeness – although that 'obsessed' and the glib 'basics of literacy and numeracy' is in itself disturbing – but by way of illustrating a particular emphasis which has emerged and will, with constant reiteration, grow stronger as the struggle within education continues. It is, perhaps, even at this relatively advanced stage, worth putting a finger on that emphasis.

Contrary to popular belief, the Start-Wells survey did not establish a *decline* in reading standards. It reported a tailing-off of improvement at all age-levels in schools – which, without being semantic about it, is something different. (Later research still has produced evidence showing that the 'trend' has changed back to 'improvement' again. But this is not the point . . .) What the research did was confirm and reinforce the *effect* of the influential preceding NFER report – 'Standards and Progress in Reading' J. Morris 1967 – which had found that teaching literacy, that is reading and spelling, 'formally and systematically' produces the best 'results' in measured reading performance and academic attainment. It is quite likely – though there is no recent research to show this – that, following such an apparent prescription for 'success', more direct, formal and systematic teaching of reading has found a place during the middle years in school and indeed has become the current orthodoxy. If so, it should give serious cause for reflection when taken alongside the recent Schools Council report (*Children and their Books* Macmillan 1977) and their earlier paper (*Children's Reading Interests* Working Paper No 52, Evans/Methuen Educational 1975) which, unlike the NFER surveys, were concerned primarily with children's attitudes towards reading.

SOURCE: DEAN, P. (1975) 'Time to get hooked: reading in the middle years' *The Use of English* Vol. 26 No. 1 pp. 297–303: this article is a modified version commissioned for The Open University

These have shown that there is a movement away from recreational book-reading as children get older.

It could be that the two kinds of finding are related – a declining rate of improvement in measurable reading performance (1972), a fall in the amount of reading being done in children's leisure-time (1975). It may be that they are indexes of the same thing – it would, after all, be logical to assume that a falling rate of success in a skill might lead to a smaller quantity of the actual exercise of that skill. However – and more to the educational point – it may be that both are, in part at least, by-products of the Morris report. 'Formal and systematic' literacy teaching, if that has indeed been increasingly the emphasis over the past decade, may or may not have produced improvement in measurable reading performance (depending on what you believe of recent accounts of this aspect); it does not, apparently, produce readers.

There is little point, however, for teachers to admit defeat over the central concern of inducing a persistent desire to read, the delight in it, which might be taken as a mark of literacy. Earnestness of application to the teaching of reading as it is generally carried out in primary schools, despite the NFER report, might not in fact be producing this. And despite the Look-and-Say versus Phonics and i.t.a. controversies which have had the merit, whatever else, of stimulating discussion and reappraisal, despite the paradox in recent years of improved facilities, more generous provision of books, materials and staff, it may be that to a certain extent in this qualitative aspect all have been, are being, counter-productive. Simply *because of* the priority accorded to it, learning to read is experienced or perceived by children as a competitive activity and hence carries a value-charge which conditions each individual learner's attitude towards it. The more we talk and hear about reading in school as a 'tool' subject, the more we banish it to the realm of strictly utilitarian matters where some kind of efficient functioning (technical competence at the decoding level) obscures the delight of real literacy.

I would not wish to attribute failure in this long-term aim of real literacy to that earnestness and systematic attention to the teaching of reading which one finds in Infants' and First schools. Certainly, young children's attitudes towards books, stories, print, working with words, are decisively influenced during these years and poor starts are notoriously difficult to make up. Even positive attitudes may not in the end be able to withstand the subtle and overt influences weakening or usurping a child's allegiance which open up for him as he grows older. If, as it seems from the Working Paper, these forces prove stronger – and the school 'culture' as well as 'outside' culture is implicated – is the middle-years period one where preserving the positive is given priority in school? Does the apparent ascendancy of non-illiterate leisure pursuits (the Schools Council survey in this respect certainly confirms a generally held impression) occur despite or because of a bias in favour of print and literature in school during these middle years? Are children given the opportunity of acquiring the reading habit? If most children do not become exposed to the possibility *during school hours*, it is not likely that they will elsewhere. Hence the importance of what goes on in school during the formative middle years.

So what does go on? Is there anything in the school situation which works against the achievement of a dynamic literacy? Two points would seem to stand out. Although it is very difficult to generalize – and the subject could well form a useful inquiry in its own right – my impression from a fair range of primary schools is that children are not encouraged or enabled to do much serious reading within the school. The organization of many (most?) primary schools sets a premium on 'quiet time' activities when protracted fiction or other reading might and ought to be done. (And if it is not done *in* schools, I repeat, the chances are it will not be done at all.) The up-and-doing involvement of activity methods would seem to exclude this unless attention and time are specifically given to it. I'm not here criticising the 'activity' approach, which I firmly support, but warning of the danger of an all-absorbing industry and bustle with such 'quiet time' as there is taken up by whole-class teacher-directed sessions. The other attendant danger of a 'production line' philosophy for a production line society seems to me closely related.

Secondly, teacher-reading of stories on a regular basis does not seem to be a widespread practice during the middle years. Yet surely imaginative enthusiasm is something caught not taught. Most children have had the experience of stories told or read to them in their infant years. Perhaps, as many teachers say, it is in recognition of their children's growing maturity that they often discontinue this practice during the middle years. There are competing priorities here, not least of which is the development towards independence.

To indicate these two areas and imply that allowing reading time and reading regularly to children themselves is all that teachers need do to contribute effectively to an eventual real literacy would be foolish. But systematic provision in these two related aspects of literacy experience during the middle years would be too much. There is no substitute for the experience of literature itself, for reading is a personal and intimate matter with regard to its choice and the pace at which it is taken. Access to leisure reading, quiet times, a variety of books in class and/or school library and the hearing of literature well read would seem indispensable items in an English programme for the middle years.

The relationship between such items and personal writing, the other major facet of a flourishing literacy, has long been clear to teachers who are enthusiastic about English teaching. If 'personal experience' has been the watchword, then literature comes with particular significance into this area: children experience it at a personal level themselves and feel through identification and sympathy the personal and creative self-commitment which are expressed on the part of the writer. And it offers them evidence of a way of *shaping* actual or imaginative experience that from the beginning of their life in school, but particularly in the middle years, they can be encouraged to emulate. Individual 'books', written by them, illustrated, made and decorated, suitably titled and bound as robustly as possible, might have a shelf to themselves among the classroom books and expand throughout the year. The typing of stories can provide a great fillip but how much can thus be converted will depend on a teacher's energies and time or willing secretarial help. Again, readings from such stories might be offered by the teacher (or child) to the class, tape-recordings made of them with simple sound effects where appropriate. ('Home-made' tapes provide a useful variant generally to the live voice of the teacher in the matter of presenting literature which is well-read.) In addition, copies of stories might be run off and used in conjunction with tapes both for the inherent interest and stimulus such a process has, and as a provision for children still needing at this stage as much discreet support in basic decoding activities as possible. The Primary Audio Set, allowing up to six headphone listeners at a time, is a most convenient and inexpensive adjunct to the tape-recorder for this purpose and others. The BBC *Listening and Reading* series consists of useful, attractive material, much of it appropriate to the younger half of the middle years, but more importantly it shows how easily 'literature' can be inveigled across the boundary into the hard technological world of 'reading material' without suffering loss. (Another similar venture, *Take Part Books* published by Ward Lock Educational, encourages children to read for themselves the original books from which the dialogue extracts are taken.)

There is no reason why literature should not form the basis of major work-effort in the classroom. While I am aware of the dangers of over-exposure, 'starting-from-story', I believe, allows a certain flexibility of exploration into background, creative doing and making, drama (whether of episodes from the books or taking cues from it) and other literature (songs and poems as well as stories sought out by both children and teacher) within a framework – that of the book itself – which is more 'naturally' coherent often than thematic or project-type work. The book points to the interest-area, which is not a narrow and confined one; discovery and effort by children in the related work deepens their experience of the ongoing story. Even under a thematic-type organization, however, I think that imaginative literature – stories for dramatization, poems and extracts for presentation and performance (whether 'live' or recorded) by children – should have place and it is important to have available as wide a choice as possible.

Book reviews written by children should form an integral part of the reading programme during the middle years. They can be short or lengthy, depending on what the individual child has to say. Many might be 'published' in a periodic magazine of class writing or separately collected under titles such as 'Critics' Choice' or 'Read a Good Book

Lately?' and so on. But children might also be encouraged to write reviews of some books they read in individual notebooks and certainly to log titles of all the books which they finish with a word or two of evaluation. Occasional talks about books by children (no coercion) also help to stimulate and sustain interest in reading. Some respond well to writing assignments of an open-ended nature – 'If Stig was living round here, where would it be? Suppose you met him. How did it happen? What did you do? Make up a story . . .' – such comments might be stuck in a book facing the last page. These must be optional and provocative, however, not obligatory, otherwise the books might be avoided or the speed of reading them retarded in the desire to postpone the (to some) uninviting follow-up. I found there to be something of this effect with rather more specific assignments on class-readers and I think any association with 'comprehension' unlikely to be helpful. A card index for storybooks in the class library, arranged alphabetically by the author and set out in a grid thus:

Author: Aiken, Joan Title: *The Wolves of Willoughby Chase*				
	Tick which comment you agree with			
Date finished	Very enjoyable	Enjoyable	Not enjoyable	Reader's name

helps to promote interest in reading and provides useful information for both teaching and administrative purposes.

Getting children into a 'library habit' is obviously highly desirable since the local authority for most people will be the supplier of books to encourage adult literacy. But they should be strongly encouraged at this age to take books home from school. A touch of formality about the borrowing, with, say, the latter part of Friday afternoon devoted to quiet time and the returning and booking-out of books, seems to me the right sort of arrangement to induce both the spirit and the habit. Naturally, the range of books for children in the middle years needs to be wide, almost within each age-group from Dr Seuss and Leila Berg's 'Nippers' to Bill Naughton, Jack London and Conan Doyle. But ultimately, given reasonable diversity it is not the number of books but the time and encouragement to read them which are the most important factors.

I come back to this: reading the books is what counts. One simple device of getting children going, that invariably meets with a fair measure of success, is to choose half-a-dozen or so storybooks of appropriate interest levels and over three or four days introduce them to the class and read an opening extract or chapter sufficient to whet appetites and heighten curiosity. Have a rota prepared and release texts to circulate. Cheap paperback sets are ideal for this. Paperback sets in the classroom; getting kids to join the local library; ceremonial class visits there if possible and return visits by children's librarians; taking books home from school; all these help in producing the necessary ethos of enjoyment. The personal-involvement element also works by reversing the direction – encouraging children to bring books in for quiet-time swap-reading sessions. Again, a touch of the 'special occasion' (it can be quite regular) serves to promote the event.

In the end, I feel, any tactics, ruses, subterfuges even, are justified in inducing the reading habit, getting kids 'hooked'. The middle years are the crucial period in which this might happen. After the, for many, halting progress through the initial stages to a basic competence it is during the next few years that the acceleration into real ease may or may not take place. Every opportunity and encouragement within the school's area of control should be provided to bring this about. The Schools Council report just published (*Children and their Books op. cit.*), now completing work begun in 1969, only two years after the influential Morris Report, records 'a marked swing away from book reading as children get older'. It calls this 'worrying', 'disturbing', 'clearly a cause for concern'. And indeed it is, although not everyone, not even everyone involved in education, would see it thus. The Secondary years close in with their unvarying, unrelieved diet of words-on-paper – textbooks, work-sheets, essays and write-ups; examinations and life-in-earnest loom. If the habit is not formed in the earlier years – and these are short enough in all conscience as an increasing examination-mindedness casts its shadow down the school – then serious disinterested leisure-reading withers. Perhaps 'habit' is not the right word – habits can change; something stronger, more committed, is needed to survive all the varying pressures, as well as time-consuming interests and distractions which develop in the later school years. In this connection, every study these days has to mention television and obviously it has been a major in-fluence. Yet the Schools Council study shows that on the whole, view-ing like reading declines, though not so appreciably, as children get older. Clearly, other things claim their attention and time. It may be during adolescence, that except for a minority they always did and always will. But, if the aim is a flourishing adult literacy, this need not be taken as an excuse for apathy. Everything depends on the quality of the experience of reading (in the middle years) before these later demands take their toll on the emotional associations which printed words hold for the indi-vidual child. Everyone, not least the politicians, is at pains to point out the importance of the relationship between developed intelligence and literacy. But Gradgrindery will not do. In a pluralist society you do not achieve a functioning literacy unless it is pleasurable, has a history, as it were, of pleasurable experiences in its making. The good signs, compared with the growing threat to it in the later years of schooling, are that the pleasure principle has entered into thinking about how children might begin to learn to read and this may provide the sustaining impulse across 'distractions'. The above, I hope, will be of some use in keeping the process going.

17 Story as an adventure for the teenager

Agnes Finnegan

We demand relevant material in education, but who is to make the decision about relevance? The problems of power are always with us and what Cicero asserted to the Roman educationists still speaks to us today, 'the authority of those who teach is often an obstacle to those who want to learn' (quoted in the Rosla Handbook Volume I, BBC Publications). We endeavour to present material which is associated with the conflicts and anxieties of social relationships and human longings, because without acute awareness of these, the pursuit of education is vain. I believe that the traditional stories that have withstood the harrowing of the centuries, image profoundly these human perplexities. Youth longs always for dignity and honour, but where he is to find them usually remains for him a mystery and growing up is at any time not an easy process.

The question asserts itself – 'Do we stay at home or go out into the world?'

The twenty-five sprawling boys pulled themselves together and began to show some attention. Should we go and look for father or stay and protect mother? Their muddled fourteen-year-old minds recognized that this might well be an immediate problem – his dad had gone off years ago but still he would like to know him; the boy next to him had never had a father, yet deep down he yearned for paternal recognition; or perhaps it was simply that his dad came in every evening but never spoke to him . . . if they could only talk to each other . . .

The story I began to tell them was about the boy with just that problem, for his father had gone away to the war years before and had never come back. Should he go seek him or stay and help his mother who was having difficulties in keeping the home together? I described the rough island where they lived and the cadgers who came persecuting them, suggesting that his mother should marry again, trying to get their hands on the farm. The youth was in a dilemma and one evening between the day and the dark, he went down to the shore and he walked beside the sounding waves, wondering what he should do. Presently an old man came to offer his help and they walked in silence together; the boy turned to him wondering whether he dare trust him . . .

Source: FINNEGAN, A. (1974) 'Story as an adventure for the teenager' *The Use of English* Vol. 26 No. 1 pp. 9–11

As the story was unfolded (*The Odyssey*, Penguin edition) the class became deeply involved and the question then arose – Where was his dad all this time? Various possibilities were discussed. I had been warned that this group was interested only in football but it was obvious that the idea of women was already a tormenting involvement in their lives, so we came quite easily to the realization that dad was on a Mediterranean island with a girl. We had a lovely time exploring her enchanting island and I gave them the name of the dream woman, Calypso, because being the name of a cigarette it was already familiar to them.

The following week they asked me the name of the youth, and when I told them they guessed that Telemachus was not English. On a map, I showed them Ithaca, his home, a real place which some day they might visit. Then I revealed to them that the story had been told about 3,000 years ago and they were amazed that people seemed to be just the same even in those far-off days. It seemed to give them a strong sense of solidarity and of confidence to know that youth always and anywhere has to confront and resolve certain basic difficulties and conflicts. We went on to discuss the dangerous enchantments of Circe, that female menace, and this of course gave rise to easy conversation about the aspects of women, and while they neither would nor could have externalized their own anxieties they could express them within the context of the story, and thus we were able to share some group counselling. They admired how Odysseus overcame his troubles and how finally he gave up his fantasies and adventures and returned safely home to his citizenship, his wife and his estranged son.

The impression in this school was that these teenagers could not care less about their education; information and project work simply went in and dropped out again. Yet every young person is hungry to learn about life, and they would soon have to face the possible misery of an empty future; there seemed to have been neither time nor opportunity to confront their own longings and fears, but their loyalty to the school, even if it was only one of resentment and rebellion, still remained a root to supplement the often inadequate home. In the old story of Odysseus, they recognized action of a more enduring quality than the doubtful glory of the street gang or the lethal speed-bike, and the three qualities that enabled the wanderer to come safely home were new to them and they found them strangely alluring.

I suggested that they write letters as from Telemachus to his absent father, to write whatever came into their heads and they need not show the letters to anyone. Some time later several of them gave me the letters; they had all urged their dad to return as quickly as possible – one said that he now had a girl friend so please, please would he hurry home and help him know what to do about it; another described how mum was a fab cook and he wanted his dad to come home quick and share their fab meals (that particular boy was living with an old grandfather, for his mother had deserted them years ago and his father had married again).

All craved for paternal acknowledgment and for the privilege of being proud of a father. The sadness of these letters made me wonder if I had given them longings of which they had been hitherto morosely unaware, but surely it is better that young people should grow up able to recognize the potentialities of life and not deprived of a knowledge of its richness, both past and future.

The pictures they painted gave a different impression and demonstrated how important it is to practise different modes of expression. The most popular subject was the huge Cyclops, sometimes with a sorely bleeding eye, usually with a great club, suggesting the utter smallness of man confronted by the power of the giant. Surprisingly there were several pictures of Odysseus clinging to his upturned boat with the little bird perched beside him; so this gentle, lyrical passage must have deeply appealed to at least some of them. There were, of course, portraits of the fair Calypso which some might have considered rather pornographic. With this class we did not have the chance of making music, but on another occasion we composed words to celebrate the endurance of the hero and sang them as a chorus to the tune of a popular song already known to them.

The Odyssey is a model for all journeys and there are endless contemporary endeavours, including the moon voyages, which may catch at the imagination of a class, but the original tale with its unfolding of initiative, of endurance and lonely leadership casts light upon all subsequent adventures. The telling of the story may be spread over several weeks or be the core of a term's group project which will include graphic paintings, songs of love, combat, the sea, fear or hope; there may be mime, role-playing and perhaps a structured dramatic performance; the most important activity arising from it is probably the spontaneous talk about human experience – parent and child relationship, street fights, fantasies, girls, the family.

18 The responses of Paula while reading a short story

James R. Squire

Paula discusses the short story 'Reverdy' with a questioner. A summary of the story appears first, followed by information about Paula and then the transcript of the discussion.

'Reverdy' *Jessamyn West*

Division 1:

Although I seldom mention my sister Reverdy, I think of her constantly. I long to tell her about the night when she left. Liked by both boys and girls, she was completely different from me. Mother was sometimes cruel to her and thought unjustly that she was boy crazy.

Division 2:

Plain and homely myself, I was proud to have a pretty and popular sister. Sometimes when my mother would warn her about girls who got in trouble, Reverdy would leave the house in anger and would walk alone in the foothills. Mother would think that she was out with boys again.

Division 3:

Once Mother made me creep into the arbor to spy on Reverdy and a boy friend. They were only practising sign language with my brother. I could not face Reverdy at dinner so I went for a swim.

Division 4:

Returning from school one evening, I found Reverdy walking up and down the driveway in a windstorm. Mother was punishing her and wouldn't let me speak to Reverdy. Then Mother called me her comfort, her girl who never caused any trouble.

Division 5:

I enjoyed being appreciated by Mother and decided to encourage her

---

Source: SQUIRE, James R. (1963) *The Responses of Adolescents While Reading Four Short Stories* National Council of Teachers of English, Research Report No. 2. 'Reverdy' was originally published in *The New Mexico Quarterly Review* No. 13 (spring 1943) pp. 21–27

affection at Reverdy's expense. While Mother was sending Father out
to scold Reverdy, I asked my brother to join in playing a musical
selection to comfort Mother. Over and over we played the selection so
that Mother wouldn't be too disturbed by the 'bad Reverdy'.

Division 6:
I was awakened that night by Reverdy who thanked me for playing
music which told her not to be sad. She had picked some asters for me.
I wanted to tell her that I was playing for Mother, but I couldn't. I
decided to tell her in the morning. But in the morning Reverdy was
gone.

Age: 16 years, one month.
School Grade: Tenth.
Intelligence Quotient: 100

Parental Occupational Class: V (semiskilled).
California Psychological Inventory: Above average on scales for Social
Participation, Social Presence, Status, Self-acceptance, Tolerance,
Dominance.
Sociometric Data: Chosen by students in a class of thirty for the social
qualities and 'good ideas'.
Observer Comments: Outgoing, talkative, vivacious, generally a frequent
contributor to discussion and a leader in group work. Feminine, attractive to the boys in the class.
Biographical Information: An only child, she has been reared by a semi-
invalid mother and an uncle. She suffers a slight curvature of the spine –
the result of polio. 'Engaged' to a boy two years older, she is afraid to tell
her mother, who keeps insisting that she go to college. Paula believes she
is not 'college material'. She objected to a unit on family life in English:
'I had enough family life at home.' 'I decided to go to summer school to
get away.'
Analysis of Responses: Paula's responses tend to be characterized by a
high degree of self-involvement as is indicated in the following transcripts. She also displays an unusual tendency to visualize events in a
story as if watching a play or a motion picture. Like many other adolescent readers, she tends to test the actions of characters against her own
experience, and the degree of her self-involvement rises perceptibly
when experiences in literature, as in the following example, suggest
problems and events of real life. Like many of the better adolescent
readers, she recognizes the need to modify her impressions as new insights are presented by the author.

In Paula's response may be found some of the same characteristics
which appear in her classroom behaviour. She is warm, sensitive,
romantic, and if her own affective desires sometimes lead her to overlook
some evidence in a story, they also lead her to vital, enthusiastic response.

Her responses to literature tend to be more sensitive and richer than those of many students whose tested intelligence quotients and tested reading achievements are far higher.

Transcript for Paula's response to 'Reverdy'

Division 1:

It's pronounced Reverdy, isn't it?

Q: Uh huh

Well ah . . . it kind of . . . right off the bat it got my enthusiasm kind of . . .

Q: Why?

And ah . . . I dunno, just the way the . . . author puts the words and everything, something and then . . . I was very let down and very disappointed when he said it was her sister . . . his sister rather . . . I think it's a boy that's s'posed to be saying it. And ah . . . she must be quite a girl, the way things go here, and she must be very pretty, for while I was reading her description I kind of pictured her as a very beautiful girl, even as a young aged child. And ah . . . but . . . kind of older for her age, but in another way, young for her age.

Q: Why do you say that?

Uh . . . well, like ah . . . the eighteen-year-old boys coming over and talking to her when she was ah . . . twelve or thirteen so she must have been able to talk older, so that older boys would enjoy talking to her. But . . . the ah . . . yet she'd go out with little . . . the little children of her brother's age, or sister's age, or whatever it was, she would be able to play with them and they'd enjoy her. And ah . . . she really must have been a terrific person and I'm just dying of curiosity why he seemed so sad and won't ever say her name [big sigh].

Q: All right, what other reactions do you have to this section?

Well, so far I like it very well . . . I think it so far is a pretty good story, and a story I'd enjoy reading more of.

Division 2:

I don't like her mother.

Q: Why?

I don't like her one bit. I think her mother is an . . . jealous ah . . . ah Reverdy's mother is jealous of her because . . . perhaps she's . . . her beauty is . . . so great and everything. Maybe her mother didn't have boys always over at her house or something, but ah . . . to me it just seems like her mother . . . it said here that she didn't hate her actually, but I think it was just plain old fashioned jealousy and I feel sorry for the girl for that and her mother thinking she's boy crazy and . . . I can kinda see how she'd feel about it when she was perfectly innocent and really wasn't because I have a girl friend myself that was just about in the same predicament. And ah . . . I found out here that it was a little sister talking instead of a little brother [laugh].

Q: Practically everybody who has read the story has made the same mistake and thought it was a boy instead of a sister.

But ah . . . I dunno . . . I'd like to know this girl myself . . . this Reverdy.

Q: You'd like her for a friend.

Uh huh. She sounds like a real terrific person, a person I'd like to be more like myself, and ah . . . I want to go on to the next part and find out what happened to her.

Division 3:

I found it rather amusing, on her mother's suspicion and then . . . the disappointment her mother had. Ah . . .

Q: Was that the section in the arbor?

Yes. Ah . . . I couldn't help but laugh about it because I could just picture her mother's disappointment when the kids weren't doing something wrong in the arbor, and I think it's very hilarious. Uh . . . I dunno I feel sorry for her though because her mother is that way and I know it can make her very unhappy and ah . . . though I think she's doing a good job of not paying attention to it, and letting it worry her. But I still want to find out what happened to her.

Q: All right, do you have any other feelings about that part?

Well, I still admire her greatly, and ah . . . I dunno it's just . . . she's the kind of a person I'd really like to know and have a good friend.

Division 4:

I even like the mother less now . . . I think she's an old hag.

Q: Why?

Oh she's making Reverdy walk out there in that . . . the . . . out in the yard. As a matter of fact I think the mother is a little bit teched . . . and then, here at the end . . . now I'm positive that she's jealous of Reverdy because of the last here she says Mother's only little dear girl who's never given her a moment of trouble . . . the little homely girl with the glasses and so now I even feel more strongly that the mother is jealous of Reverdy and ah . . . I dunno . . . it's sort of bewildering, this story in a way. You don't . . . some things you don't know what to think about 'em, and other things you have definite feelings.

Q: What did you have in mind there?

Well . . . ah . . . I like Reverdy and all that but I wonder if she could be doing things that were you know . . . being a bad girl, not necessarily with boys or anything like that but just doing things that irritate her mother. Besides her mother being jealous . . . I do think her mother's jealous of the girl.

Q: So you think she was right about Reverdy.

Uh huh . . . if she does little things to be bad and not trying . . . I wonder . . . I don't think she does, but still I kind of, you know, that little suspicion. And ah . . . I dunno, all through the story the way the author has written it, you feel more or less as if, you're the little girl.

Ah . . . from ah . . . her point of view, you kind of feel as though you're her and that's the way she does. And ah . . . I like the way the author wrote it very well I think it's very interesting.

Q: What other observations do you have to make about that part?

Uh . . . oh dear . . . uh . . . I think it's a very true to life story myself . . . ah . . . some parts of it because ah . . . a lot of mothers are jealous, or I have seen mothers who were jealous of their daughters that were more beautiful than they are, but I don't think there are many of them. I think there are very few . . . I think more mothers will ah . . . be proud of their daughter if their daughter's more beautiful, they feel proud, or happy for them.

Division 5:

Well, I was quite surprised a couple of times, them using the word, hell. In the story . . . it kind of . . . it . . . you know, comes as a sudden shock coming out of a school story . . . that you read at school. Ah . . .

Q: You think it should be an outside-of-school story?

Yes, in a way. But ah . . . oh, I think the mother's an old hag [laugh]. But she . . . I dunno, I don't think it's fair, the way she treats Reverdy, as a matter of fact, I don't think it's fair the way she treats anybody. It sounds to me like she's got everybody in the family all henpecked and ah . . . more or less, you do things the way I want you to do, or I'll drive you crazy nagging at you, or sump'n/ And ah . . . the way she's got the father . . . and she goes in and talks to him and then he goes out and . . . it kinda gives the impression that he gives Reverdy heck too. And ah . . . even though in a way it seems as if he doesn't want to. And ah . . . I dunno . . . I don't understand this mother, and why she is the way she is. I think she's got a mere grudge against life or something . . . And ah . . . I don't think this'll work back here where Clare is . . . and her little brother Chummie start playing, I think the mother's just in a mere bad mood and nothing can make her happy . . . in fact I think she's in a . . . isn't the word, habitual . . . bad mood. Right word? And ah . . . and I just don't like her at all. I don't think it'll work though, about those two kids playing and trying to make the mother happy . . . I think it's an impossibility.

Q: Oh.

Division 6:

I'm sad.

Q: Why?

Oh, it's just . . . I dunno . . . it's . . . oh, it's a terrific story, but the way it ends it is just . . . the next morning the little girl wakes up and . . . and ah . . . there was the flowers there . . . the asters and they'd grown fresh over night and Reverdy was gone and ah . . . I dunno. In a way though it kinda gives you an impression . . . it makes you wonder where the poor kid went but I guess she just couldn't stand her parents giving her heck all the time and bellyachin' and nagging at her and ah . . . at least that's the impression I got from the story and I think it's a . . . well, I dunno, I think it's a true to life story. I think there have been a lot of experiences like that, in a way . . . a parent . . . most parents are more loving and everything but there always are the ones that have to be different and difficult and ah . . . the poor kid, I just think her mother's a little bit off in her head myself because the way she acted towards the children and ah . . . I thought it was awful sad though where Reverdy thought that her little sister Clare was playing for her, but she really wasn't . . . she was playing for her mother and ah . . .

Q: What are your feelings about that other than sadness?

I dunno . . . I could just see the ah . . . kinda feel the very same feeling that Clare would have you know, when her sister was thanking her for that . . . she'd feel kinda like a heel in a way and ah . . . though her sister . . . her older sister appreciated it, but yet her mother didn't and ah . . . oh, I dunno, I think it's . . . I think it's a wonderful story.

Q: Do you have any other feelings or reactions . . . ?

Well, right now I . . . I can't think of any but ah . . . I . . . I've never read a story like it and I think the schools should have more stories like this 'cause I think it would help a lot, because some kids do have problems like this, in their homes.

Directed cumulative response

Q: What do you think this story is about?

Well . . . I think it's about a young girl . . . a teenage girl . . . it kind of bewildered me though about whether she was actually an older teenager about eighteen or so or a younger one, about my age . . . fifteen or sixteen. I didn't quite understand it but . . . ah . . . anyway, it's about the girl Reverdy and her younger sister who is telling the story from her point of view I think and ah . . . Reverdy is beautiful and has looks which her younger and I don't think her mother have, and ah . . . a great personality that people just naturally go for and ah in the family I think there's a lot of jealousy and ah . . . ah . . . no warmth and loving and . . . I think any family, in order to be a happy family, needs that definitely and ah . . . the young girl is being criticized by her mother and her . . . for the boys liking her and all of them flocking around her all the time and . . . actually her mother refuses, I think, to understand . . . doesn't want to understand and just thinks that her daughter is boy crazy and probably calls her names like Chippy and stuff like that and here she is just a sweet girl trying to be a good girl. And ah . . . I think it's a very warm story and a story with . . . not much understanding on the other parts of the family . . . the other members of the family.

19 Asking questions

Penny Blackie

When *Language, the Learner and the School* (Barnes *et al*.), came out in 1968, I had been teaching for two years and it threw me completely. Page after page I saw, with guilty recognition, how it all applied to me. It was little comfort to know that it also applied to most other teachers I knew. For weeks I was unusually self-conscious in the classroom – everything I said seemed to ring louder in my ears and I started leaving a tape-recorder running to see how much I did actually talk. The tapes bore out my fears – I like the sound of my voice too much.

Being aware of the problem didn't help . . . enough. I became increasingly interested in the now-often quoted paradox about asking questions. When we, as adults, want to know something, we ask someone who might know the answer. In schools, when we, as adults and teachers, often (though not always) know more than our pupils, it is we who ask the questions. The answers we already know, or, even if the question is genuinely open-ended, there is a range of possible answers in our minds. There is much evidence, in *How Children Fail* (Holt 1964) especially, to show that teachers somehow indicate to their pupils which is the right or most acceptable answer, by leaning towards it, by an inclination of the head or a particular tone of voice. In my case, this is a hypocritical acceptance of a given answer, followed shortly by a hopeful 'Anything else?' I find myself saying this time and time again. So, in fact, what we are asking children to do is to play a game called Read My Mind.

Teaching in a secondary school has made me notice that whereas the eleven- and twelve-year-olds are often prepared to ask questions, the natural curiosity and exuberance of most children die away in the next year or two. One can only speculate about the causes for this, but at quite an early age small children find their parents fobbing off their questions because they cannot cope with the interminable 'Why?' It is likely that in their first years of schooling this crushing of questions becomes more widespread until, in the setting of the more rigidly structured secondary school, teachers find the questions irritating: they are asked just as the bell goes, or there isn't time anyway – we have to get through the

Source: BLACKIE, P. (1971) 'Asking questions' *English in Education* Vol. 5 pp. 77–96, also in Melnik, A. and Merritt, J. (1972) *The Reading Curriculum* pp. 360–77 The Open University Press

syllabus. Another factor that might affect this directly is the greater willingness of younger children to put themselves at risk. The adolescent will go to enormous lengths to avoid any kind of threat, whether it be making a fool of himself, or risking direct scorn and wrath or polite dismissal from his teacher. Richard M. Jones (1968) says:

> Teachers know that the proofs of well-composed and well-conducted lessons are more often found in the questions raised than in the answers given. Moreover, one has only to spend some time as a professional outsider in an elementary school to know that children will share their answers with almost anyone who asks the right questions; but they will only share their questions with their own teachers – and then only if they love them. After all, there is little risk in giving an answer, it is either right or wrong and that is usually the end of it. But to share a question is often to invite inspection of one's tenderer parts. Like other loving acts this is not something we do with strangers.

It was with great interest and something like relief that I decided to follow up a suggestion for a possible group study in Bulletin 7 of the 'Children as Readers' project (NATE 1971):

> One of the more disappointing aspects of the traditional classroom is the relatively small number of questions asked by the pupils themselves; and these probably become even fewer as children move into adolescence. This has two implications for any study of children's questions: it raises the problem of what determines the rate of question-asking; and it makes it impossible to collect children's questions just by recording ordinary lessons. Thus it becomes necessary to design situations that positively encourage children to ask questions – both because the habit of questioning is educationally valuable to children, and for research purposes.
>
> What is required is a collection not just of children's questions, but of questions gathered in a prearranged sequence of teaching.

The 'Children as Readers' Panel, with the approval of Dr W. P. Robinson (Director of the Schools Council Project on 'Children's Questions'), then suggested a procedure for following up this idea. I have used this procedure (slightly adapted for convenience) with a first-year class, two third-year classes, a fifth form and more frequently with the sixth-form A level group. In describing some of the work I should like to stress that any conclusions or hypotheses are very tentative as I have only worked on this for one term and have several tapes which I have not yet examined very closely.

After some preliminary work I thought that the procedure for 'Training Pupils to ask Questions about Poems' was particularly suitable for the sixth form. I teach in a girls' comprehensive school in a rural area, and although we have a group of twenty-three in the lower sixth taking A level English, few of them will go on to university and only one or two to read English. Many of the students might be included in what is loosely termed the 'new' sixth form, in that it is not important for their future careers that they pass A level but they either want to, or are required to, follow an A level course. For this reason we try to make our A level course as flexible as possible – set books are chosen to fit into themes and we have lectures, play-readings, poetry readings, seminars, smallish tutorial groups twice a week and a good deal of individual work based on worksheets.[1] The tutorial groups range from six to nine students. We have been studying the theme of 'War' with the Henry IV plays, Graves, *A Farewell to Arms* and war poets including, recently, Wilfred Owen. Because of the departure of a member of the English department, I found myself with three lower sixth tutorial groups all studying Owen. Much as I like his poetry, I was somewhat daunted by the prospect of six sessions a week, two with each group. Therefore, to experiment with the 'Children as Readers' suggestion of asking questions about poems seemed a good way of tackling the problem.

This account will deal with three or four lessons (of thirty-five minutes each) with two of the groups. Group I contains six students, grouped according to their subject choices, containing only one student likely to go to university. Four students in the group have very little chance of passing A level. Group I started by splitting into two groups of three, with copies of two poems by Owen: 'Shadwell Stair' (an early poem) and 'The Promisers' (written shortly before Owen's death).[2] They were asked to look at and talk about the poems, either or both, and set out to formulate questions about them. The stipulation was made that the questions should be (a) questions to which they did not already know the answers, and (b) questions to which they would *like* to know the answers. They took one lesson to formulate their questions, to be followed by a discussion by both sub-groups of all the questions.

Group I Questions
Sub-group A:
1 Where/what is Shadwell Stair? Is it a real place or is it somewhere imaginary?
2 What is the point of 'Shadwell Stair'? He is trying to say something, but what?

Sub-group B:
3 Where or what is Shadwell Stair?
4 Is it a ghost or memory or what?
5 What does 'and after me a strange tide turns' mean?
(At all stages I shared with the students the approach to this work as an experiment, and at appropriate moments we had very full 'post mortem' discussions [to which I shall refer later], quite separate from the work

183

itself, about what was happening to them and how and what they were learning.)

The next lesson the questions were put on the blackboard and the two groups discussed them all while I acted as an impartial Chairman. My explicit aim and intention was to act as Chairman, not as a teacher and not to intervene unless it was absolutely necessary. As will be seen to some extent from the transcripts, I find this extremely difficult to do. The transcript of Group 1 that follows is made from detailed notes as the students were not happy about recording it. (I did not think to identify speakers at that time.)

Group 1 – the whole lesson (from notes)[3]

    Teacher: Which questions are most important?
    Student: 1 and 5.
    No response
    Teacher: Well, if it's real . . . ?
    Student: Hotel stairs.
    Student: It might be coming up from an embankment.
    General agreement
    Silence
    Teacher: What time of day is it?
    Student: Evening.
    Long silence
    Teacher: What sort of mood is he in?
    Student: Reflective.
    Student: Pensive.
    Pause
    Teacher: Why does he go out?
    Student: To think about something.
    Pause
    (This part of the transcript took ten minutes and was very slow)

a   Teacher: (with some frustration) I refuse to barrage *you* with questions. Start talking through your questions.
    Student: Why does he go out every night?
    Student: Possibly he's a tramp.
    Student: In the third stanza it says 'always' – gives the idea that he *lives* there – and 'I walk' as if it *always* happens.
    Student: Is he waiting for something or somebody?
    Student: What does he do during the day?
    Student: Perhaps he's escaping from some world . . . wants to be alone.
    Pause
    Teacher: What about the last two lines? What are the 'crowing syrens'?
bi Student: Work syrens?
    Student: Bombing syrens?

Rest: No.

Student: When the rest of life wakes up he disappears 'like a ghost'. Perhaps he can't stand the daily life.

Student: If it's a person why does he call himself a ghost?

Student: He might be comparing . . .

Student: If it's a ghost, it can be a shadow . . .

Student: Do you think he's mad?

bii Student: We still don't know what he's doing?

c Student: Someone suggested he was waiting.

Student: Why the last line?

Student: Perhaps inspiration only comes at night?

Student: What is 'the other ghost'?

di Student: That part of his life is finished.

Student: Can't be.

dii Student: Perhaps the part of life he doesn't want to know about is during the day?

Student: Is he asleep all day?

Student: There must be two ghosts.

Student: Which is the other ghost?

Student: Look at the notes, it says 'For "crowing syrens" in the last line but one, "morning hooters" is written in another version'.

Student: Night has put a stop to people working on ships. Everything is still except for him waiting.

e (After this, four out of five students thought Shadwell Stair was a real place. All thought they hadn't got anywhere – yet the first four questions had been answered after a fashion.)

Teacher: Let's sum up: Where is it? [Bank of Thames].
What is it? [Steps leading up from embankment].
A real place? [Yes].

Student: Couldn't it be imaginary?

Pause

Teacher: Therefore we have answered 1 and 5. Have we answered 2?

Students: No.

Teacher: Have we answered 6?

Students: Yes – he is not a ghost or a memory.

(One student disagrees.)

Student: He is a troubled man out walking.

Teacher: Let's look at question 2.

Student: In the morning he has to live like others, at night he is someone else.

Long silence

f Teacher: Why is it more difficult to answer question 2? What is it about the question?

Student: In question 1 there is more to go on.

Student: Greater possibilities.

Student: This drift ... becomes a thought in his mind ... other things are definite ... We won't know how his mind works ... we can think but we can't know.

Student: Yeah ... we can't generalize.

g { Teacher: Can we imagine it? Can we each interpret it our own way?

Silence

Teacher: What will affect the way we interpret it?

Student: The mood you're in.

Student: Whether you've done it yourself.

h Student: Yeah ... your past experience.

The next week we talked about 'The Promisers'. In fact I am only going to deal with 'Shadwell Stair' in detail, but include this linking piece:

j Sue: If he's dead, at night, the ghost comes back when it's dark and then it links up with 'Shadwell Stair'.

Jeni: Yes it does, he's waiting for something.

Faith: The man in 'Shadwell Stair' is always out at night.

Liz: He's been expecting him all day.

BELL (for end of lesson)

Teacher: What about the other questions? (on 'The Promisers') Are they important?

Jeni: No, not really.

Teacher: Why not?

Jeni: We seem to have got at the poem more.

Teacher: Which parts?

Jeni: The bits that were puzzling us.

Group 1 find it difficult to talk. After the first stultifying ten minutes up to (*a*), it became much easier, because I abdicated my role of impartial Chairman and took over the habitual role of the teacher, i.e. choosing or directing questions to act as starting points. More of this later. Looking at contrasting questions helped (I certainly wouldn't have thought to ask whether 'Shadwell Stair' was an imaginary place) and we would not have had *this* discussion without that question. The choice of the question raises important points because it appears that the teacher does not always choose the question the students would most like to know or talk about.

In our post-mortem discussion, the group said that if I had gone on asking the questions they would have been silent (as indeed they were at the beginning) or would have given monosyllabic answers, often using the opt-out 'I don't know'. As they became more relaxed as a group, the answers became fuller, although it was noticeable how short the answers still were. It would have taken us longer perhaps to get round to the purposeful and insightful observations, but I am sure that this is because a measure of exploratory talk had already taken place and had an important function for the students' learning. Sue had been away for the formulation of the questions, and came into the session feeling it was all rather strange. She thought she wouldn't 'catch on, but it was better than I expected – I didn't feel I'd missed anything'.

I haven't space to discuss the talk about 'The Promisers' in detail, but this was even more useful and relaxed. I should like now to take up some specific points marked *a* to *j* on the transcript.

a   This sort of statement might normally be expected to have the opposite effect on a group than that of making them talk more freely. The only reason why I think it did not have this dampening effect is that in four previous tutorials I had opted out of the discussion completely because of their reluctance to talk to each other. Each student had chosen a poem and led discussion on it, and therefore this statement was what they had come to expect of me at this time.

bi to *bii*   At first sight this appears to be a series of unconnected thoughts with no one listening to anyone else or taking up points that are made. There is certainly none of the sort of organized sequence that a teacher might have encouraged when taking an active role. However, this may be a very necessary kind of 'talking around' the question, exploring through talk.

c   This is the first indication that any student has actually taken any notice of what has already been said, but even this is not pursued.

di and *dii*   Both of these are the sort of statement that are just bordering on the verge of an insight into the poem. A teacher who did not have my aims in this situation would probably have followed up both these points, making more of them. In this kind of talk, how can we ensure that important observations are not left floating? Does it matter if they are? Perhaps George Kelly helps here:

> The confirmation of our local predictions, equivocal as that may be, is about the most we can expect. No, there is one thing more, vastly important – our ability, while alive, to pose further questions by our invested behaviour, and thus to enter the stream of nature's fluid enterprise as an entity in our own right (Maher 1969 p. 39).

e   The tentative nature of the talk and the lack of a very clear directive had led the students to think that they had achieved nothing, whereas in fact they had had some purposeful discussion and had certainly answered some of their questions. Once they became used to this sort of working, it might be reasonable to think that they might explore certain points more deeply because they thought they were getting somewhere and achieving something positive.

f   Question 2 is a much larger question than the others, and this has affected the group's ability to handle it profitably. They should, with practice, be able to work towards tackling questions like it more successfully.

187

g Teachers often use this method of asking questions – rephrasing the question when there is no immediate response. Students don't appear to do it in their own questioning – what effect does it have?

h Here the student is coming to terms with an important way of approaching literature. She is making explicit the realization that one's own experience affects one's interpretation of literature and from that follows the corollary that one's experience of literature in some way changes, as Kelly puts it, 'one's perception of himself and his world' (Maher 1969 p. 39). This seems to be continued from what they were saying earlier, and not to be entirely due to the teacher's question.

j This lesson a week later shows the link the group made after their discussion on the questions about 'The Promisers'. Here, two important things seem to be happening – the first part of their talk is more confident and assertive once they have understood what this method of working is all about (they decide the priorities); and they are also making the point that they are tackling the bits that puzzle *them*, not the parts that the teacher would necessarily have emphasized or thought they ought to know.

Group 2 consists of nine students, who although they are also grouped according to their other subjects at A level, contain most of the really able students. At least four will probably go on to university, three to colleges of education and only one is likely to have any real difficulty passing 'A level' English. I had taught this tutorial group all through the year (and several of them for four years previously) and knew them very well. They had had no difficulty up till now in talking freely and openly.

Group 2 started asking questions about three other poems by Owen – 'The Show', 'Mental Cases' and 'Spring Offensive'. The questions, I was interested to see, were very different from those of Group 1 on 'Shadwell Stair' and 'The Promisers'. I did not know why. Was it because the poems were intrinsically of a different nature? Were three poems too many? Was it because these students were more able? (Although they had the option to talk about one or two poems, all three sub-groups talked about all three poems.) The first full group discussion on 'The Show' was a disaster – we all ended up knowing far less about the poem than we had to start with, and we were all thoroughly confused. When we discussed why this was in a post-mortem, we started to analyse the questions. We developed the categories of (a) imagery; (b) semantics; (c) whole poem – background. Out of eighteen questions, ten were category (a), five were category (b) and three were category (c). At the time I did not comment on this, but we all decided that to pursue these poems would do more harm than good. Therefore it was in this rather dispirited and muddled frame of mind that Group 2 came on to 'Shadwell Stair' and 'The Promisers'. Instead of having three groups of three as we had had before, this time we had one group of three and one of six. The larger group recorded their discussion, and the full group discussion of 'Shadwell Stair' was also recorded.

Group 2 Questions
Sub-group A (three students):
1 Who is the ghost?
2 Where is Shadwell Stair? In London, but what is it?
3 What do the last two lines mean?

Sub-group B (six students):
4 What was his job?
5 What does 'after me a strange tide turns' mean?
6 What does the last line mean?
(The similarity in the questions between sub-group and sub-group and, in fact, between group and group does not need labouring – but would I, preparing that poem to teach, have asked those questions?)

Here follow certain extracts from the transcript of the full group discussion on 'Shadwell Stair', which I feel have interesting points to offer.

Group 2 – extract A of lesson transcript
Talking about Question 1:
Teacher: (summing up) So, it's this person anyway who looks like a ghost because he's seen from a distance, but who is he do you think?
Sue: A watchman.
Teacher: A watchman?
Several: Mmm
Long pause
Teacher: A night watchman? What an interesting idea. What do you think of that? I never thought of that. . . . Go on.
Susan: We talked about it last week . . . being a watchman.
Teacher: What, among yourselves? Yes, of course, Vicki wasn't here and I wasn't here. You talked about it yourselves. Margaret wasn't here either.
Pause – followed by discussion about absence
Teacher: So you decided he was a watchman did you?
Susan: We talked a lot about it and thought he probably could be . . .
Marion: Because he goes *through* the slaughter-house and not round it and he'd . . .
Teacher: Oh, yes . . .
Marion: He's just in one part all the time.
Yvonne: Stays in one place . . . 'where I watch *always*'.
Teacher: Yes . . . 'where I watch always'.

I am particularly interested in this piece of talk for two reasons. First, at the time, I felt very excited about this idea (the night watchman) and the detail with which its exponents tried to convince us. I no longer felt myself to be in the role of the Chairman, nor did I feel remotely like a teacher, but was with them as a member of the group. (The intrusiveness comes out as excitement on the *tape* although I realize that it is not so evident from the words of the transcript.) Although we were discussing a minor point in the poem (and it was quite probably an incorrect assumption to make about the 'ghost'), the teacher here was clearly a learner in every sense as much as any other member of the group. If the teacher can be seen to be learning with the group this must have important effects on the atmosphere and relationships within the group. By extending the discussion on Question 1 in this way, we partly answered Question 4.

Secondly, the extract makes me feel simultaneously ashamed and interested. When I played the tape of the group formulating their own questions, I found that I had not remembered participating in that discussion right at the end when I returned to take away the tape recorder. In fact, the tape shows that we talked, then, about the watchman and that I had tentatively suggested framing a question on that idea as the group was puzzled about it. Yet a week later, when the question arose, I felt I was genuinely learning something and had no recollection of the previous conversation. Nor, from their tone, had the group remembered that I had been there. This has implications for learning – possibly self-evident ones. The mood and attitude of the learner directly affect how much he retains. On the first occasion, I had felt like an intruder in their group discussion and was loath to be drawn in: I therefore somehow shut out the part I had played in their formulation of that question. What implications does this have for how children learn – or don't learn?

Group 2 – extract B

Teacher: What do the last two lines mean? Are you happy about them?
Vicki: Well, I can get the bit when he's the night watchman and he's tired when morning comes and his work ends and he goes home to sleep and the ordinary people come out to do their ordinary work . . . you know, in the day time . . . normal, more or less . . . and he has to go back to sleep; that's the wrong way round isn't it, for human beings who should sleep at night . . . but I can't, I still can't see the ghost – 'another ghost' fits in . . .

(never resolved)

(In answer to the question 'Who is the ghost?')

Yvonne: Well, I looked at it like this, like down there at night and anybody watching from a fence, that sort of thing, would only see sort of shadows, a dark thing moving and wouldn't be able to identify it really, so he's just got a ghost-like appearance.

These pieces are by far the longest speeches that were made in a tape that lasts twenty-five minutes. It is worth noting that both of them are the sort of exploratory talk that tries to build up a context in which the poem might fit. The West Suffolk 'Children as Readers' group has been studying transcripts of tapes of children talking about poems when the teacher is not present. In two tapes of eleven-year-olds, the children use this technique of building up a context much more often and it does help them to see how the poem might work. Why, with seventeen-year-olds, is there so little of it?

Group 2 – extract C
Teacher: (as Chairman) Right, then, what does 'after me a strange tide turns' mean?
Yvonne: Could it mean when a ship goes past and sends a sort of tidal wave type thing as he turns away to go back home?
Teacher: In what sense 'turns' and 'tide'? You mean literally?
Yvonne: It's the only thing I could see clearly.
Carmel: I don't think the tide's turning literally . . . on the whole it's a 'strange tide' . . . in his mind.
Long pause
Teacher: Well . . . yes . . . well, let's carry on with that idea.
Long pause

This extract raises a point we have discussed earlier. Carmel is making a significant and insightful observation which is not taken up by any of the others. After her interjection, made very quietly and hesitantly, there is a long and unresponsive pause. The teacher, unable to resist the potential of a comment like this, tries to get the group to consider it still further; but within the brief of acting as an impartial chairman, insistence on it cannot be justified. Therefore, the insight is not pursued and all discussion of this point collapses. How can this be overcome? (Should it be?)

Group 2 – extract D
Teacher: Do you feel happy with the poem now looking at it like that?
All: Yes
Vicki: What do you think 'dolorously' means though?
Teacher: Anybody? Dolorously?
Susan: Grief
Teacher: Something to do with grief, sadness, very depressed, yes. Well, I think this is very interesting you know, because we've spent now three, some people have spent four sessions on these two poems and certainly with *this* poem ['Shadwell Stair' – we hadn't yet discussed 'The Promisers']. I think we wouldn't have got anywhere near where we've got if we hadn't been working in this method? What do you think?
Jane: Mm
Pause
Teacher: Because, let's face it, you thought of things which I didn't

think of, and if you, if I had been asking the questions I would have been asking questions of things that *I* was thinking about whereas you were asking questions that *you* were thinking about . . . right?

Yvonne: Yes.

Teacher: It never occurred to me perhaps to say 'What is his job?' whereas you formulated that question because you had talked about what his job was which confirms me in my belief that half of the time, probably all of the time, I am asking the wrong questions.

Long pause

Teacher: What do you think?

Reflective pause

Teacher: What do you feel about this asking questions? Do you feel sceptical about it or do you think you've learnt something? Do you think it's a useful thing to do?

Several: Yes
Mmm/Yeah

Teacher: Is it?

Susan: I was a bit muddled at first but we've got the result now. I thought, you know . . . the first couple of times we were thinking differently . . .

BELL

Teacher: Yes, I'm very interested in this you see because as a group you have not liked doing this at all, or up till now perhaps; I don't know if you even like doing it now but at least you feel a sense of achievement . . . or do you?

Several: Mmm

Teacher: Does everybody?

Several: Yes . . . I do . . . Mm

Teacher: But I sense that you didn't until now. And I certainly didn't with you till now. Right? With the other groups, particularly one group I'm thinking about, they felt it was important right from the start, very exciting . . . and they felt it was a new way of looking at things and felt very satisfied the very first time they did it. Now I wonder if we can account for at all why you took such a long time.

Pause

I really don't know the answer. I'm just wondering about this . . .

Yvonne: I don't think we've . . . *I've* never disliked doing it.

Teacher: You didn't dislike doing it?

Yvonne: No

Teacher: (to the rest) Did you?

Sandra: I didn't mind.

Teacher: You felt indifferent?

192

Several: Yes
Teacher: All of you?
Marion: We had to start off without any questions whereas usually we start off with something to work on.
Teacher: What, from me?
Marion: Yes
Teacher: Did you find starting off, then, very difficult?
All: Yes
Carmel: We've got to think what to look at first.
Teacher: Yes. Well, in that case, do you think you've progressed because the questions you've asked in the first lot of poems ('Mental Cases', 'The Show' and 'Spring Offensive') were in fact very particular questions? They were all sort of imagery or semantic questions. And remember that we talked about this on Monday [3rd session] that it wasn't until you started finding questions on *these* poems [nearly all category (c) questions] that you started looking at the key parts of the poem . . .
Student: Mmm
Teacher: And it's on your own (I mean I hope I didn't point this out to you, I spotted it at the beginning and was a bit worried about your kind of questions . . . which is in fact why I got you to categorize them but I don't think that at the time I drew any conclusions from it, did I?)
Student: No
Teacher: Until after you'd done those questions. Now somehow on your own you got these questions which were what was needed to break it open, which I think is very interesting.

I am not at all happy about the intrusive role played by the teacher here. In explanation I must point out that this whole conversation took place in three minutes at the end of the last lesson before school examinations, and in the knowledge that there would be no opportunity to come back to it for three weeks. This is not offered as an excuse because I feel very conscious of its limitations – for example, many of the affirmative mutters could simply be the sort of agreement one finds in polite society. The reason for bringing the extract in at all at this stage is to point out how seriously I took the factor of awareness in what was happening. I wanted the students to be critical and analyse what was happening to them in this situation. It also reveals a misunderstanding on my part – in the earlier work when we had achieved little, I had been disappointed and thought the group shared this feeling. They obviously didn't, at least not to the same extent. Possibly this more positive viewing of events by the students happens more than we think it does. Sometimes teachers are disappointed in lessons that students may have found more rewarding. However, the key point is made by Marion when she says, 'We had to start off without any questions', and by Carmel when she says, 'We've got to think what to look at first'. This has been exactly the situation found to exist in the transcripts of the tapes of younger children studied by the West Suffolk 'Children as Readers' group. There, we found that there is either a panic response, where the only way out is to examine bits of the poem in isolation (as Group 2 did in their earlier work on 'The Show') or a more ordered response where the group talks through the problem slowly and carefully, not feeling threatened if they cannot reach immediate conclusions. In 'Shadwell Stair' and 'The Promisers', the questions were much more 'background' questions than 'meaning' questions in the sense of merely pertaining to imagery or semantics.

General observations

Group 1, ostensibly the weaker group which had always had difficulty in talking easily, coped much better at first with this work. Why? Does the size of the group affect this? Or their relationship with the teacher? (I had worked with Group 2 for a year, and Group 1 for six weeks.)

All the tapes show horrifyingly and abundantly clearly that I tend to pause for far too short a time between question and answer, or statement and follow-up. The pressure for someone to say something (*anything?*) leads to embarrassed and uncomfortable silence which might account for the rather slow and dead response in the first part of Group 1's discussion. Worse still, this anxiety to have someone talking cuts down the opportunity for exploratory thought and talk. This is shown to be crucial in the tapes made of the groups discussing alone, where points are often discussed slowly and thoughtfully with many long, relaxed pauses. This carries implications for all forms of teaching and Douglas Barnes in his latest work is further emphasizing this need for exploratory talk (NATE, 1971) – it is depressing to find that one makes too few allowances for it, even when trying consciously to opt out of the role of teacher.

Many times in the tapes of full group discussion I find that I repeat the students' contributions. Why is this? Is it necessary for reinforcement or consolidation or reassurance (mine or theirs), or is it for the benefit of the tape-recorder? A more serious possibility – does this repetition destroy the students' own language, especially if the teacher paraphrases their contributions?

Is there any pattern in the initiation of responses after a pause? If the pause is uncomfortable *and* too short, it is usually the teacher who interrupts it. If a student assumes this role, does it happen in the same way as when a teacher interrupts? If the pause is not threatening, what is the nature of the initiation of the next point? I know little about this.

There are places where the teacher could (and normally would?) help by providing information, but this does not occur here because of the impartiality of the teacher's role. For example, a copy of the *A to Z* (which most of our students, living in Suffolk, don't know) would have told them where Shadwell Stair was. By not having recourse to an authority, in the shape of person or book, they worked it out for themselves and I feel sure that this was of greater educational value in the end. However, it is important that this authority (where it exists) is eventually recognized and that we don't rely only on guess-work. I did, in fact, show both groups where Shadwell Stair was on the map after they had reached their conclusions. Points which did not come out in full group discussion sometimes do in the smaller sub-groups; e.g. in one full discussion the assumption was made that 'Shadwell Stair' must be a war poem since Owen wrote war poetry, and the fact that 'Shadwell Stair' is an early poem was not raised. However, in one of the Group I sub-groups, this very point was discussed fully by some of the students with references to technique to back up their conclusions. The teacher might have pointed out this fact in a traditional lesson – here again the students work it out for themselves, a fact which was not immediately apparent until the tape of their own discussion was played. All these processes take a great deal of time. In a normal study of Owen, a poem like 'Shadwell Stair' might be lucky if it were discussed for one thirty-five minute session. *In fact, this work in both groups took four times as long as this.*

Asking questions of themselves and each other seems to ensure that the questions discussed are those the students really want to know about, rather than those the teacher might think they want/ought to know about, although usually one could expect certain questions to straddle both choices. This is not merely a question of relationship with the teacher – in many cases the students did not themselves know what questions they would like to ask until they had discussed the poems at some length.

Certain levels of enquiry do not seem to be satisfactorily achieved with this method. Insights are not thoroughly pursued, and sometimes seemingly trivial data overshadow the key points. However, I feel reluctant to do more than state this as a problem at this stage. The work the Leeds 'Children as Readers' group has done points to the possibility that this 'sorting-out' process may be a necessary stage for students working on their own. Furthermore, more practice in this kind of independent work might well lead to a deepening response to the real insights that occur.

I throw out questions and problems deliberately, and do not attempt to attach weight to the few conclusions I draw. Carried out as a serious research project, the whole problem of children asking questions will be sure to raise important implications for teaching. I do not pretend to do that here, but simply raise a few points which I found to be interesting in a very limited study.

Appendix
Shadwell Stair
I am the ghost of Shadwell Stair.
   Along the wharves by the water-house.
   And through the dripping slaughter-house,
I am the shadow that walks there.

Yet I have flesh both firm and cool,
  And eyes tumultuous as the gems
  Of moons and lamps in the lapping Thames
When dusk sails wavering down the pool.

Shuddering the purple street-arc burns
  Where I watch always; from the banks
  Dolorously the shipping clanks
And after me a strange tide turns.

I walk till the stars of London wane
  And dawn creeps up the Shadwell Stair.
  But when the crowing syrens blare
I with another ghost am lain.

Wilfred Owen

From *The Collected Poems of Wilfred Owen*. Reprinted by permission of Chatto and Windus Ltd.

Notes

1 Since worksheets are another way of asking questions, it might be worth saying a word about those we use. The idea of the worksheets for our sixth form course is that they should provide an occasion for writing – it is always stressed that although there are certain minimum requirements, the students are free to use or reject the worksheets as they wish. As long as they do write, they are invited to formulate their own questions or write about any aspect of the text or theme that interests them. However, few of them take this opportunity, so we try to provide a variety and range of questions. For example in a worksheet on *The Rainbow* by D. H. Lawrence, the students are required to prepare notes for discussion on a few questions such as:

> Examine the three major symbols of the novel. Make notes on their significance and effects:
>
>   the arch (pp. 65, 202)
>   the rainbow (pp. 97, 202, 496)
>   the cathedral (pp. 200 +, 456)
>   (page references are always a guide).

Also, along with a fairly wide choice of other questions there are traditional A level-type essay questions, and also questions like:

> Lawrence is very concerned with the place of woman, both in her relationships with men and in society as a whole. Examine this concern. You might like to compare the position he takes with Women's Lib., but find out about Women's Lib. first (there are newspaper articles available if you ask for them, or read *The Female Eunuch* by Germaine Greer) (pp. 9, 11, 19, 334, 343, 353, 406).

2 For the text of 'Shadwell Stair' see Appendix, p. 195.

3 The letters *a* to *j* will be referred to later in detailed comment.

References

BARNES, D., BRITTON, J. and ROSSEN, H., (1968 rev. edn, 1971) *Language, the Learner and the School* Harmondsworth: Penguin Education

HOLT, John (1964) *How Children Fail* New York: Pitman

JONES, Richard N. (1969) *Fantasy and Feeling in Education* London: University of London Press

MAHER, Brendan (1969) *Clinical Psychology: the Selected Papers of George Kelly* New York: John Wiley

NATE/Schools Council Project (1971) 'Children as Readers' Bulletin 7

NATE (April 1971) from a talk to the Projects Commission Annual Conference on 'Language across the Curriculum'

20 Responses to reading: how some young readers describe the process

Jean Blunt

The reading process – is it so indefinable?

What happens in the mind of the young reader as he engages with the ebb and flow of narrative as it is retold in print? How does he respond to the fiction – if he responds at all?

Still we go on teaching literature not knowing what the young readers are really making of it. The direct response is a nebulous, untouchable area perhaps conveniently best left alone. Frank Whitehead's interim report on the mammoth investigation into 'Children's Reading Interests' is self-consciously evasive when the question of what children take from their reading is raised:

> This section will inevitably be more speculative and impressionistic than has gone before since (as our interviews with individual children confirmed) the young reader seldom finds it possible to be articulate in any very specific way about what he has liked or valued in his reading. (Whitehead 1975 p. 40)[1]

Do we really have to go on living in hope? Is it fair to continue basing hours of our teaching time on mere speculations and impressions? Can we not somehow probe a little more into the question of what teenage readers bring to and take from their reading?

Certainly, the tools for such analysis are close at hand.

The theory and its provision of useful reference points

The much-quoted D. W. Harding has tried to suggest a definition of the processes involved in the reading of fiction. Identifying the salient features of the reading process might help in an analysis of responses said to be made during an engagement with a novel. To consciously search for the 'theoretical' elements of response in the replies of young readers might be a revealing exercise.

What are the components of the full response seen to be?

Firstly, the reader of fiction must accept *the role of onlooker* if he is to savour human interactions from a detached vantage point. Then, those

Source: BLUNT, J. (1977) 'Response to reading: how some young readers describe the process' *English in Education* Vol. 11 No. 3 pp. 35–47

other requirements, says Harding, should come more easily as the reader becomes absorbed in educating reading:

1   Willing attendance to the work.
2   Elementary perception and comprehension.
3   Empathy with the characters of the novel as imaginative insight is gained.
4   Distanced evaluation of the participants.
5   Reviewing the whole work as the author's creation.
6   Wish formulation as varying possibilities are imaginatively explored in print.
7   Analogizing and searching for self-identity.

The notions of 'identification' and 'vicarious satisfaction' are certainly inadequate, but are these more sophisticated definitions of any real use to the teacher in the classroom and his refractory young readers? It may be interesting to see how much or how little a group of particular teenagers take from their reading in the light of such theories.

Choosing the readers

From two schools, one being a direct grant grammar school in a suburban area, School A; and the other a secondary modern taking pupils from the industrial neighbourhood, School B, sixteen pupils were interviewed about their reading. The sample was made up of eight pupils from each school, and each group of eight contained two boys and two girls, randomly selected, from a 'top' ability group, and two boys and two girls, again randomly selected according to position on class register, from a 'bottom' ability group.

These sixteen had already filled in questionnaires and profile sheets about their own reading habits, and I had also obtained information about family circumstances and measured ability. But it was during the discussions with each group of four readers that the real advance was made. I found nine of the sixteen interviewees to be explicit and definite about what the process of reading held for them. After Whitehead's warning about possible reticence and bewilderment, I found the readers needed extended interview time. I returned to schools to listen to the upper ability groups elaborate on such propositions as 'getting involved' in a book and getting 'bored' with one. For the pupils of School B's lower ability group, all having an IQ falling below 90, the questions were baffling as the Schools Council's researchers had forewarned. Yet this in itself may give some clues about the nature of the response. Still, I had nine talkative fifteen-year-olds from different social and educational backgrounds:

The readers of School A: Vikki, Tina, Peter, Brian, Richard.
The readers of School B: Melanie, Wendy, Jeremy, Ian.

Space does not allow the detailed biographical information obtained concerning each to be reproduced; neither does it allow the hours of transcription to be adequately represented. However, perhaps selections from the discussions and my own reflections after all the talk had subsided might be interesting to other teachers who, like myself, wonder what goes on inside the heads of our teenagers as they turn to their own reading. Can the activity of private reading throw any light on the vexed exercise of classroom reading?

Levels of response
The role of the spectator
One of the elemental conditions of responsive fiction reading is that the reader accepts the role of the onlooker. How did the sample of young readers define their stance to story reading?

Vikki's reading response is evidently a developing one. She has the capability of becoming a sophisticated reader if Harding's contentions are to be believed:

> I try to imagine what people would be like/ I do relate it to my life/ I'm not actually in the story/ I think I'm in the room with the characters/ but I'm not actually one of them/ if you like/ er/ I'm like a dumb friend/ they don't know you're there/ I'm an invisible visitor who doesn't change the story/

Quite unprovoked, one sees Vikki here expressing the process of imaginative, distanced onlooking, almost duplicated in Harding's own words:

> . . . the reader of a novel is in the position of a ghost watching unseen the behaviour of a group of people in whom he is deeply interested; he can imagine what they are feeling, he takes sides in their conflicts, regrets this bit of behaviour, applauds that, and he has hopes and fears about the outcome but can say nothing and do nothing to affect it. (Harding 1968 p. 12)[2]

Now Melanie's novel reading involves her in a process of role creation. She somehow imaginatively projects herself into the fiction and deludes herself into the belief that she is responsible for the course the narrative takes:

> I become another character/ well/ like if it's a mystery/ or something/ I become another detective and I'm/ like/ helping the person to work it out/ and giving him the ideas/ I'm in the book/ the author's writing about me/ as well/ inside the book like/ 'Murder on the Orient Express'/ I was with Hercule Poirot/ and/ I was/ I told him all the answers/ I was another detective with him/ I gave him one of the ideas for solving the mystery/

Melanie has moved to a rather curious role creation cleverly devised to allow that priceless fuller view. She is both in the novel and out of it.

Tina is much less attracted to book reading. Like Wendy, she prefers her stories to have happy endings and reads magazine serials and romantic novels which meet her wish for contentment. Tina's reading may perhaps be largely idyllic excursions which allow but little of that distanced evaluation of possible events and circumstances.

For Jeremy appreciation of detached spectatorship probably allows a keener adherence to the recognition of the book as a technique of communication to be observed from a distance. He relishes the opportunity for withdrawal which an observer of a second-order experience is given:

It's like in a cinema/ you see it going past/ you're on the outskirts of the story and you get some of the/ you know/ . . . interest/ but you're just far enough away to not get too involved/ in case anything happens you don't like/ you're just there/ on the outside/ you're in the story as you imagine yourself in a film/ but you're on the outside as well/ watching them do everything in the book/ and you see all of them in it/

In Peter there stirs a somewhat immature response to reading. He seems to be confused by the techniques of novel writing and again one sees the breakdown of detachment from the narrative as he recalls his stance to novel reading:

You can actually take part/ you sometimes think of alternative endings that might have been better for that book/ or worse/ I like to change it round a bit/

Brian, the highly intelligent boy who holds book reading in very low esteem, was rather scornful in his replies to enquiries about what reading meant to him. Adolescent lethargy hung heavily as he volunteered his reaction to reading a novel:

I just read it and don't go right into it/ I just read it and that's it/

Books have no real value within his peer group or his home and laconic replies reaffirmed his disregard for reading as a pleasurable pursuit.

Ian, with his paucity of remembered reading to draw upon exacerbated by unpleasant memories of early failures at mastering the basic skill, found talking about the response a little more difficult than the others. Book reading was not a favoured occupation. However, what he did say hinted that he had at least seen the advantages of distanced onlooking:

I'm reading/ 'Day of the Triffids'/ I'm just standing up a corner/ watching it all happen/ I can see them/ they can't see me/ but I don't think I could change things/ I just stand there/ and watch it all happen/ I don't have any feelings/

The third boy claiming to have little interest in books, Richard, is concise in his definition of the role he plays during his reading of his own chosen fiction:

> I'd say I was looking in through the window/ hearing what the characters say/

Again, spectating, rather than participating, is the primary concern.

Vikki, Melanie, Jeremy, Ian, and Richard are undoubtedly spectators at the fictional events. Brian may also adopt such a stance though he preferred to leave the processes of his reading unexamined. Wendy, Tina, and Peter seem to have not yet fully mastered this elementary level of response. Though they may look at events from a distance when it pleases them to scan the scene, they remain anxious to intervene and set the fiction right when it displeases them. If, as Harding suggests, this spectating role is so all-important if newer levels of a mature reading response are to be reached, it will be interesting to see how the readers advance through the other phases of the reading process.

The elements of the full response

Attending willingly
The attitude set of the reader must be positively oriented towards the pleasure which novel reading can offer if the response is to be a full one. All were talking of reading to which they attended willingly. All, that is, except Brian. He suggested that he had 'enough of books' in school and only read them at home when there was nothing else to do.

> It's less effort to watch television/ you don't have to concentrate as much/

Elementary perception and comprehension

The readers all chose material which was not likely to endanger comprehension. Certainly reading was not pitched at too high a level, though perhaps the notable low-level reading of Peter (comics and supernatural stories) and Tina (women's magazines) leaves little room for a mature response to emerge. None of the readers really challenged his own powers of perception: they were mostly happy to choose a book with a sense of story, however crudely told. Vikki, for instance, chose historical romance to the exclusion of all else, and Melanie had worked her way through the murderous entanglements of Agatha Christie.

It may be dangerous to despair of such a reading choice, and it should be remembered that wide reading provides the raw material for discerning reading. Yet, if reading levels chosen influence the development of responsive reading, then it is crucial that these young readers should receive guidance. They need to be offered prose which is neither too exacting nor too easy: prose which will hopefully feed the growing response.

Empathizing

Harding's warnings that empathy comes in varying degrees ranging from virtual indifference to delusional participation must be heeded. Empathizing with the personae of a novel is a delicate affair, and the young, unpractised reader must strive to reach a balance of imaginative appreciation which does not blur distanced evaluation. It will now be seen how the readers were able to strike this balance or topple it.

In her reading of Catherine Cookson's *The Dwelling Place*, Vikki's extreme involvement may well have endangered the detachment so important to a mature response:

> In 'The Dwelling Place'/ you feel you want to help Cissie in the story/ and/ er/ it's just so true-to-life/ I think/ I would have liked to have lived in those days/

One can only suggest that the response is growing through empathy which occasionally runs too deep for objective evaluation of the work of fiction as a whole.

Melanie empathizes with the characters by joining them as an imaginary fellow sufferer created for her own convenience.

Tina, Wendy, and Peter enjoy easy empathy with the heroes and heroines of fiction.

A much more structured empathy allows Jeremy to stay firmly within the contraints of the book:

> You're in the story as you imagine yourself in a film/ but you're on the outside as well/ watching them do everything in the book/ and you see all of them in it/

Here, empathic insight is used to appreciate more fully the novel, rather than indulge the imaginings. The business of reading, not dreaming, is paramount.

The reluctant imagination within Brian directs him towards reading non-fiction where empathy may be less demanding. Yet, even in his comment on the process of reading biographies, one can detect the arousal of what may be seen to be a dormant imagination:

> You imagine yourself in the place of the hero/ the/ er/ star of the book/ I like reading biographies about people's lives/ you can see what happened to them/ what you would have done in their situation/

The following pronouncement of Ian's reflects that a high degree of empathy has yet to develop to enhance the reading response. He may still be too suspicious of print to invest too much of himself into its reconstruction.

> I just stand there and watch it all happen/ I don't have any feelings/

Richard again succinctly proposes that his empathy with a character from fiction is nicely poised to allow him to appreciate the situation more fully or withdraw at whim to evaluate and speculate:

> Hearing what they say/ sort of/ commenting to yourself/ the justice of the situation/ telling yourself as you go along/ you think it's a shame/ or/ you're happy for somebody else/

For most of the readers empathizing with the characters of novels creates no real problems.

Perhaps at this stage the analysis of the reading response takes a new turn towards more sophisticated considerations. So far the readers have, generally speaking, met the requirements of Harding's defined response. Occasionally they have only partly fulfilled a condition: it will be recalled that three of the readers had some difficulty in extracting themselves from the fiction to place themselves at a distance most suited for judging the work as a whole – but more of this later. Yet the emerging response may just have been recognized even in apparent contradictions. *Stage One*, then, has, fairly successfully, been passed. Now in *Stage Two* where such considerations as analogizing, distanced evaluation, and reviewing the whole work as the author's creation are called up for examination, the dissenters begin to be identified.

Analogizing and searching for self identity

Using the analogies taken from one's reading to enhance the significance of one's own life is a less evident trait of the reading responses of this sample of fifteen-year-olds.

Busily discovering the criminal before the final denouement of Agatha Christie's suspense stories gives Melanie real satisfaction. She sees herself as the seeker of truth, the astute adult rather than the impressionable adolescent. While she was obviously growing tired of Agatha Christie and the murder story as an intellectual 'whodunnit' exercise in which her supremacy over the writer had become tedious, she was also awakening to the novel as a pattern of events from which analogies could perhaps be drawn:

> I like to get away from it all/ but/ er/ I don't want to get too far away/ because you can't/ sort of/ interpret it with your own life/ cos you don't know whether it's true/ it can be actually possible/

Jeremy, too, is discerning enough to demand psychological feasibility of his science fiction stories. To upset physical probability is acceptable to him, but he is not so easily duped that he does not demand a wider convincing probability which will ultimately allow him to analogize and educate himself into reinterpreting his own beliefs and values.

The only other reader to suggest that analogizing was a part of his response to reading was Richard:

> I read *Lord of the Flies* and enjoyed that/ it's as if you're an observer outside it all/ but still feeling revulsion/ I was working out whether it could happen/

Richard here takes the picture of imagined experience and tries to fit it into the vision and knowledge he has of real experience. With the merging of first- and second-order experiences the business of self-education has begun. One returns to an oft-quoted truism with renewed interest:

> To obliterate the effects on a man of all the occasions on which he was only an onlooker would be profoundly to change his outlook and values. (Harding 1961 p. 136)[3]

Only three readers stated that they have consciously experienced the need to analogize as they interact with a chosen novel. The field narrows.

Distanced evaluation of the participants

Only two readers provided evidence to suggest that they perhaps comment to themselves on the doings and sufferings of the characters.

Tina's reading of *Valley of the Dolls* had caused her to reflect again and again upon the situations retold in the drama and the predicaments of the fictional characters as they succeeded or failed in pursuit of a loving relationship:

> I usually put myself in the place of one of the main characters/ and imagine how it would be for them/ I keep thinking about them/

The heroines reverberate in her mind and she moves out from the fiction to review them.

Richard's conversation revealed that he evidently upholds a running commentary on the events of the narrative:

> You comment to yourself as you go along/ you think it's a shame/ or/ you're happy for somebody else/

It seems that Richard is reacting *to* the behaviour and feelings of the characters as much as he imaginatively reacts *with* them. He both empathizes and withdraws to evaluate.

205

Now, only two readers advance to the full response, and it has to be admitted that Tina's words are much less explicit than are Richard's.

Reviewing the whole work as the author's creation

The ultimate requirement of a mature response is the ability to recognize that an author presents an evaluation of possible human experience in his own written style. The book is finally seen as an artefact, a convention to be rejected or applauded by the reader.

Vikki certainly stated that she had some feeling for style, and she chose books written by favourite authors:

> I think the storyline's important/ but I think the way the author approaches the book/ and/ explains it helps/ the atmosphere that Catherine Cookson builds up/ I think she probes your mind/ and so all the exciting things are brought out by her words/

There is here a crude recognition of the authoress's part in the proceedings and an approval of the style employed.

Melanie's developing discrimination is best illustrated in her rejection of a novel:

> The way it was written was er/ very worldly/ too permissive/ brash/ I liked what it was about/ but I stopped reading it because the way it was written spoiled it/ the same words over and over again/

At this point Melanie is criticizing a novel for its linguistic exaggerations and her jettisoning of such stories leaves room for optimism.

Jeremy spoke of his appreciation of the novelist's technique of giving a book form, texture, credibility, and interest. He listed his favourite authors. He talked of 'good' science fiction as that in which he could 'get involved' imaginatively with the people in the story. He valued a book which made him think of the real possibilities held within it.

Richard, too, spoke of stepping back from the book to scan the whole work and test the integrity of the author against his own knowledge of the world. When he makes the aside to reaffirm his interest in *Lord of the Flies*, 'it was great, I'd read more of his books', one realizes that the business of discrimination is also brought into play.

Only Richard, who professed to have no interest in books, has fulfilled all the requirements of the full response. He had willingly listened to and comprehended representations of experience, imaginatively entered the drama, evaluated the sufferings and doings of the actors, and accepted the created personae as pawns manoeuvred by the writer for the purposes of communicating what he conceives to be worthwhile reflections.

Jeremy and Melanie almost provided evidence of mature, responsive reading. For these two only distanced evaluation of the participants was the missing component.

Vikki managed to somewhat crudely recognize the importance of a writer's style, and Tina somehow gave life to a sustained consideration of the characters of a chosen novel.

For Wendy, Peter, Brian, and Ian the response was apparently never so well formed, though they still had specific information to impart which led one to believe that a fuller reading response needed only gentle tending from an informed and sensitive tutor – perhaps the school could help bridge a formidable chasm which may well exist between the elementary response of *Stage One* and the sophisticated process reached in *Stage Two*.

Emergent patterns discovered during examination of the reading response

Several important points begin to present themselves during such an analysis of response.

1 One has to suggest that the pupils of very low ability in this sample (those with an IQ falling below 90) found any articulation about the psychological processes called into being whilst reading a work of fiction a baffling proposition. What they did say pointed to the existence of a very elementary and cursory response. On the other hand, a very high IQ did not guarantee a full response especially when the attitude set to reading was not a favourable one.

2 A readiness to imagine, daydream, and invent one's own fictions may be an advantage as far as responding to the fiction created by someone else is concerned. It may be no coincidence that Vikki, Jeremy, Melanie, and, significantly, Richard, were regarded by their teacher as *imaginative* and *inventive* where their own writing was concerned.

3 A conscious awareness of the role of the author as creator of the fiction is less manifest in this sample of teenage readers than their willingness and evident desire to discover characters in the novel with whom they can empathize in some depth. In adolescence it seems that such emotional responses may come more easily than the cognitive ones.

4 One must comment on the high degree of empathy which the girls of the sample invest in their reading. The ready interest in imaginatively experiencing the joys, the disappointments, the frustrations of heroes and heroines may perhaps be nurtured by the cruder romance stories of the magazines and popular paperbacks. The two pupils reluctant to admit to accommodating empathy whilst reading were both boys, and both were opposed to reading in their own time.

5 The more practised, wide reader may be nearer to achieving the fuller response than his non-reading companions.

6 Though the quality of reading matter may not be a determinant of response, the ability to discriminate and recognize weaknesses in certain works of fiction, however trivial, may be important to the development of fuller psychological activity during reading. Comics,

magazines, supernatural tales, and thrillers may well form the seedbed for the germinating response.

7 Lastly, one must observe that at this stage the response to the reading of fiction is in evolution. Mostly the readers are at different stages of growth, and one has to consider how far these delicate, incipient reactions are accommodated and tended in the English classroom.

Such an analysis, then, suggests two very important things which may be of use to the teacher of English. *If* the reactions of these young readers are at all typical, then: firstly, one must recognize that the level of response reached is not always inextricably linked to ability. Sometimes a very intelligent pupil may find responsive reading an evasive proposition, and sometimes the less able may readily find the empathy to at least ensure an elementary response, always providing that there is no blockade to comprehension. Certainly the weakest pupils of the sample need help, but so also do the brightest – seeing the novel as a writer's construct, a form of communication to arouse the reader to deeper contemplation of possible human experience is no easy task. Yet these young readers provide evidence to suggest that such a reaction may not be completely out of reach. Secondly, one also has to bear in mind the individuality of the reading response. It is a personal affair developing hesitantly and requiring the very gentlest of encouragement if a mature, worthwhile engagement with fiction is to result. The direct response can hardly be transmitted from teacher to pupil.

Deepening the response
Perhaps we, as teachers of English, should explore ways of deepening and articulating this response. Again and again, one has to pay heed to the young readers' anxiety to 'get into a book', 'to get carried away', 'to get involved', 'to imagine you're there'. The desire to empathize is seemingly ever-present as far as voluntary reading is concerned. It is the distanced evaluation which results in reflection on the fuller pattern of events and the author's part in directing them that is so much more elusive – and it is this very aspect of literary study which has for decades been so heavily and dangerously emphasized in school. The readers of the sample were not complimentary in their remarks on the novels chosen for them in school and the accompanying discursive activities. There is clearly a need for re-thinking classroom practice if we are to liberate the dormant, direct response.

How do we cater for educating the response?
Firstly, it seems to me, that more opportunity for individualized reading, especially for older adolescents, must be given. Class libraries of alluring paperback novels covering wide interests and varying levels of difficulty should be provided. Readers might be encouraged to choose in a discerning manner from both modern works (Townsend, Zindel, Garfield and

many others are providing quality novels for young adults) and some of the classics. Their own private choice needs to be valued, for a full inter-action with a chosen novel has been seen to be a highly personal affair. Here the teacher must have a knowledge of modern children's and adults' fiction as well as older literature, and he must also have some idea of books which are likely to both please and extend temperamental readers. Perhaps several books by a single author might be included so that readers would be given the chance to choose a writer rather than a title. Work in such an individualized scheme might involve the readers in giving their honest, immediate reactions to episodes in the book and the work as a whole. This might simply amount to a recorded conversation with a fellow pupil. Always the *direct* response would be encouraged. After reading several books, the pupils might be asked to choose one which made the greatest impact and say why such a choice had been made. Here, reflection on fuller patterns of events might be given hearing time.

Imaginative recreation of aspects of fiction gives ideal opportunities for deepening empathy. It is also invaluable in requiring young readers to return to the text, to structure a response so that it remains true to the author's intentions. If it has been seen that occasionally readers of the sample empathize to a dangerously high degree curtailing detachment, then requiring pupils to reconstruct their reading by imagining them-selves in particular and specific predicaments which remain closely faith-ful to the writer's words might helpfully nurture insight and detachment. In this way a more distanced evaluation and contemplation of the participants – an aspect of the response most lacking in the readers of this sample – might be encouraged.

Private reading time given over to reading chosen works should not be underestimated. The teacher does not always need to intrude and dictate the pace of the the activity.

Perhaps, above all, the teacher should talk much more with his pupils about the books and magazines they read and *why* they choose them.

It may be that we need to recognize that the full response to reading is highly charged with personal, affective concerns not always allowed for in school-based activities and consequently sometimes over-indulged in voluntary reading. The teacher of English may need to redress the balance by working towards a disciplined approach to good quality, appropriate novels which allows the personal emotional response, how-ever crude, to grow to maturity.

Notes

1 Schools Council Working Paper 52 (1975) *Children's Reading Interests* Evans/Methuen Educational, London

2 HARDING, D. W. (1968) 'Considered Experience: The Invitation of the Novel' in *English in Education* 1968

3 HARDING, D. W. (1961) 'Psychological Processes in the Reading of Fiction' in *The British Journal of Aesthetics* Vol. 2

21 Modes of response: some interactions between reader and literature
Mike Torbe

Literary response is a complex activity. I begin with D. W. Harding's comments about reading literature:

> Any but the most naïve kind of reading puts us into implicit relation with an author. A novelist (or a playwright) may be directing our attention mainly to the action and experience of his characters and part of our job is to enter imaginatively into them. But he is at the same time conveying his own evaluation of what is done and felt, presenting it (to mention simpler possibilities) as heroic, pathetic, contemptible, charming, funny . . . and implicitly inviting us to share his attitude. Our task as readers is not complete unless we tacitly evaluate his evaluation, endorsing it fully, rejecting it, but more probably feeling some less clearcut attitude, based on discriminations achieved or groped after.
>
> ('The Bond with the Author' *Use of English* 22.4 summer 1971)

I have always found the teaching of literature the most difficult of businesses. For many years I taught *about* literature, and shied away from the central questions I was posing myself all the time: what sort of sense are my pupils making of this piece of literature? how am I helping them to approach nearer to that essential centre of the work that first made me feel I wanted to place it before them? Like most English teachers of my generation, I found the conventional modes of literary criticism unsatisfactory. What was available to me when I started teaching and for years afterwards did not seem to help me in my search for something dimly seen: classroom discussions, literary critical essays, out-of-class chats with enthusiastic pupils, visits to theatres and museums – none of this seemed to help in assisting pupils towards the feeling centre of the work. When recently I read Barbara Hardy's essay on 'Teaching Literature in the University' (*English in Education* 7.1 (Spring 1973)) I felt a strong flow of recognition:

> There are three sets of human particulars in a teaching situation: the

Source: TORBE, M. (1974) 'Modes of response: some interaction between reader and literature' *English in Education* Vol. 8 No. 2 pp. 21–32

particularity of the work and the author, the particularity of the teacher, and the particularity of the student . . . Too often there is only one voice in the lecture and even the seminar and the tutorial – that of the teacher. More commonly there are two, the voice of the teacher and the voice of the author, but the teacher may . . . drown the author's voice.

What was missing from my teaching, I came to see, was any recognition of the interaction between the voice of the author and the reader, which did not necessarily, or even usefully, involve the teacher. The teacher's role, which I had seen as being to mediate between literature and reader, could in fact be obstructive and harmful to the pupil's active engagement with a text. I needed to find some kind of teaching structure which would remove the teacher from the centre, and focus pupils simultaneously on their reading, and on their response to the reading. It was because of these concerns that I designed the course I will describe.[1]

Because of recent reorganizations, the English Department in this Primary College of Education had devised a unit-based course, with compulsory and optional elements. My course was a second-year, five-week option course, three hours a week, with all three hours blocked on one morning. I decided we would concentrate on Twain and Hemingway, especially *Huckleberry Finn, Farewell to Arms,* and *The Snows of Kili-manjaro.* The structure of the course included powerful constraints; apart from my choice of particular authors, and particular books of theirs, I drew the following limits.

(a) The whole group (fourteen opted for the course) must work in sub-groups of three to four.
(b) The sub-group would, during the first week, make a tape-recording of itself talking about whichever of the books it had chosen to explore.
(c) The sub-group *must* listen to this tape of the discussion.
(d) Each individual must keep a personal logbook in which she was to jot down both what happened in the course and also what she thought and felt about what she was doing and reading.
(e) The sub-group had to decide on a final piece of work, the only criterion for which was that it must *not* be a conventional literary critical essay. This product could be either individual in design and execution, or group-based.

Later, at the group's suggestion, we added another requirement – that we all meet together for the last hour or so of the morning.

My own role was left vague. I was around during the morning for consultation, and I tried to spend a session each morning with whichever group happened to be around, particularly when they were listening to their discussion on tape, because I felt (rightly, it turned out) that most

H 211

of them would have difficulty in listening to their tapes with any real understanding and would need help in attending to what was actually there, rather than to what their predispositions led them to expect to be there.[2] On two occasions, I had long sessions with individuals at their request. In the whole group discussions I tried to mediate between the work the different groups were doing – because working apart, they lost contact with each other – and to suggest ideas for general consideration.

I was concerned not only with literary response but also with the fact that these students were teachers in training, and it seemed important to me to consider literary response as an example of one kind of learning. In the College of Education it is possible to teach and learn and simultaneously to make the process of that teaching and learning the subject of enquiry, so that student-teachers can analyse the learning process to illuminate their future behaviour as teachers. Thus, I felt it necessary to explore the whole question of *languaging* – the choosing of forms and modes of language appropriate to what one is doing rather than those modes of language expected by academic custom or by conventionalized thinking about writing. Douglas Barnes suggests in 'Classroom contexts for Language and Learning' (*Educational Review* 23.3 (June 1971)) that most teachers 'see language in terms of performance instead of in terms of learning'. The fact that the written work students in this college do is mainly in essay form supports Barnes's contention. An essay is, of its very nature, not the process but the product of learning, where the writer has to structure and organize what he previously learnt: thus most students and perhaps most school pupils too are being asked to learn and organize simultaneously. Simply, this is not possible. One organizes for public utterance what one has already learnt. In this context 'learning' involves the whole question of the image one has of oneself as a learner, and of oneself in relation to others; and one learns in this sense most successfully, it seems, in what James Britton calls 'expressive language'.

> Expressive language is language close to the speaker: what engages his attention is freely verbalized, and as he presents his view of things, his loaded commentary upon the world, he also presents himself. Thus it is above all in expressive speech that we get to know one another, each offering his unique identity, and (at our best) offering and accepting both what is common and what differentiates us.
>
> Secondly it is in expressive speech that we are likely to rehearse the growing points of our formulation and analysis of experience.
>
> ('What's the Use?' *Educational Review* 23.3 (June 1971))

There are several modes, private and public, appropriate for any learning situation, and for the learning to become meaningful the learner must decide for himself which mode to employ, why that and not another, and what demands this mode makes upon its user. The logbook was intended to offer a situation in which the student could use expressive language rather than the formal transactional modes she was used to being asked for in College. The kinds of response possible in this mode differ greatly from those possible in conventional modes.

Another problem for the students in encountering these modes was to define their audience. We discussed together whether the logbooks should be made public to the rest of the group: the decision, because of the way each individual had chosen to define the audience for their writing, was that they should not share their logs, because they had identified me as the reader, not each other, nor an impersonal marker-of-essays. Once they had made this decision, the logbooks, for many of the group, took on a particular intensity, in which the explorations of the group work and the literature became a searching out of new dimensions of response, which emerged with a growing coherence and confidence from the vagueness and aimlessness of the early entries in the logs. With their permission, I quote some entries from logs, to show what I mean.

Kath – a mature student – first: her first entry is merely a record of the first meeting: after that dots show entries omitted.

Monday 5th June 1972. a.m. Meeting with English group. p.m. Started to read *A Farewell to Arms* – this will be no hardship –

Tuesday 6th June: Group decided to 'do' *The Snows of Kilimanjaro* so read that – missed it the first time I read Hemingway – surprise ending – must think about it.
11.30 a.m. In car – reread book (Snows) made some notes on it
Like his directness (Hemingway's) there are no unnecessary words – no padding – also his simplicity

. . .

Wed 7/6/72. Am enjoying F to Arms although I prefer the male characters to Miss Barkely and the other women.
Hemingway is confident and completely in control of his *masculine world*.
When he writes of women it is from a male viewpoint – he makes little attempt to give them depth of character – for me they are very flat and not quite true?? Unlike Lawrence he doesn't try to *think* like woman – so everything is from a male point of view.

There follow some days (till the next Monday) of records of pages read, some notes about the symbolism of 'Snows', some comments on *Farewell*, and other of Hemingway's work, interspersed with quotations, some typed out, from what she is reading. Then there is a page and a half of much more personal comments on 'The Short Happy Life of Francis Macomber'.

She [Mrs Macomber] like the wounded lion and buffalo will charge intending to kill when cornered, and she is certainly cornered & retaliates in an effective way . . .

More pages of notes, comments, quotes, up till Saturday, 24 June. And suddenly something very different happens. The entry for that day begins 'Bought and started to read *The Sun Also Rises*', but what follows is eight pages of very intense and engaged writing. She writes:

> I first read this book when I was 17 (1949) and on the fringes of a similar group in Brighton, the most marked difference being their lack of money.
> My involvement began quite simply by being picked up . . .

Her reminiscences flow, sketches of the people, hints and explicit comments about her relationships with them, and above all a penetrating and honest appraisal of what she was then as a person (and is now? she doesn't say so). She concludes her 1,000-plus words (written over that weekend):

> It seems strange that rereading a book should start me writing at such lengths – haven't thought about the members of the crowd for a long time and never visit the old haunts when in Brighton – it all belongs to another life that.

A week later there is an interaction between her reading and her reminiscence, in a comment which grows out of the feelings created by the autobiographical writing, and synthesizes personal retrospection and literary response:

> Have been very surprised – Hemingway is so enthusiastic about mountains & writes so many beautiful descriptions of scenery that I expected him to do so in 'The Flight of the Refugees' [in *By-Line*]. He covers such beautiful country with really magnificent scenery that I know well & always react to – & never mentions it. But then the people were the important things there – doesn't this contradict what he was getting at in *The Sun Also Rises*, that whatever happens to people the earth carries on and triumphs?
> I particularly liked the episode in the mountains when Jake and Bill Gorton are fishing in the Burguete. It is reminiscent again of the raft in the middle of the river with Huck and Jim cut off from all that is distasteful – civilization – there is comradeship – all male.

I have spent some time with Kath's logbook: Alethea's now. She is twenty. Her first entries, like so many of the logs, are tentative and rather conscious of the situation.

Monday June 5th. Read couple of chapters in the evening, had to put the book aside through lack of interest and concentration. Began to seem unreal.

I mentioned above that I expected students to have some difficulty with listening to the tape of the discussion. Alethea comments:

Not too bothered by the tape-recorder however found it difficult to speak about the book. Points were brought out but not further developed.

Three days later, the group listened to the tape:

Listened to the tape. Better than I thought it would be. We had mentioned some good points but not discussed them deeply we tended to skip the surface. For my part I think I lack understanding of the book and am having to explore different aspects.

This is a radical change for Alethea; before the *book* was seen as being the barrier: now she sees the barrier as being within herself, and needing an active effort on her part to overcome it.

A week after making the tape:

Listened to the tape with Mr Torbe. Listening to it brought up many points we had not previously thought of. What makes us say the things we do? It became obvious in one point how in trying to help Sue with a particular point she was making I cut off all line of thought – mine and Sue's. I couldn't carry on the idea as it wasn't mine, Sue wasn't thinking what I had thought. What would happen in a teaching situation? Became obvious how we drifted from the book as art form to the book as part of real life. We saw the characters as real people. Many points had just been passed over on the tape could now be considered.

I have just discovered how much easier I am finding it to talk in lectures. It has taken me two years to overcome it.

That something important happened to the way Alethea evaluates her reading, and therefore, perhaps, to the actual quality of her reading, is suggested by a later entry about *The Old Man and the Sea*, very different in its openness from the simplistic comments of the early entries in the log:

Haven't as yet managed to sort out my ideas. I suppose I don't really know what it is about. An old man battling with a fish, to overcome it. What has he to show for his trouble? He risked his life to overcome it with merely the skeleton to show for it. Everyone could see the result but nobody could know what he went through. He was alone except for the boy, who cared for him. What meaning is behind this story, prompting its writing?

At the end of the course, trying to evaluate what happened to her reading of *Huckleberry Finn*, she concludes:

> I am gaining a slow liking for the book. The slowness of movement in the book reflects itself in my slowness of understanding. I am now determined to look further into it, a progression from my first disregarding of it.

It is useful to place Alethea's notes on listening to the tape with those of the other members of that group, Liz Walker and Sue. Liz writes:

> Listened to the tape again, this time with Mike Torbe there. (Now I do have to decide who I'm writing for, because if it's for you, there's not much point in writing about what we said, only about how I feel now.) How do I feel now?! I feel as if for the first time I've actually consciously thought about the process of learning and how little one really learns from a conversation at that moment. Its only afterwards, and then only if you make an effort to think about what you've been discussing.

Because of the requirement to keep a logbook, Liz has been led, through reflecting upon what has happened, into new thinking. By having to write – also, by *wanting* to write – Liz has clarified her thinking and raised to consciousness what might otherwise have remained only a vague feeling. The most important aspect of the course to Liz became the realization that she herself was in control of her own learning, something she had not previously recognized.

Sue's comments throughout her log are longer and more relaxed and personal than many of the others. It was as though she found this mode offered a way of handling thoughts and feelings which had been denied to her in the conventional mode she was used to. I am not certain why this should be so: but part of the reason is that she finds the logbook writing afforded a relief from the feeling she is familiar with when she usually writes – that her thoughts are on public display, with all their inadequacies paraded to be mocked and belittled. In her log she moves steadily towards deeper understanding of the book, and of the process of literary response. Her entry for the day on which we listened to the tape:

> We did not have the discussion after all but talked about our tape instead. I really believed that there was not much on the tape that was really relevant but as parts were pointed out I could really see their significance. The main thing that came out of the discussion was that,

although we had all said that we hadn't liked the book much as we talked about it the more we realized (when hearing it) that the more we liked the book. How strange! I really wish that I could have a discussion after every book I read because I am sure it would iron out a few points and I would understand it more. One reads a book, enjoys it, puts it down and then usually forgets about it even though there are parts of the book that could be stretched and talked about further. I don't think it would do me much good writing about my thoughts on paper because my thoughts do not develop as much as when I'm talking and discussing them. Also when I write things down I feel that they are no longer part of me because the words i.e. my thoughts are now staring me in the face and therefore they are no longer part of me – they are no longer private – they have been made public for everyone to see and comment upon. Whereas when one is speaking, these ideas and thoughts are still yours even though they are being spoken – they still belong to me and are part of me because they are being spoken directly by me. This is very hard to explain. When writing it down – I really must talk about it. Other people have no difficulty in writing down their thoughts, but I do because they come out all disjointed and with not much order or sense to them – I think I'll have to take a course on writing down one's thoughts.

Sue's self-deprecation shows that it is possible for an intelligent girl to reach the second-year of higher education without ever having been shown that this problem is not uniquely hers, but is common to all writers – 'trying to learn to use words . . .' She has been led by her experience of writing to feel that it must be of necessity structured and public, instead of being helped to discover that it may be a powerful learning mechanism. When the pressure of public display is removed, as it was in the logbook, what she writes shows a constant exploration of the new thoughts that come to her. It was this early, relatively unstructured stage of formulation that she had needed. The importance of this stage is immense: Vicki's log throughout shows thoughts at the point of formulation. Freed from the need of satisfying anyone but herself, she is able to speculate in ways that would have been impossible in the formal essays, in a language that is inconsequential, mazy, and implicit.

How can some people teach the rest of the group anything? How do you point out to people what they have learnt? I suppose they could pick them up & say you wouldn't have said that before or you didn't have any ideas at all on that before. I think the trouble is that a lot of people have learnt an attitude towards the teacher & so don't want to know what they have learnt as it would not be in context with their attitude to the teacher. Its no good saying this is what I have learnt as they'll pick out lots of silly reasons to say why you have learnt & give lots of silly reasons to say why they didn't want to. The fact is they just don't want to face what they have learnt & some perhaps haven't learnt at all.

Liz Hatton, on the other hand, engages in a different kind of formulation, facing in her log powerful emotions, and coming to terms with them by writing about them.

> Read *Farewell to Arms* in the train going home. Finished it. I thought I was going to faint at the end – it made me feel really bad. I have never felt so disturbed by a book before. I am still suffering from shock. The trouble with being such an optimist, or perhaps with reading too many second rate novels, is that I couldn't believe it was going to end with her death. It was too hurtful. Her death meant the end of everything . . . Its awful writing this – it isn't making much sense because everything I write is subjective – I suppose the experience of the book is too near to be anything else. I was full of a sense of injustice.

Not all the writing in the logs is tentative or in process of being formulated. Pauline Marriott asks herself what she has learned from the course, and answers her own questions impressively:

> I thought [when I started College] that English meant studying authors' lives and their work. I know now that it means much more than that. English is everything, it is our response to everything we read, it is the relationship between the way we feel and what we read and what we write . . .
> What happens when I read a story? Just a few thoughts:
> (*a*) I involve myself in a series of happenings and incidents.
> (*b*) I'm not conscious of looking at words.
> (*c*) A story adds a new facet to my experience.
> (*d*) A story is always there to be looked at again.
> (*e*) I never forget completely a story that means something to me at the time I read it.

It would, then, be wrong to suppose that the logbooks can only produce one kind of writing: they were used in different ways by different individuals. Margaret Pemberton, writing a sequence of poems about Time, generated by her thinking about the River in *Huck Finn*, found it unnecessary to do more than chart dates; Jane called hers 'Portrait of a self-engrossed adolescent'; while Liz Hatton was concerned with refining for herself a theory of Art. 'All cases are unique, and very similar to others': what is unique to each log is the individual response of that person to the total situation of the course. There was no demand for some kind of conformist reaction confined by a known structure; and thus the similarity of the fourteen logs is in the sense of their release into the freedom of felt and expressed response.

It is more difficult to talk of the taped discussions, because of their length. I want to concentrate on one tape only, and suggest general trends which apply to the others, and perhaps to any discussion of literature among adults. Kath, Jane, Vicki, and Liz discussed *The Snows of Kilimanjaro*. The transcript of the tape runs to thirty-six pages, and the tape lasts over an hour: the first thing to note, then, is that the discussion was found profitable enough by the participants for them to want to expend this much time on it. Why? There were, I think, two factors: one is the warm, strongly supportive feeling in this self-chosen group, which enabled a high degree of tentativeness and hesitancy to exist without demanding resolution; and the other is that this atmosphere encouraged the group to explore certain areas of their response to the story that they might otherwise have held back from, and by so doing to attain to simultaneous insights about the literature and about themselves as people. Thus the response to the story, both individual and shared; each person's honest appraisal of herself, supported by the group; and the group's interrelationship: all enrich and deepen the discussion. It is the intimacy and shared experiences of the discussion which lead the group to wish to extend it.

Here is an example of this sharing and mutual support going on. Liz has asked a question about the women in the story.

Liz: But is this, is this his wife, the one who's in the story now?
Kath: I don't know, I shouldn't think so.
Liz: I couldn't quite work that out, you know, who was who.
Jane: I it sounds as though it's something she might do, which is sort of his way of describing *all* women, isn't it?
[General agreement]
Jane: He doesn't use there's nothing special about his sort of, the words he uses about his wife as to other women.
Liz: Mmm
Kath: He doesn't make that clear at all, does he?
[Pause]
Jane: Perhaps it *is* sort of true in a way, though, because I think we do see people who we love – our children, our, you know, adults who we do love – as um images of ourselves. They're sort of a bit hung on to us, aren't they? We only see them from this point of view of loving them.
?: Mmm
Jane: And like people want things for their children, they don't want them for their children, they want them for *them*. And –
Liz: They want to see their children sort of in a certain way, don't they?
Jane: Yes. Yeh, because they're starting out from this position only in viewing their children and just as we view –
Liz: Do you think this is what's wrong with relationships, then, that people *do* this?

[General agreement]

Vick: Well, you can't do it any other way, can you?

Jane: You can't no, really.

Vick: Cos um you can't see other people from any other eyes but your own.

Liz: No you can't but there's a difference between seeing them only in relation to you and seeing them as a sort of a whole person. I think you can see 'em as a whole person if you try hard enough. I think it's very hard to sort of to not think of yourself when you are looking at 'em, but I think perhaps you can do it.

Jane: Yeh.

Vick: But you've got to put *your*self in their position then and live and try and live their lives.

Liz: Sorry? I didn't hear.

Vick: You've got to put yourself into, make yourself become them, then, and see how they live and how they look at the world and how they react to different people.

Liz: Mmm

Kath: It's very difficult, um, this business of children, I find. Er you have ideas and theories on life and things, theories that you've proved for yourself to be true. And er it's marvellous for other people, it might, okay, be alright for yourself, but um it's only up to a point that probably you can accept it fully for your children.

?: Yeh

Kath: You have to start um thinking very very deeply and um and hard about whether, you know, this *is* right for your children. I don't – I have to fight this one constantly . . .

At this point, Kath's tentative contribution, following her lengthy silence, suggests this a subject of some importance to her. Indeed, it becomes clear later that she is thinking of her relationship with her own children. (This extract is on pages 11–12 of the transcript; on page 27 Kath returns to the matter.) The rest of the group give support in two ways at this point – by allowing Kath to talk her way through a difficult and complex preoccupation, and by trying to reformulate the problem in such ways as to give a different, more generalized, perspective on it, without in any way being hostile to Kath's formulations. Thus:

Liz: I think probably that the hardest part about being a parent must be realizing that your children have *got* to make their own mistakes and battle through it on their own, cos really

[Two talk at once]

Kath: This is futile, this business of um – only I know it has to happen – I I was exactly the same. It's so damn futile though, when, if only people would benefit from other people's er

[Several talk at once]

Kath: No, I know this. I know this. I I I've always said the same thing.

Liz: There's nothing real unless you've experienced it yourself.

Kath: Quite

Liz: People can tell you till they're blue in the face, but unless you know yourself it doesn't

Vick: The more you find out from other people, you can find out if you're going, people will tell you something, and you do it and you make mistakes, then you realize that other people *are* telling the truth and then you learn from them.

Kath: But it's a it's a great pity, in a way, that people have to get hurt and kicked in the teeth and battered around um but on the other hand, if you don't have these things happen to you, then you're not really a a

General: person.

Jane: No.

Kath: I suppose the more kicked in the teeth and battered around you get (laughter) the more of a person you are.

Liz: Character building's the phrase isn't it?

Kath: Character building. Yes, I suppose so.

Vick: Some people have to cut themselves off.

Jane: Like he has. I think *he's* cut himself off. He doesn't seem to feel does he? He doesn't have the sort of irrational, emotional behaviour.

And the group has achieved a new insight into the piece of literature which is serving as the catalyst and focus of their discussion. This weaving in and out of the story, the seeing of the interrelationship between life and art, is the dominant feature of the discussion. Thus, there is a long stretch on the transcript where the discussion has apparently moved completely away from Hemingway, and is debating very personal morality, and the standpoints of the four towards violence; but that it is ultimately derived from the literature is clear, because the examples chosen are bullfighting, boxing and warfare. The conversation ranges over these into very intimate comments about personal behaviour, out into the question of integrity and personal honesty, and love-affairs. Then suddenly, right at the end of the tape, the group returns to *The Snows of Kilimanjaro* with an unexpected insight of real power:

Liz: Probably because you've got a picture of how you would die even though you've no idea about death, you know, you sort of envisage what your death will be like and it's always perhaps a little bit romantic a romantic view.

Jane: Perhaps that's the illusion. But I think he *does* have an illusion about it.

?: Yeah. Mm.

Jane: I think that's his own illusion in it, about his death.

Liz: And that's why that's why it's the mountain, because it's searching for s, you know, like the leopard, it sounds so noble that he was up, found on the moun – er what was it? 'Close to the western summit there is the dried and frozen carcase of a leopard. No one has explained what the leopard was seeking at that altitude.' You know it's as if as if nobody will know what he was seeking, isn't it?

Jane: Yeh, it is yeh, and this petty squabbling and irritability between them is – he doesn't want that, it's too honest for him, isn't it? He wants something more, that is his illusion

It is only because of the nature of the discussion that has preceded this moment that such responses can be made.

The taped discussion raised for us all two important matters. The first is a commonplace: that the way in which groups operate together is an important part of learning, and that a group can be either supportive or destructive of learning. The other is more fundamental, and returns me to my original concern with literary response. What happens in a discussion like this is different from what happens in the usual teacher-controlled discussion; the stress here falls not on the individual response, with a certain competitiveness with one's peers to see who can reach nearest the 'correct' response; it is a shared, supportive discussion which returns us to a pre-Romantic notion of a sharing community who work together, rather than the inspired isolate, trusting in his talents to set him apart. The group-concept that a discussion can generate is of potentially greater strength than any individual's concept, and the satisfaction of working with a group, the exhilaration of feeling that one sees all sides simultaneously, is a rich reward. The sharing which goes on in these tapes does not stop at a simple relationship-bond, but means much more than that, as Vicki commented:

> Our group's discussion brought the four of us together and made us form a group relationship – it was a good one in which we eventually formed a trust in each other to admit honest personal opinions and attitudes. In our discussion we abstracted from the book ideas and feelings which seemed significant to our own lives. Our own experiences helped us to understand what was going on in the story, whilst the story illuminated our own experience a little more. In this way our understanding of different concepts could be deepened and widened. Similarly, if something did not have much significance to one person, it was given a relevance by the experience of the discussion and the relationship of the listener and the person who was offering to share their experience and the relevance of it with them. We used the other people to bring us closer to the meaning of the story and we used the story to bring us closer to the people in the group.

This work supports all the evidence of the *Children as Readers* project: that readers can reach the heart of a piece of literature without the presence of a teacher, and may go further in honest, perceptive response when the teacher is absent. But it is also likely that the ways in which readers are expected or allowed to *express* their response, actually alter the nature of the response itself. As Stratta, Dixon, and Wilkinson say in *Patterns of Language* (Heinemann 1973): 'Response is inseparable from the words in which the response takes place.' These students had to find ways of both coping with their responses, and learning to *value* them, to be secure and confident in their shared opinions, instead of diffident and vulnerable as they had been often before: it was through the tentativeness and hesitant early formulations of what was only indistinctly felt, in talk and in writing, that they worked through to the confidence of opinion and evaluation.

I am conscious that despite the length of this essay, I have left unmentioned and unquoted, most of what went on in the course; and what is unquoted might well have been more eloquent than my words here, especially since I have quoted none of the more formal outcomes – story, poem, essay – produced for requirement (*e*). The most satisfying outcome, for us all, is that we feel, student and tutor alike, more confident in what we have to say, and perhaps more willing to say it. We have found our voices. Alethea commented, 'The work was difficult in that it was a fight with understanding': and Vicki wrote afterwards:

The main thing is that it isn't finished as I thought it was. Now we are together again we carry on discussing and thinking and learning . . . I felt during the course as though something important had been shared. Things are always better when they are shared.

I began with D. W. Harding. I finish with Ronald Morris:

It is, I think, profoundly if paradoxically true that only by beginning with responsive reading, with the alive awareness that may result at immature stages of development in the subordination of exact meaning to the distractions and distortions of personal associations, that we can hope to achieve a more mature level where the reader can maintain a balance between responding freely as a person to the message of the text as he first reads it and reaching out more critically in his search for the exact intention of the author.

('What children learn in learning to read' in *Success and Failure in Learning to Read*, Ronald Morris: Penguin 1973)

My thanks to the students who worked with me on the course:

Group 1	Group 2	Group 3	Group 4
Barbara Cope	Liz Hatton	Pauline Marriott	Alethea Hutchinson
Janet Oldham	Vicki Maffia	Margaret Pemberton	Sue Ogden
Pauline Tallet	Kath Marriott	Margaret Price	Liz Walker
Jane Withington	Jane Warrender		

Notes

1   Much of what I say about the course will be hindsight: I was certainly not conscious at the time of all threads I was trying to draw together, and have only been made aware of them since by discussion with the students who were on the course.

2   Behind this feeling was everything I had learnt from *The Anatomy of Judgement* (Abercrombie: Penguin) and particularly her comment: 'How to tell students what to look for without telling them what to see is the dilemma of teaching.'

Additional Reading

The books listed below are a selection from recent publications which relate to different themes and topics in this Reader. We have tried to indicate the ways in which they contribute to and extend the ideas of specific sections and chapters.

1 General reading
These first three books are listed separately as they have been a major influence on the formation of this Reader.

BRITTON, James (1970) *Language and Learning* Penguin
The theme of this book is one which has become widely accepted – that language is a means by which we organize our representation of the world. Professor Britton handles this deceptively simple and yet dauntingly complex and speculative theoretical area by exploring and relating the work of linguists, philosophers and psychologists to the real experience of children, parents and teachers. Chapter 3 is particularly relevant to readers of *Literature and Learning* as it looks at the theory, first put forward by D. W. Harding, which places literature among other language uses. Professor Britton distinguishes the spectator and participant roles, outlining and illustrating the theory which informs the thinking behind the chapters in Sections 3 and 4 of this book, and in particular the work described by Jean Blunt and Mike Torbe.

MEEK, Margaret, WARLOW, Aidan, BARTON, Griselda (1977) *The Cool Web: The Pattern of Children's Reading* The Bodley Head
This is the major recent work in the field of children's literature. It offers a comprehensive collection of essays by many of the best current writers and critics of children's literature in this country, supported by academics, teachers and publishers from the world of education. The book contains comments on a wide range of books and authors, and presents a series of approaches to the nature and purposes of children's literature, starting with the clarifying statement of its introduction:

> It would be difficult to justify another collection of essays such as this, unless it opened up a way forward from the minority cult which children's literature can so easily become if the authors and the critics,

mutually sustaining as they are, lose sight of the readers. The adult's response and the child's cannot be the same; the former has a memory of childhood and categories for delineating experience and judging it. The latter has childhood itself, passing every day, and memory is one of the things that a reading experience creates.

WHITE, Dorothy (1954) *Books before Five* New Zealand Council for Educational Research
Suzanne Walker's observations and recollections of her children's reading development echo the much earlier and more extensive record of a child's reading by her mother. Dorothy White, a librarian with an interest in child development as well as literature kept a record of the books which she read to her daughter from the age of two. It is a fascinating account of one child's interaction with stories. It is full of splendid detail, Carol's reaction to pictures in specific books: 'her face goes dull and she turns over quickly', Dorothy White's own reactions as a parent rather than as librarian: 'Now I have a child of my own, my sympathies – or rather my antipathies have changed . . . in choosing the books I realized how much one needed to know about the vocabulary of a little child *at the moment*. At present any book about an umbrella would be popular with Carol for she can say the word and is obsessed with the thing itself.' The diary records the part books have played in helping the child come to terms with her world; their contribution to her social, emotional and intellectual development. What is exciting is to observe the way that the meaning of things as it has been revealed to her through literature constantly influences the way she interprets the things that happen around her:

> The experience makes the book richer and the book enriches the personal experience. Even at this level, I am astonished at the early age this backward and forward flow between books and life takes place.

This is a marvellously readable account of the effect that literature can have on a growing child and demonstrates the importance of stories in the early years.

2 Books and children

FOX, Geoff, HAMMOND, Graham, JONES, Terry, SMITH, Frederic, STOCK, Kenneth (ed.) (1976) *Writers, Critics and Children* Heinemann Educational
This is a collection of articles from the journal *Children's Literature in Education*, many of them written by successful writers for children. Many of the chapters contain information about the way the writer approaches his task and teachers will find many insights into particular books that will be of help when introducing them to children.

There are two outstanding chapters. The first, 'Myth and Education', by Ted Hughes, is an essential accompaniment to Section 1 of the Reader, **Becoming a Reader,** and the second, 'Reading Children's Novels: Notes on the Politics of Literature', by Fred Inglis, provides a clear and condensed but rigorous theoretical structure that will inform the rest.

The book also contains chapters on the organization of literature in schools and on the teaching of specific books. It is a set book for Module 3 (P333) of The Open University Reading Diploma.

TUCKER, Nicholas (ed.) (1976) *Suitable for Children?* Sussex University Press

The section 'Fairy Stories' which begins this collection of extracts and articles on aspects of children's literature quotes from early nineteenth-century writing, interestingly demonstrating that a feeling of unease about these tales is not a contemporary phenomenon. In 1802, Mrs Trimmer, who is quoted here, was an early objector to fairy stories but, Nicholas Tucker observes, 'There have always been attempted encroachments on children's literature, and in our own time dentists have objected to sweet-eating in books, feminists to sexism, socialists to middle-class backgrounds . . .' and he quotes a splendid piece from Charles Dickens's *Household Words*, about interference with the freedom of literature and the reader. The book is a collection of writing (mostly short and readable articles from journals and magazines) by various authors and critics of children's literature, grouped in such a way that Nicholas Tucker can present areas of controversy, fairy tales, comics, fear, what the 'classics' have to offer and the value of fiction at all.

DIXON, Bob (1977) *Catching them Young, Volume One and Volume Two* Pluto Press

Bob Dixon takes on too many big issues (Volume One is entitled *Sex, Race and Class in Children's Fiction* while the second volume deals with *Political Ideas*) but his reference to over two hundred specific books and authors, particularly ones which have become part of the corpus of 'good' children's fiction, provides an alternative view to the accepted one of critics and prize givers. The chapter 'Class: Snakes and Ladders', has a discussion of historical fiction which provides a useful footnote to Anna Davin's chapter in this book. Both volumes are a deliberate attempt at consciousness-raising – Volume One makes generalizations about the ways in which attitudes to sexism, race and class are embedded in the language and content of children's fiction, while the second looks at comics, Enid Blyton and, in an extensive historical account, shows how attitudes and values have remained fairly constant since the nineteenth century. Both volumes contain material which should stimulate discussion of important issues.

CULPAN, N. and WAITE, C. (1977) *Variety is King, Aspects of Fiction for Children* A symposium School Library Association
This is a collection of articles on various aspects of children's literature which have all appeared in different journals for librarians, teachers or parents and are usefully grouped together here. Most of them were written between 1970 and 1976 but some may seem familiar or even rather dated, like Nicholas Tucker's 'Can literature solve problems?' or David Shavreen's 'Reading and imagination in the junior school'. All the articles, which are short, because of the constraints of writing in magazines and journals, tend to be rather thin, raising issues which they then cannot take up in depth. The section ' "Young Adult" Novels' is particularly frustrating as it deals rather superficially with an area that needs much more discussion. However, a comprehensive list of available and recently published books for this age-group emerges and ideas for discussion are positively presented.

FIELD, C. and HAMLEY, D. C. (1975) *Fiction in the Middle School* Batsford
This book is a useful companion to the Reader for teachers of seven- to thirteen-year-old children. The first part justifies fiction in school: the writers establish objectives, arguing that the case for teaching fiction is 'to sharpen the perception of those to whom it is addressed, to enable them to see what was not seen before, or to make them see differently what they had already seen'. They explore the need for fiction and, in particular, for fantasy, in relation to the emotional and cognitive development of children within this age-range, paying particular attention to responses to scenes that are potentially disturbing.

The second part contains detailed recommendations of books for the ages seven to eight, eight to nine, ten to eleven, and eleven to twelve. The books recommended were written at various times in the past 100 years, and the authors make imaginative reappraisals of many children's 'classics', including *The Wind in the Willows, The Little House on the Prairie* and *Moonfleet*. There is also comment on plenty of the best recent fiction; all the books are given sympathetic criticism together with advice on how best to read them aloud. There are collections of stories as well as full length works for the younger children and fantasy is given a special place.

WHITEHEAD, Frank, CAPEY, A. C., MADDEN, Wendy, WELLINGS, Alan (1977) *Children and their Books* the final report of the Schools Council research project on Children's Reading Habits, 10–15 University of Sheffield Institute of Education Macmillan Education
This research report is a thorough and systematic account of the pattern of children's reading. The study was largely of the social and educational situations which best promote reading, and the findings relate to parental occupations and types of school, but they also concern areas within the

teacher's control, particularly in connection with the availability of books.

The research provides substantial evidence for the provision of class libraries in secondary as well as primary schools, and for the positive promotion of books. There are useful lists of the most popular books at different ages; due acknowledgment is given to the influence of availability and the preferences of parents and teachers.

The research is disappointing in its inability to make a convincing assessment of responses to literature (cf. Jean Blunt's chapter of the Reader), although it summarizes thoroughly work on the satisfactions to be derived from reading. Its general findings of a move away from reading at 12+ and 14+, especially among boys, as compared to 10+, are interpreted as evidence for the need for increased provision of narrative and fiction in the middle and secondary years, a proposal that is further developed in this Reader by Margaret Walden and Peter Dean.

3 Books and the classroom

TORBE, Mike and PROTHEROUGH, Robert (eds) (1976) *Classroom En-counters: Language and English Teaching* Ward Lock Educational in association with The National Association for the Teaching of English

This book contains a series of articles from *English in Education*, the journal of The National Association for the Teaching of English. The writers included share a common concern for the process of learning and the language that enables it to happen. There are many transcripts of children talking to their teachers and to each other and the book is full of children's own stories and poems with extensive explanation of the context of their work.

The chapters that relate particularly to this Reader are: Nancy Martin, 'Children and Stories: their own and other people's'; John Alcock, 'Students' questions and teacher's questions'; Margaret Mallett, 'English in projects'.

It would, however, be difficult to single these out from the book as a whole. All the work on children's and teachers' language strategies contributes to an understanding of the linguistic contexts in which stories may best develop and be read and listened to. Fiction and poetry appear as central features of almost every chapter.

The book provides a collection of ideas and experiences of teachers working in all sections of education, from five-year-olds to adults. It is full of the experience of learners and teachers; the writers between them develop convincing evidence for the promotion of children's own language, including their stories and poems, as an intergral part of their learning.

JONES, A. and BUTTREY, J. (1970) *Children and Stories* Basil Blackwell

This book describes the practical application of theories about the importance of story. The authors begin with a subject which tends to get little attention; 'Television shares a place in the child's imaginative life with gossip and play and books and stories that he hears from his parents and teachers'. They see stories and story-telling, as one of the most important functions in the provision of an environment in which children can play many parts and develop in all of them. Television contributes alongside books and people to children's store of common experience. The authors suggest that 'when we are trying to assess what children will be capable of responding to in their stories we should take into account the extensive and diverse experience they may well possess through watching television'. Their chapter 'Responses' looks at children's own storywriting and the way in which the child brings together and organizes in his own story, material both from his actual and imagined experience. Using examples of children's writing they explore the extent to which children project their experience into the stories they make up while expressing responses to stories that they have heard and read. Further chapters deal with the problems and criteria for the choice of books for the classroom looking in detail at the provision of books in the classroom, the child's private reading, and the telling and reading of stories aloud. Underlying all the practical advice is the authors' belief that stories have always been of vital significance to man as a social being.

ROSEN, C. and H. (1973) *The Language of Primary School Children* Penguin

This book is rich in detailed observation of children and teachers in the classroom. The chapter 'Some Comments on Learning to Read and the Encounter with the Printed Word' contains a transcript of a small group of girls reading a poem which can usefully be read alongside the transcripts in this reader. The authors write about this group of girls 'We can hear their talk developing and absorbing the poem as they surround it with their experience of language and of life and their readiness to project *outwards* from it into their own imaginings in order to penetrate *inwards* to its meaning for them.' A subsection of this chapter, *Storying*, looks at 'the whole business of storytelling', stressing that for young children:

> receiving, retelling and composing stories can be seen as different parts of the same process. The receiving of stories is part of a child's cultural inheritance providing him with models, patterns and symbolic figures for his personal story-making ... To a very large extent reading and writing are indivisible and nowhere is this more evident than when children are engaged in what we must call storying, the taking and giving of stories.

The chapter describes and exemplifies different ways in which the authors observed children and teachers engaged in 'storying'.

Jones, Anthony and Mulford, Jeremy (eds) (1971) *Children Using Language: An Approach to English in the Primary School* Oxford University Press
Like *Classroom Encounters*, this book's origins are in work carried out by the National Association for the Teaching of English; it is based on the work carried out in a project on 'Language in the Primary School'. There are chapters on all aspects of language work in the primary school, containing extensive accounts and illustrations of work in progress. In particular, 'Object Lesson', by Connie Rosen, and 'What Are They Up To?' by Nancy Martin, should be read in connection with Section 2 of the Reader, **From Experience to Literature,** and the chapter by Margaret Spencer on 'Stories in the Classroom' is further important evidence for the potential of literature as a central element in the curriculum.

The book is given its theoretical framework in a chapter by James Britton called 'Words and a World' and by a series of linking commentaries by the editors, part of the function of which is to relate this chapter to the rest. The result is a close and convincing association between the theory and evidence from the classroom, making the book a stimulating and practical accompaniment to any teacher's own work.

Burgess *et al* (1973) *Understanding Children Writing* Penguin
The title of this book is deliberately ambiguous and takes as its focus the fact that children are called on to write an incredible amount during the course of their school career. It presents a range of different kinds of writing, inviting the reader to consider what is happening to the writers during the process. The chapter 'Sharing Experience' shows children of different ages dealing with their own fiction and fantasy – the authors comment, 'one may wonder why it is that young children seem to develop their understanding of the purposes implicit in the poetic function of language so much earlier than their understanding of the transactional . . . Is it simply that they encounter the stories which are read to them at an earlier age?' Later in the book, in 'Contexts', teachers comment on transcripts and writing produced as a result of talking and reading, particularly poems, together.

4 Tales and legends

Briggs, K. M. (1970) *Dictionary of British Folktales* 4 Volumes Routledge & Kegan Paul
The dictionary is in two parts, each part comprising two volumes. The first (part A) is devoted to British folk narrative or folk fiction proper, the second (part B) to folk legend, that is, to tales once believed to be true.

Complete or abbreviated short tellings are given, a good proportion collected from oral sources. Part A distinguishes between different forms of folk narrative. Volume 1 (part A) is largely devoted to the magical tale – the equivalent of the German *Märchen*. Tales otherwise similar in incident but from which magical occurrences are absent, are designated

Novelle, and appear in Volume 2, together with a small collection of nursery tales. A large section of jocular tales appears in Part A Volume 2. This includes drolls, and noodle stories from the thirty-six places in England and Wales reputed to be inhabited by simpletons, of which Gotham is the most famous, and Cambridge perhaps the least expected. Legends in part B are subdivided under such headings as Black Dogs, Devils, Giants, Ghosts, Fairies, Witches and Local Legends.

An index of tale-types appears in Volume 2 of each part, and a separate index to story titles for each part is also included, together with a comprehensive bibliography. (H.M.L.)

COOK, Elizabeth (1969) *The Ordinary and the Fabulous* Cambridge University Press
This is a very individual and committed assessment of myths, legends and familiar stories; the books in which they are collected, and the importance of telling and reading them to children and young people.

Readers will find the extensive cataloguing of published sources of the stories most useful and the book as a whole is an excellent practical guide. Elizabeth Cook's enthusiasm for her subject does perhaps lead her to needless disparagement of 'realistic' stories and fiction. She is also over-prescriptive in her recommendations, and her preference for the Greeks is reflected in an undervaluing of other mythologies.

However, the great virtue of the books is her insistence on letting the stories speak for themselves:

> The problem of 'reality' should never be forced upon children. Their curiosity should be satisfied as it arises, but they will not continually want to know 'What does this particular story mean?' as long as they are interested in it as a story ... Stories should be left to make their own imaginative effect with as little interference as possible by the storyteller.

Students and teachers approaching the chapters in the Reader by Bruno Bettelheim and Heather Lyons will find Elizabeth Cook's book a valuable preparation.

BETTELHEIM, B. (1977) *The Uses of Enchantment* Thames & Hudson
Dr Bettelheim's interpretations of fairy tales are along conventional Freudian lines but the main contention of the book is that children are powerfully affected by fairy tales, whether they fully understand them or not and that these tales make an important contribution to their maturation. He explores and illustrates the functions of fairy tales, demonstrating that, far from being harmful – insofar as their content may be violent, frightening and even distasteful – these tales are positively therapeutic. In an extensive analysis of many familiar tales, Bettelheim suggests that they may reflect the child's inner imaginative life and that they may convey a sense of order. It is interesting to relate Bettelheim's claims to the chapters by Ralph Lavender and Agnes Finnegan in this book.

Index